DRINKING FRENCH

The iconic cocktails, apéritifs,
and café traditions of France,
with 160 recipes

DRINKING
FRENCH

DAVID
LEBOVITZ

Photographs by Ed Anderson

TEN SPEED PRESS
California | New York

CONTENTS

AUTHOR'S NOTE

The recipes in this book are given in cups, ounces, and metric measurements. In some cases, I've rounded amounts up or down slightly, if the precise conversion to metric is too persnickety and won't affect the results. Because liqueurs, spirits, and even fruit juices can vary in flavor and strength, it's not always imperative to be ultra-precise with drinks. So, if a cocktail recipe calls for 22ml (¾ ounce) of a spirit or another ingredient, just aim for the midway point between 20 and 25ml in your measuring cup or jigger. In many instances, I've kept measurements in teaspoons, as the French do, calling for a *cuillère à café*, a coffee (or tea) spoon. The metric equivalent of a teaspoon is 5ml, and a tablespoon is 15ml.

Cocktails are traditionally measured in ounces (or the metric equivalent), whereas other beverage recipes, especially non-alcoholic ones, are usually expressed in cups as well as ounces (and the appropriate metric equivalents). Because the recipes in this book range from hot chocolate, lemonade, and marshmallows to apéritifs, infusions, and cocktails to candied nuts, home-cured salmon, and homemade syrups, please accept any variations in measuring methods that you might notice from one chapter to the next. Like the French, I'm fond of rules, but also know when to diverge from them.

1 | CAFÉ DRINKS

Un P'tit Verre, SVP 6

Café au Lait 8

Café Express 11

Chocolat Chaud
Hot Chocolate 12

Chocolat Chaud au
Caramel Beurre Salé
Hot Chocolate with Salted
Butter Caramel 13

Chocolat Chaud
aux Épices
Spiced Hot Chocolate 16

Guimauves à l'Armagnac
Armagnac Marshmallows 17

Infusions and Tisanes 21

Tisane 22

Thé à la Menthe
Mint Tea 23

Vin Chaud
Hot Mulled Wine 26

Frappés 27

Café Frappé
Coffee Frappé 27

Chocolat Frappé
Chocolate Frappé 28

Café Frappé
Glacé Irlandais
Coffee Frappé with Irish Cream
Liqueur 30

**Citronnade and
Limonade** 31

Citronnade
Lemonade 33

Citron Pressé 33

Citronnade
Gingembre-Romarin
Ginger-Rosemary Lemonade 34

Juste un Verre 34

Limonade
Sparkling Lemonade 36

Menthe à l'Eau
et Grenadine
Mint and Pomegranate Syrup
Drinks 37

Diabolo Menthe
Classique
Mint Lemon Soda 39

Diabolo Menthe
Fait Maison
Homemade Mint Lemon Soda 39

Where's the Ice? 40

Blanc Limé
Lemon-Flavored Wine 41

Beer 43

**Deck & Donohue
Brewery** 44

Pananché
Lemon-Flavored Beer 46

Monaco
Lemon Pomegranate–Flavored
Beer 46

Tango
Pomegranate-Flavored Beer 48

Picon Bière
Beer with Picon 48

Kir
White Wine with Black Currant
Liqueur 49

Kir Royal
Champagne with Black Currant
Liqueur 49

The Colors of Kir 50

La Bicyclette 51

Playing with Pastis 52

On the darkened streets and sidewalks of France, the flicker of lights in corner cafés signals the start of the day. Whether you're in a city like Paris, Lyon, or Marseille, or a village in the countryside, once the lights are on, the next order of business is to flip the switch on the coffee machine. With that simple action, the day begins.

While the machine is warming up, the beige ceiling lights cast a warm glow on wicker chairs stacked one on top of the other, along with the café tables, waiting to be set up on the sidewalk outside. Baguettes picked up at the local bakery on the way to work are propped up against the bar in a paper sack, and will eventually be sliced for breakfast *tartines*, served with butter and jam. But first things first: coffee.

Le barman (or woman) releases a sputtering blast of steam from the milk-warming wand, an indication that the machine is ready to go, as people start to wander in. In the wintertime, the warmth is definitely part of the attraction, as are the free morning newspapers on wooden spindles. But any time of the year, locals gather at their neighborhood bar to stand and drink a short, dark *café express* while reading the paper or catching up on *commérages* (gossip) in the neighborhood. Most of the customers have just woken up. Others are heading home after a long night of work—or play. But it doesn't matter: There are no judgments in a French café; everyone is welcome to gather there, whether you spent the night sweeping the streets (or working the streets), are on your way to a business meeting, or are a timid tourist, hoping to get your first taste of France.

I fell into the latter category. On my first visit to Paris, zonked after the long flight from California, I walked into a nearby café and ordered a coffee at the counter. After the barman strong-armed the filter holder into place, he hit the switch and the espresso machine dribbled a trickle of murky dark liquid into a cup placed underneath the spout. When the flow of coffee stopped, he slid the cup and saucer toward me. I dutifully picked up my coffee, walked over to a table, and sat down to drink it. Within seconds the barman barked something at me that I didn't understand (with my nonexistent comprehension of French, and French café customs), but eventually I deduced that I'd made a grave error by taking my coffee from the bar to a table, where the price of a cup doubles. I slunk back to the bar, embarrassed by my *gaffe*, finished my coffee, and left. That was my first lesson in how to drink, and behave, in a French café.

There seems to be a code of conduct for everything in France, from the *salle d'attente* of the doctor's office, where you're expected to greet each and every person in the waiting room when you walk in, to not calling a café waiter *garçon* (boy), which is a mild insult. One should say *monsieur*, because everyone is *égal* in France, and service here is about serving you, not being at your service. (You can thank the French Revolution for this mind-set, or blame it, if you've ever had a less-than-optimal customer service experience in the country.)

Later that afternoon, refreshed from a nap, I decided to go for a walk and take in the city. I had finally made it to Paris, the place I'd always dreamed of visiting, and didn't want to spend my first day snoozing on the so-small-my-feet-were-hanging-over-the-edge bed in my hotel room. (Were French people *really* that tiny?) After meandering around for a while, stopping to admire the window of each and every chocolate and pastry shop I passed (there were so many of them—it was paradise!), I decided to try my luck again at a café. Being a sunny afternoon, I chose one where people were sitting at tables outside. And this time, I knew enough not to get my coffee at the bar first, and bring it to the table.

Still reluctant with my faltering French, I wove myself between the closely packed tables to squeeze into the only available seat I had spotted on the terrace. I did my best not to bump into or jostle anyone (after all I'd heard about Parisians before my visit, I was afraid to incur any wrath). I did, however, know how to say *pardon*. When I grazed someone and uttered a nervous "Uh, *pardon*," no one looked at me or paid any attention. They kept on chatting with friends, reading their newspapers, or staring off into the distance, looking at nothing in particular with a cigarette smoldering in the ashtray.

Once seated, my anxiety climbed when I saw there was no menu or list of drinks on the table. Nothing I could point to and say, "I'll have that." I had no choice but to ask for my drink in French. *Café* was one French word that I found easy to master, but there's only so much coffee you can drink in a day, and I was ready for something more relaxing. Fortunately, I spotted a blackboard on the wall that listed wines available either by the *verre* or by the *pot*, at prices that seemed too good to be true (three dollars for a glass of wine?!), and it seemed only right that I order one. I didn't think I could drink a whole pot of wine by myself—and later learned that a *pot* is a refillable bottle with an extra-thick bottom so it doesn't tip over—but I wouldn't

have a problem with *une verre*. Or was that *un verre*? My worries were mounting. I finalized the order in my mind, with a little help from my guidebook, and memorized the phrase in advance: "*Je voudrais un verre du vin rouge, s'il vous plaît*," so I'd be ready.

When the waiter finally came to take my order, I was suddenly on the spot and completely blanked on my plan of action. Flustered, I stammered and stuck with my usual "... *uh* ... *um* ... *un café*," barely remembering to add a "*monsieur*" to the end of my less-carefully crafted phrase. A minute later he placed the little cup of coffee in front of me with two paper tubes of sugar resting on the saucer, as well as a separate burgundy-colored plastic dish with a built-in clip on it, holding *l'addition* (the check). I was no stranger to strong coffee, but after my first

few cups in France, I understood why everyone added all that sugar. I ripped off the end of one of the sugar tubes and dumped it in. Then I added the second, and sat back to watch the world go by.

■   ■   ■

I often refer to cafés as the living rooms of Paris. Historically, artists and writers used their local café as a place to work, attracted by the heat they didn't have at home in the winter. They also benefited from the alcohol being served, which most writers deem a necessity after laboring over words all day. (Hence, entire chapters devoted to apéritifs, infusions, and cocktails in this book.) Cafés are also places to meet friends, especially in cities, since many people live in apartments that are too small to host guests,

or they don't want to go through the bother of tidying up. (With clothes dryers not very common in France, there are invariably a few unmentionables hanging in your apartment to dry, that you don't necessarily want everyone else to see.) Also, who wants to stay at home when you can sit on an open-air terrace and have whatever kind of drink you want, served by a dashing Frenchman? Not me.

I've come to love the café culture in France, and the drinks and customs that are part of the rhythm of daily life. The wines, beers, coffees, infusions, apéritifs, liqueurs, distillations, cocktails, and digestives also tell the story of France. If you want to understand the French, watch how they eat, and see what they drink. After being in France for almost two decades, I'm no longer wary of cafés. And, like the French, I can be found in a café at all hours of the day, to meet friends, to write, or to conduct a little business (but nothing *too* serious). Once you're seated at a table, it's yours until you're ready to leave. I used to wonder how people could sit in one place and do nothing for hours, as the French do. But after just a few years of living in France, I learned how to just *be*, too.

You can re-create the feeling and flavors of a French café at home, no matter where you live. I can't prove this, but to me, French drinks taste better in traditional coffee cups and cocktail glasses. Over the years, I've amassed quite a collection of tableware and glasses by scouring flea markets and thrift stores. Most of my *café au lait* bowls and vintage glasses had stood up to decades of use before I got them, and I plan to use them for many more years to come.

You'll rarely see anyone measure the ingredients for a drink in a café in France.

Most of the drink-making is done *au pif*, or "by the nose." A bar person simply adds a splash of syrup and fills the rest of the glass with water or beer, pours in what looks like the right amount of pastis, or adds some lemon juice for a *citron pressé* and lets you do the rest yourself. The one exception to this rule is that some French café glasses have faint rings around them so owners don't have to worry about employees being overly generous with their pours.

Some of the drinks in this book may be as unfamiliar to you as they once were to me, but I've re-created versions of them using measurements so you can make them at home. Things like mint syrup may not be available where you live, although everything these days seems to be available online, and I've provided a Resources section on page 283 to help you find them. I've also included homemade versions of syrups, infusions, and liqueurs in case you're anything like me and want to make your own. Be aware that ingredients differ from place to place, and from brand to brand, so even if you've measured something precisely, your beer may be stronger than the one I used, or your store-bought sparkling *limonade* might be sweeter than my homemade version. Feel free to adjust the ingredients in all of the drinks in this book, to suit your taste, or your nose.

UN P'TIT VERRE, SVP . . .

To feel a little more like a local, it's fun to learn a few words of café slang before visiting France. I wouldn't try some of these out at an upscale café on the Boulevard Saint-Germain, but in a neighborhood joint, they'll likely elicit a smile. Or in my case, a laugh at my expense when I get one wrong!

- To ask someone to have a drink with you, invite them to *boire un coup* (get a drink) or *prende un verre* (take a glass).

- A café can be a *bougnat*, originally a reference to the hardworking owners, often from the Auvergne (called *bougnats*), or *un zinc*, referring to the zinc bar. If you're meeting someone at a *troquet*, don't bother to dress up; it's a dive bar (or café).

- A *café express* gets shortened to *un noir, un p'tit café,* or *un p'tit noir*. With a "nut" of steamed milk, your *café express* becomes a *noisette* (hazelnut). If you want a bigger cup of coffee, *un allongé*, also known as *un americano*, is made longer by adding extra hot water, a custom that goes back to U.S. soldiers adding water to their coffee to dilute the strong French brew during WWII.

- If you get a bad cup of coffee, French people refer to it as *jus de chausettes*, or "sock juice," an expression that's best not shared with the person who made your coffee.

- For an overview of the drinks available in a café and the prices, check the *tarif des consommations*, which every café is required by law to post. Note that there are several prices: the *prix comptoir* (the less-expensive one) is for drinks consumed standing at the bar; the *prix salle* and *terrasse* are the prices if you sit at a table.

- The standard sparkling water to order in a café is *un Perrier*. If you want sparkling water with a lemon wheel, ask for *un Perrier-rondelle*. San Pellegrino has become trendy in France and shortened to *San Pé*.

- When locals want a 1664, a well-known lighter beer, they ask for *une seize* (the number sixteen, the first half of 1664). A regular Kronenbourg is *un Kro*. A glass of white wine is a *blanco*, and table wine is known as *jaja*, but unless you're a local, I'd go with *vin de maison* or *vin du moment*.

- To use the restrooms, don't ask where *les chiottes* are (unless you're French), as it's somewhat vulgar. Asking for *le vécé* is more polite jargon for the W.C.

- If you end up drinking too much, you'll wake up with a *gueule de bois* (wooden snout), i.e., a hangover. It might merit a trip to the *pharmacie*, not the *droguerie*, where one shops for cleaning supplies.

CAFÉ AU LAIT

Makes 1 serving

Moka pot, or your
preferred coffee maker

Freshly ground coffee
(not too finely ground if
using a moka pot)

Whole or low-fat milk

The most misunderstood drink in France is the *café au lait*. Actually, I should say, it's the most misunderstood drink *outside* of France. The literal translation is "coffee with milk," which it is: hot coffee with a good amount of warm milk. But the French drink their morning coffee from a footed bowl (or a large mug), at home. What visitors are thinking of when they order a *café au lait* is a *café crème*, or *un crème* in café-speak, which is the French version of a cappuccino.

I don't know where the idea of drinking coffee from a footed bowl came from, but it gives me something to collect in France, which is how several cabinets in my kitchen became devoted to vintage *café au lait* bowls. I suspect the bowl gives people a wider space in which to dunk their butter-and-jam-slathered baguette at breakfast, like my French partner, Romain, does every morning with a gusto (and mess) that still surprises me.

There's no trick to making *café au lait* at home. Contrary to popular belief, the French are not necessarily fans of strong coffee, and they add a lot more milk than I do. I like my morning brew to be very strong, with just enough milk to lighten and take the edge off it, but not enough to diminish the coffee flavor.

My preferred coffeemaker for a *café au lait* is a Bialetti Italian moka pot. Other people use a French press, but after a few morning incidents (or accidents, I should say . . .) wrestling with a stubborn plunger that blew hot coffee and coffee grounds across my kitchen, my allegiance remains with the pot that our neighbors in Italy safely use for their morning brew. The moka pot requires no special techniques, nor do you need to fear any mishaps. I prefer to start my day without a lot of drama (because there's usually enough of that later on), and find the moka pot's ease of use to be very morning-friendly.

For me, the stronger the beans, the better. However, I avoid "French roast" coffee; the technique is used by some roasters to hide the taste of poor-quality beans by overroasting them. When coffee beans are overroasted and shiny, the flavorful oils have risen to the surface, where they can become oxidized, rather than allowing them to remain inside the bean, where they belong.

To make a *café au lait*, prepare a moka pot of coffee. When making a *café au lait* just for myself, I use what's called a 6-cup moka pot, which yields about 1 cup (250ml) of coffee. (The "6-cup" designation refers to six cups of espresso.) Fill the lower chamber of the pot

with water to the mark inside (some say you should start with preheated water in the pot; however, boiling a separate pot of water is too much effort for me in the morning), insert the filter, and add coffee to the top of the filter. Level it off, but don't tamp it down. Twist on the top, and set the moka pot over medium-high heat. While the coffee is brewing, warm some milk in a small saucepan over medium heat until it starts to steam. If you prefer a little bit of *mousse* (foam) on top, either steam the milk with the wand of an espresso machine or use a handheld milk frother, an inexpensive device that acts like a miniature electric whisk and makes quick work of the task without a lot of fuss. A small whisk works, too; place it in the warm milk and rapidly roll the handle of the whisk back and forth between the palms of your hands to froth the milk.

When the coffee has passed through the filter and into the top chamber of the moka pot, pour the coffee into a footed bowl. Top off with warm milk, spooning in extra foam, if you like.

CAFÉ EXPRESS

If I had *cinq centimes* for every time I've been reprimanded for writing *café express* by people pointing out: "It's not *express*, it's espresso!!" (usually with a few more exclamation points), I'd be able to afford one of those fancy top-floor apartments with a flower-laden terrace overlooking the Seine, where I could sip my afternoon demitasse of coffee. *Espresso* is correct if you're in Italy, but in France, a shot of dark coffee is a *café express*, which the French (who like to combine their fondness for apostrophes, and the word *petit*) shorten to *p'tit café* or *p'tit noir*.

Much has been written about the not-especially-delicious coffee served at French cafés because, historically, the quality of the coffee wasn't a primary concern. The priority was coffee that was dark, cheap, and caffeinated. It was something to slug, not savor. During the last decade, however, cafés have sprung up in several cities in France that could easily trick you into thinking that you were in Berlin, Brooklyn, or Brisbane if it weren't for the patrons speaking French, where a barista carefully weighs out just the right amount of coffee, then pours temperature-controlled water through a spiral-shaped filter into an individual cup.

In Paris, their coffee tends to be supplied by local roasters such as Belleville Brûlerie, Coutume, L'Arbre à Café, and La Caféothèque, and most of these roasters lead workshops and master classes so locals (and professionals) can learn how to make and appreciate coffee. There's even an annual competition amongst French baristas called Frog Fight, a good-natured event that pits them against each other.

In a country that values tradition, especially French tradition, it used to be unthinkable that France would have cafés with intentionally weathered floors lit by exposed-filament lightbulbs hanging from the ceiling and tattooed baristas wearing pegged jeans obsessing over cups of single-origin coffee. But the new wave of coffee shops is one change that coffee-lovers like me are happy about. That said, from time to time I still like standing at a curved zinc counter in a traditional café, sipping a *p'tit noir*, and drinking in the atmosphere.

CHOCOLAT CHAUD
Hot Chocolate

Makes 2 regular or 4 *p'tit* servings

2 cups (500ml) whole milk

5 ounces (140g) bittersweet or semisweet chocolate, chopped

1 to 2 tablespoons raw granulated or light brown sugar (optional)

Whipped cream or Armagnac Marshmallows (page 17), for garnish (optional)

The secret of rich, unctuous Parisian hot chocolate isn't an overload of cream; it's regular milk and lots of chocolate. This *chocolat chaud* gets thicker the longer it sits, so feel free to make it in advance and then rewarm it—if you can wait. I like my hot chocolate on the bittersweet side, so I use chocolate with a cacao content of around 70 percent. If you prefer it a little sweeter, you can use semisweet chocolate or add sugar. Raw granulated or light brown sugar gives the hot chocolate a little toffeelike edge. Parisians tend to drink *chocolat chaud* in modest portions, about a teacup's worth, rather than serving it in generous-sized mugs. But it's sometimes offered by the pitcher, so you can have seconds (pictured on page 19).

In a medium saucepan, warm the milk and chocolate, whisking occasionally until the chocolate is melted. Bring the mixture almost to a boil, paying close attention; if you let it come to a full boil, it will quickly boil over. Reduce the heat to the lowest setting possible and gently simmer the hot chocolate, whisking constantly, for 3 minutes. Remove the pan from the heat. When the chocolate is cool enough to sip, add the sugar to taste (if using).

To serve immediately, pour the hot chocolate into cups and top it with whipped cream (if using). Or, for an even better flavor, let it *reposer* (relax) for at least 15 minutes, then rewarm it over low heat. You can also make this up to 2 days in advance and store it in the refrigerator before rewarming; it'll get thicker the longer it sits.

CHOCOLAT CHAUD AU CARAMEL BEURRE SALÉ

Hot Chocolate with Salted Butter Caramel

Makes 2 or 3 regular or 4 to 6 *p'tit* servings

½ cup (125ml) heavy cream

¼ cup (60g) salted butter, cubed

¾ cup (150g) sugar

½ teaspoon flaky sea salt, such as fleur de sel or Maldon

1¾ cups (430ml) whole milk

4 ounces (115g) unsweetened chocolate, finely chopped (see Note)

Whipped cream, for garnish (optional)

NOTE

If you have difficulty finding unsweetened chocolate where you live, Lindt makes a 99 percent dark chocolate bar that works well, too.

Of the many brilliant ideas I've had over the years, one was a project with my friend Régis, who comes from a family of salt harvesters who work off the coast of Brittany. I wanted to create a mix for making salted butter caramel hot chocolate using their *fleur de sel* and sell it globally. The trick was to get enough salted butter caramel flavor into a cup of hot chocolate without making it overly sweet. I cracked the code by using unsweetened chocolate, called *100 percent pâte de cacao*, which isn't easy to find in France. (Americans use it for brownies, so it's readily available.) The short-lived project was also thwarted by the challenges (and costs) of international shipping, so I kept the recipe to myself, until now.

Unsweetened chocolate can be more stubborn to melt than bittersweet chocolate since there's no added fat. (This fact may also explain why the French don't use it.) But a few moments in a blender will smooth things out perfectly.

This is like drinking a delicious salted butter caramel chocolate candy bar, so you might want to break out some demitasse cups and serve this in delectable, but modest-sized portions.

In a small saucepan over low heat, or in a bowl in a microwave oven, heat the cream and butter together until the butter melts. Cover to keep warm while making the caramel.

Spread the sugar in an even layer over the bottom of a wide 5- to 6-quart (5 to 6L) saucepan. Heat the sugar over medium heat. As the sugar at the edges begins to melt, watch it carefully. When the melted sugar starts turning a light amber color, use a heatproof silicone spatula or wooden spoon to gently stir the melted sugar from the edges toward the center of the pan, mixing it with the undissolved sugar. Continue to cook, stirring gently to keep the sugar melting and coloring evenly. When the sugar is a deep amber color, about the color of an old penny, and starts to smoke, turn off the heat.

continued

Wait a few seconds until the sugar smells as if it's just about to burn, then gradually (not too quickly) add the cream-and-melted-butter mixture, stirring constantly, until it's completely incorporated. If the sugar clumps a bit, keep stirring it off the heat until it smooths out. Don't worry about any stubborn bits that resist melting; they'll get taken care of later.

Add the salt, milk, and unsweetened chocolate to the caramel. Rewarm the mixture over medium heat, stirring, until the chocolate has completely dissolved. (It may look somewhat grainy at this point, which is normal.)

Use an immersion blender to smooth the mixture, or let the mixture cool to room temperature, pour it into a standard blender, and blend until smooth, about 10 seconds. (Never fill a blender more than halfway full with hot liquid as it can create a vortex in the machine and blow the top off, which is hazardous.) Return the mixture to the saucepan and rewarm before serving. Pour into cups and top with whipped cream, if desired.

CHOCOLAT CHAUD AUX ÉPICES
Spiced Hot Chocolate

Makes 2 regular or 4 *p'tit* servings

2 cups (500ml) half-and-half

4 ounces (115g) bittersweet or semisweet chocolate, coarsely chopped

2 ounces (60g) milk chocolate (preferably with at least 30% cacao solids), coarsely chopped

Pinch of salt

¾ teaspoon freshly ground cardamom

¾ teaspoon freshly ground cinnamon

½ teaspoon freshly grated nutmeg

At Maison Aleph in Paris, a pretty little pastry boutique in the Marais, Myriam Sabet eloquently serves contemporary, bite-size pastries made using French techniques, incorporating Middle Eastern ingredients. And when I say "pretty *little* boutique," I mean that there are maybe four seats and a counter.

The first time we met was over pastries in the shop. After chatting a bit, she offered me a cup of hot chocolate, which I tried to decline since I was enjoying my fill of her delicate sweets. But after the first sip from the steaming cup she insisted I try, I was powerless to stop. It was so good that I went home immediately after and came up with my own version so I could enjoy it whenever I wanted, which is more often than one might consider prudent. But I can't help myself.

The secret is the spices. The French believe so much in using freshly ground spices that when you buy nutmeg pods at the supermarket, a teensy metal mini-grater is included in the jar so you have no excuse for not grating your own. To grind the cardamom and cinnamon, I use a mortar and pestle, but if you don't have one, use a rasp-type zester to grate the cinnamon and nutmeg to a powder, and crush the cardamom seeds in a sturdy ziptop freezer bag using a rolling pin or hammer.

In a medium saucepan, warm the half-and-half, bittersweet chocolate, milk chocolate, and salt over medium heat, whisking until the chocolates are melted.

Turn off the heat and add the spices. Use an immersion blender to smooth the mixture, or let the mixture cool to room temperature, pour it into a standard blender, and blend until smooth, about 10 seconds. (Never fill a blender more than halfway full with hot liquid as it can create a vortex in the machine and blow the top off, which is hazardous.) Rewarm the mixture before serving.

GUIMAUVES À L'ARMAGNAC
Armagnac Marshmallows

Makes 25 to
36 marshmallows

⅓ cup (80ml)
cold water

1½ tablespoons (15g)
unflavored powdered
gelatin

4 large egg whites,
at room temperature

⅛ teaspoon kosher
or sea salt

6 tablespoons (90ml)
plus 6 teaspoons
Armagnac

1 cup (200g)
granulated sugar

3 tablespoons (45ml)
golden syrup or light
corn syrup

½ teaspoon vanilla
powder or paste, or
pure vanilla extract

1½ cups (180g)
powdered sugar

¼ cup (40g) cornstarch

NOTE

Due to the Armagnac,
these may be on the
damp side. If after a
few days they become
sticky, dust them
with the reserved
powdered sugar
mixture.

I knew I'd fit right in when I discovered that the French love
marshmallows as much as I do. Originally they were made from the
mallow plant, considered to have medicinal properties. Pharmacies
would dispense "medicine" in the form of marshmallows from large
apothecary jars. Like dark chocolate, also considered medicine in
France around the same time, marshmallows weren't taxed, which
certainly added to their popularity.

But marshmallows aren't all that taxing to make at home. Since
these have a shot—actually, a couple of shots—of Armagnac in them,
they'll be softer than other marshmallows, so plan on leaving a little
extra time for them to dry. But you're welcome to float one in your
Chocolat Chaud (page 12) as soon as they're cut, if you just can't wait.

Lightly spray an 8- or 9-inch (20 or 23cm) square cake pan with
nonstick spray. Line the bottom of the pan with a square of
parchment paper and lightly spray the inside of the pan and
the parchment with nonstick spray. Wipe with a paper towel to
sop up any excess oil.

Pour the cold water into a small bowl and sprinkle the gelatin over
the top. Set aside.

Put the egg whites and salt in the bowl of a stand mixer fitted with
the whip attachment.

In a small saucepan with a candy thermometer attached, combine
6 tablespoons of the Armagnac, the granulated sugar, and golden
syrup over medium-high heat. Let the mixture cook, stirring
only as necessary if the sugar needs help incorporating, until the
temperature reaches 225°F (107°C).

Begin beating the egg whites at medium speed. As the temperature
of the syrup climbs toward 245°F (118°C), increase the mixer speed
to high. When the syrup reaches 245°F (118°C) and the egg whites
are stiff and hold their shape, with the mixer running on high speed,
slowly pour half of the syrup into the beaten whites. Pour the syrup
directly into the egg whites between the side of the bowl and the
whip, not directly onto the whip.

continued

Scrape the gelatin from the bowl and add it into the remaining warm syrup in the saucepan, stirring until it's completely dissolved. Slowly pour the syrup-and-gelatin mixture into the egg whites while the mixer is running on high speed.

Continue beating on high speed until the marshmallow mixture is no longer hot, but tepid. Add the remaining 6 teaspoons Armagnac 1 teaspoon at a time, letting each one completely incorporate before adding the next. Add the vanilla and beat until the outside of the bowl feels room temperature.

Using a silicone spatula, scrape the marshmallow mixture into the prepared pan and smooth the top. Let the mixture rest at room temperature, uncovered, for at least 3 hours.

Sift together the powdered sugar and cornstarch into a large bowl. Sift an even layer of the mixture over a large cutting board, and another layer over a baking sheet.

Run a knife around the outside edge of the marshmallows and turn them out onto the sugar-dusted cutting board. Depending on how large you want them, cut 25 or 36 marshmallows using a chef's knife or pizza cutter. (For a cleaner cut, rinse the knife blade clean in hot water after each cut and wipe it dry before making the next cut.)

After cutting the marshmallows, separate them and toss a few at a time in the bowl of powdered sugar mixture so they're well covered. Use your hands to shake off the excess sugar mixture and place the marshmallows on the dusted baking sheet so they're not touching each other. Reserve the leftover powdered sugar mixture (see Note, page 17).

Let the marshmallows dry, uncovered, for at least 8 hours or overnight. After they've dried, toss them again with more of the powdered sugar mixture. Shake off any excess powdered sugar.

Float a marshmallow on top of a cup of *chocolat chaud*, or nibble on them as an adults-only treat. (Another bonus of these marshmallows: You don't have to share them with the kids.) Store in an airtight container at room temperature for up to 5 days.

VARIATION —— Substitute another liquor, such as whiskey, dark rum, calvados, or cognac, for the Armagnac.

INFUSIONS AND TISANES

I avoid correcting visitors to France who are doing their best to speak the language (since even the French sometimes have trouble with their own language). But when people order herbal tea, and the perplexed waiter doesn't have a clue as to what they're talking about, I politely intervene and explain that herbal "tea" doesn't exist in France; it's called *infusion* or *tisane*.

Tea, or *thé*, refers to black tea, which contains *théine* (pronounced *tay-ee-enn*), a caffeinelike stimulant that I've read is the same thing as caffeine (though people in France insist otherwise). The French language is rich in words and meaning, with extremely specific vocabulary (such as *thé* versus *infusion*), so I guess someone figured, Why not add one more word to the mix?

The French drink infusions and tisanes (sometimes served *en sachets*, or in "tea bags," although—of course—they don't use that phrase, because the bags aren't filled with tea) during the day at cafés and in the evening, after dinner. Since tisanes are herb-based, and the French believe strongly that herbs are *bonne pour la santé* (good for one's health) and can do everything from help you sleep to unblock you if you're blocked, they're always eager to partake.

The one exception to the "nonherbal only" rule for *thé*—because there are always exceptions to rules in France—is *thé à la menthe*, fresh mint tea, served in North African cafés and restaurants. I didn't understand why mint tea was referred to as *thé* until I found out that it's brewed with green tea, which contains *théine*, which is the same thing as caffeine, even though it (supposedly) isn't.

If all of this makes you want to sit down with a relaxing cup of tea, or *infusion*, or *tisane*, or *thé à la menthe*, the following instructions and recipes should help.

TISANE

Each makes 6 servings

FRESH SAGE

2 cups (6g) fresh sage leaves with 4 cups (500ml) boiling water

DRIED LEMON VERBENA

Scant 2 cups (1.5g) dried lemon verbena leaves with 4 cups (500ml) boiling water

FRESH MINT LEAVES

2 cups (11g) fresh mint leaves with 4 cups (500ml) boiling water

DRIED CHAMOMILE FLOWERS

¼ cup (2g) dried chamomile flowers with 4 cups (500ml) boiling water

FRESH THYME

20 sprigs of fresh thyme with 4 cups (500ml) boiling water

In all of my time living in France, I've never seen anyone measure anything when making tisane. They just place herbs in a pot, pour boiling water over them, and let them steep until the tisane takes on a delicate green or amber color, usually between 3 and 5 minutes.

Herbs used to make tisane include *verveine* (lemon verbena), *tilleul* (linden), mint, and chamomile flowers, but sometimes more obscure ingredients are used, such as dried cherry stems, which are said to make you slender. (And here I've been eating all these cherries over the years and discarding the stems. If I only knew! Think of all the pastries I passed up. . . .)

Often the herbs are dried, but fresh herbs, such as thyme, lemon verbena, sage, or mint, can be used when available. A little fresh thyme goes a long way, whereas fresh mint can be used more liberally. Be your own judge of how much fresh or dried herbs to use, but keep in mind that tisanes are meant to be on the light side.

It's a ritual at every French dinner party to watch the hostess or host pour a little of the tisane out into the first glass, give it a look, and pour it back into the pot if it's not quite ready. Guests invariably chime in as well, because no one wants to pass up a chance to express their opinion. I like to serve tisanes in clear glasses, which show off the beautiful color the plants lend to them, which of course, people comment on as well.

Infuse the herbs or flowers in the boiling water for 3 to 5 minutes, until the flavor is to your liking. If you prefer a lighter-flavored tisane, infuse the herbs or flowers with 6 cups (.75L) of boiling water.

THÉ À LA MENTHE
Mint Tea

Makes 6 to 8 servings

1 tablespoon green
gunpowder or black
Ceylon tea leaves

6 cups (1.5L)
boiling water

2 cups (80g) fresh
mint leaves and sprigs
(use only the tender
stems), plus more
for garnish

3 tablespoons sugar

Toasted pine nuts,
for garnish (optional)

A typical drink at North African restaurants and salons *du thé* in France is *thé à la menthe* served after dinner to aid digestion, often with a selection of almond- and pistachio-scented pastries. My favorites are the ones from La Bague de Kenza pastry shops in Paris, which are made with top-quality ingredients and go remarkably well with a glass of mint tea as an afternoon break, too.

I use a metal teapot that I found in one of the multicultural food and housewares shops in Belleville. It goes directly on the burner and is made for simmering mint tea. When I bought it, I didn't realize there was a whistle hidden in the handle of the lid, and the first time I used it, it startled the heck out of me when it suddenly went off. (It sounded like an air-raid drill in my kitchen.) Because most people are likely to have a ceramic or porcelain teapot, I've written the instructions here for using a standard teapot with a built-in or removable strainer, and a saucepan.

There is a bit of ceremony in making and serving *thé à la menthe*. Once the tea is finished, the teapot is lifted high above the table as the very hot tea is poured into little glass cups. This bit of showmanship, and distance, helps to cool the tea down so it's drinkable sooner, and adds some attractive foam and bubbles to the surface.

Put the green tea leaves in a teapot. Bring the water to a boil in a saucepan. Pour 1 cup (250ml) of the boiling water over the tea leaves in the teapot and let the tea steep for 30 seconds. Pour the liquid out into a cup and set aside; leave the tea leaves in the pot.

Pour another 1 cup (250ml) of the boiling water over the tea leaves in the teapot. Swirl the leaves around a couple of times, then drain and discard the liquid. (The first steeping is to retain the "character" of the tea, and the second is to remove any bitterness.)

Add the green tea leaves, fresh mint leaves, and sugar to the saucepan with the remaining 4 cups (1L) boiling water and the reserved tea-infused liquid from the first step. Cover, leaving the lid ajar, and

continued

simmer for 10 minutes. After simmering, pour the mixture back into the teapot.

To serve, pour the mint tea into small heatproof glasses. (If your teapot doesn't have a built-in strainer, pour it through a strainer into the glasses.) Garnish each glass with a sprig of fresh mint and a few toasted pine nuts.

VARIATION —— To make *thé à la menthe express*, steep the green tea and fresh mint with the sugar in a teapot for about 5 minutes, or until you're satisfied with the flavor. The taste will be less traditional and not as complex, but the fresh mint flavor will be more prominent than in the classic version.

VIN CHAUD
Hot Mulled Wine

Makes 4 to 6 servings

1 cinnamon stick

4 cardamom pods

4 whole cloves

2 wide strips
orange zest

2 slices fresh ginger

1 bottle (750ml) fruity
red wine, such as
Merlot, Pinot Noir,
or Gamay

¼ cup (80g) honey

¼ cup (60ml) brandy or
eau-de-vie (optional)

In the dark days of winter, there's nothing more inviting, and warming, than a glass of spiced wine. French cafés offer up their own homemade version of it, announced by a hasty scribble on a blackboard hung outside, beckoning those braving the cold to come in and have a glass.

———————

Lightly crush the cinnamon stick, cardamom, and cloves in a mortar and pestle, or in a ziptop freezer bag using a rolling pin or hammer.

Put the spices in a medium nonreactive saucepan along with the orange zest, ginger, wine, honey, and brandy (if using). Warm over medium heat until the wine just starts to bubble. Turn off the heat, cover the pan, and steep for 15 minutes, or until the taste of the spices is to your satisfaction.

Strain out the solids, return the mixture to the pot, and rewarm. Serve in heatproof glasses.

FRAPPÉS

The French don't share America's zeal for tall, icy drinks. That said, where there's coffee, the French have their own versions of coffee-flavored milkshakes, called *frappés*. Frappés, which come in a variety of flavors, are served in modest tumblers in France, rather than supersize pint glasses. I make mine in a cocktail shaker to get them really frothy, but if you don't have one, you can also use a large Mason jar. Or get out the blender and whiz them up in that. There's no debate, though, when it comes to the coffee used in a frappé; it must be espresso. If you don't have an espresso machine, brew up some very strong coffee and add additional powdered coffee or espresso to ramp up the flavor.

CAFÉ FRAPPÉ
Coffee Frappé

Makes 1 serving

3 to 4 shots (3 to 4 ounces/90 to 120ml) espresso, cooled to room temperature

¼ cup (60ml) whole or low-fat milk

¼ cup (60ml) cold water

2 teaspoons sugar

3 ice cubes

Sweetened coffee drinks always feel like a treat to me. Feel free to add more or less sugar to taste. Or leave it out.

———

Put all the ingredients in a cocktail shaker and shake for 30 to 45 seconds. Remove the lid from the shaker and pour the frappé into a chilled glass. (You can include any pieces of ice that remain, or strain them out.) Spoon any *mousse* (foam) left in the shaker on top of the drink.

VARIATION ——— Shake the ingredients with a scoop of chocolate or coffee ice cream, or add a scoop to the finished frappé after pouring it into the glass.

CHOCOLAT FRAPPÉ
Chocolate Frappé

Makes 1 serving

½ cup (125ml) whole or low-fat milk

2 tablespoons unsweetened Dutch-processed cocoa powder

1 tablespoon sugar

3 ice cubes

Whipped cream, for garnish (optional)

Chocolate shavings, for garnish (optional)

If you're going to eat, or in this case drink, chocolate, it should be the best you can get your hands on. For this frappé, I use Dutch-processed cocoa powder, which tends to be ground finer, so it dissolves more readily in drinks than natural cocoa powder would. To keep this frappé French, use Valrhona or Cacao Barry Extra Brute cocoa powder, both of which are stronger in flavor than other cocoa powders. Top this off with a dollop of *crème Chantilly* (whipped cream) and chocolate shavings, if you wish.

Put the milk, cocoa, sugar, and ice cubes in a cocktail shaker and shake for 30 to 45 seconds. Remove the lid from the shaker and pour the frappé into a chilled glass. (You can include any pieces of ice that remain, or strain them out.) Spoon any *mousse* (foam) left in the shaker on top of the *chocolat frappé*. If desired, garnish with whipped cream and chocolate shavings.

VARIATION —— Shake the ingredients with a scoop of chocolate or coffee ice cream, or add a scoop to the finished frappé after pouring it in the glass.

CAFÉ FRAPPÉ GLACÉ IRLANDAIS
Coffee Frappé with Irish Cream Liqueur

Makes 1 serving

1½ ounces Irish cream liqueur, such as Baileys or Kerrygold

1 scoop (2 ounces/55g) vanilla, chocolate, or coffee ice cream

1 shot (1 ounce/30ml) espresso, cooled to room temperature

3 ice cubes

Nothing surprised me more than when I found out that the French love Irish cream liqueur. I learned this when I was gifted a bottle of it in Paris, and then kept it (unopened) on the shelf, not quite sure what to do with it. But every French friend who came to my apartment would stop when they saw it and remark, *"Ah, j'adore le bay-lèze!"* At first, I didn't get what they were talking about when they said *bay-lèze*, just like I didn't understand the French fellow who, when he found out I was American, told me repeatedly that he adored *"iss-okay."* It took me several minutes to figure out that he wasn't telling me "it's okay" over and over again; he was talking about ice hockey.

If you haven't tried *bay-lèze* in a while, I think you'll agree that it's better than just *okay* when shaken up in this frozen frappé.

Put all the ingredients in a cocktail shaker and shake for 30 to 45 seconds. Remove the lid from the shaker and pour the frappé into a chilled glass. (You can include any pieces of ice that remain, or strain them out.)

CITRONNADE AND LIMONADE

While it's not entirely clear who invented lemonade, many trace it back to 1676, when vendors in Paris called the Compagnie de Limonadiers walked the streets carrying tanks of lemonade on their backs, doling out liquid refreshment. The lemon-based beverage they served is considered the world's first soft drink.

Today, you might notice that some cafés in France have signs announcing themselves as a *limonadier*, which has become a term for any beverage vendor, whether they sell lemonade or not. Almost every café in France still carries on the tradition of serving lemon-based drinks, although the nomenclature may be confusing at first. Lemonade without carbonation is called *citronnade*, and is made with lemon juice, water, and sugar. *Limonade* is sparkling lemonade, made with lemon juice, carbonated water, and sugar. Because there are exceptions to everything in France, you may also see *citronnade gazuese* or *citronnade pétillante* used to describe sparkling lemonade.

There are different types and brands of *limonade*. The most widely known, commercially available brands of artisanal French *limonade* are Belvoir, Lorina, and La Mortuacienne, which are available in and outside of France. (Lorina and La Mortuacienne are sold in thick glass bottles closed with wire stoppers.) *Limonade* can also refer to store-bought lemon or lemon-lime soda. So, if you order one at a café, you may get a bottle of soda, such as Sprite, Gini, Pulco, or the unfortunately named Pschitt, which you won't likely ever see for sale in an English-speaking country.

When *limonade* (sparkling lemonade) is mixed with beer, it becomes a Panaché (page 46). If grenadine syrup is added, in addition to the *limonade*, it becomes a Monaco (page 46). You can use one of the above-mentioned brands, or any good-quality lemon or lemon-lime soda, one that notes a high proportion of real lemon juice on the label, for any recipe in this book that calls for *limonade*.

CITRONNADE

Lemonade

Makes 1 quart (1L), about 4 servings

3 cups (750ml) water

⅓ to ½ cup (65 to 100g) sugar

Zest of 2 lemons

1 cup (250ml) freshly squeezed lemon juice

Lemon wedges or wheels, for garnish

I make *citronnade* by the pitcher, especially during the summer. It keeps in the refrigerator for a few days, and it's a relief to have it on hand to beat the heat. If you like your lemonade on the tart side, use the smaller amount of sugar.

Heat the water, sugar, and lemon zest in a medium saucepan over medium heat, stirring, until the sugar is dissolved. Turn off the heat and let the mixture cool to room temperature. Add the lemon juice. Strain into a pitcher and chill thoroughly.

Serve the *citronnade* in tumblers with a handful of ice. Garnish each with a lemon wedge.

CITRON PRESSÉ

One of the most iconic drinks in France is the *citron pressé*. Part of the enjoyment of this drink, made with freshly squeezed lemon juice, is that you get to assemble it yourself at the table. After you place your order, the server will reappear with a tall glass partially filled with fresh lemon juice (about 2 ounces/60ml) and a pitcher of *eau du robinet* (tap water), to add as you wish. A *doseur à sucre* (sugar dispenser) will probably be brought out, or sugar in little packets, so you can temper the drink to your liking. Ice may or may not be offered. If not, ask for a few *glaçons*, and the server will oblige with a separate glass of ice cubes.

CITRONNADE GINGEMBRE-ROMARIN
Ginger-Rosemary Lemonade

Makes 1 serving

One 1-inch (2.5cm) piece of fresh ginger, unpeeled

2 tablespoons freshly squeezed lemon juice

1 tablespoon plus 1 teaspoon rosemary syrup (page 272)

½ cup (125ml) sparkling water

Citrus wheel or wedge, for garnish

Small sprig rosemary, for garnish

He'd probably wince—or if you know him, blush—at the term, but Guy Alexander was an integral part of the "hipster" wave of coffee shops that have spread across Paris and are here to stay. Being half French, half English, Guy took cues from both cultures and opened Café Oberkampf and Café Méricourt, both located in the unabashedly *bobo* 11th arrondissement. While I'm always the least hip person in either of his places, they're still some of my favorite hangouts in Paris. Guy always greets guests with a generous smile, no matter how busy he gets, so it's no surprise that I'm not the only one who likes to spend time in his cafés.

Making me feel especially unhip was when I had to stop drinking coffee for health-related reasons. Thankfully, the *interdiction de café* didn't last long, but it was fortuitous because during that time I discovered Guy's house-made lemonade spiked with a heady dose of ginger and a touch of rosemary. If you can't make it to one of his cafés, drinking this lively libation is the next best thing.

Grate the ginger using a rasp-type grater into a small bowl. Use your hands to squeeze 1 teaspoon of ginger juice into a tumbler. Add the lemon juice and rosemary syrup to the glass, then add the sparkling water. Stir briefly, and add a small handful of ice cubes. Garnish with the citrus wheel and rosemary sprig.

JUSTE UN VERRE

Although I usually make lemonade (Citronnade, page 33) and sparkling lemonade (Limonade, page 36) by the pitcher at home, sometimes I want just a glass. To make a single glass of either one, mix 2 tablespoons simple syrup (page 270) with 3 tablespoons freshly squeezed lemon juice in a tall glass. Add ½ cup (125ml) still or sparkling water, then add ice. Garnish with a lemon wheel or wedge.

LIMONADE
Sparkling Lemonade

Makes 1 quart (1L), about 4 servings

⅓ to ½ cup
(65 to 100g) sugar

Zest of 2 lemons

1 cup (250ml) freshly
squeezed lemon juice

2½ cups (625ml) cold
sparkling water

Lemon wedges or
wheels, for garnish

Shortly after I moved into my current apartment in Paris, an anonymous package arrived holding a sparkling water machine that, oddly, was shaped like a penguin. There was no note to explain who had sent it, and I thought it was a dumb thing to have. That is, until I used it. Since then, I have stopped buying bottled sparkling water, something that I always felt guilty about doing. Bottled water is very popular, but it generates too much plastic for this former, but still very green, Californian. I eventually found out who sent it, and my friends told me they chose the kooky contraption because it used glass bottles, rather than plastic. My penguin and I have been happy together ever since, and he (or she?) fuels my sparkling lemonade *fait maison.*

Due to the carbonation, *limonade maison* is best served shortly after it's made. It can be stored in glass bottles with rubber stoppers and swing-top wires to hold them in place, if you want to keep it longer. As with non-sparkling Citronnade (page 33), if you like your lemonade on the tart side, use the smaller amount of sugar.

Combine the sugar with the zest and ½ cup (125ml) of the lemon juice in a small nonreactive saucepan and heat over medium heat, stirring, just until the sugar is dissolved. Remove the pan from the heat and let the mixture cool to room temperature. Strain into a large pitcher and chill thoroughly.

To serve, add the remaining ½ cup (125ml) lemon juice and the sparkling water to the pitcher. Stir and pour the *limonade* into glasses, adding a handful of ice to each. Garnish each serving with a lemon wedge.

MENTHE À L'EAU ET GRENADINE
Mint and Pomegranate Syrup Drinks

Makes 1 serving

Two drinks that are fixtures of French cafés are the *menthe à l'eau* and the *grenadine*. To be completely honest, I was initially skeptical to try them because of their vivid colors. Romain, my partner, who enjoys one every once in a while, kept telling me that the emerald-tinted *menthe à l'eau* was *très rafraichissante* (very refreshing). But I wasn't entirely convinced.

It reminds me of the first time he tried to get me to try andouillette, a pungent sausage with a filling so coarse that bits and pieces of the actual organs used to make it spill out onto the plate when you cut into it. That, coupled with the smell, keeps me politely declining whenever he offers me a taste.

But I took a sip of his *menthe à l'eau* and had to admit that it *was* very refreshing. Admitting you're wrong doesn't happen very often in France, but Romain didn't gloat about it. (Well, not for very long.) I learned to love the *menthe à l'eau*, as well as the *grenadine*, its rosy cousin made with pomegranate syrup in lieu of mint.

There isn't a fixed recipe for *menthe à l'eau*; you simply mix water and mint syrup in a glass, using five parts cold water to one part mint syrup if using store-bought syrup, or two parts cold water to three parts homemade mint syrup (page 272). For a *grenadine*, use one part homemade grenadine syrup (page 274) to four parts cold water. If using store-bought grenadine syrup, start with one part grenadine to five parts cold water and add more syrup to taste, if desired, since the sweetness of store-bought grenadine syrup varies by brand. Ice is optional, but there's no disagreement that cold water is obligatory. (Both drinks pictured on page 38.)

DIABOLO MENTHE CLASSIQUE
Mint Lemon Soda

Makes 1 serving

2½ tablespoons store-bought green mint syrup

1 cup (250ml) cold store-bought sparkling lemonade, or lemon or lemon-lime soda

Pass by any French café in the afternoon, and you'll see an *arc-en-ciel* (rainbow) of colorful drinks on the tables. One of the most popular is the Diabolo Menthe, made with a generous splash of green mint syrup topped off with sparkling *limonade*, or lemon soda.

In order to make a true Diabolo Menthe, you'll need to use a luminously colored green mint syrup, such as those made by Monin, Teisseire, or Védrenne, or a crème de menthe syrup, as they are sometimes called outside of France, even though they have no alcohol in them. You can find them online or in specialty stores (see Resources, page 283).

———

Pour the mint syrup into a glass. Pour in the lemonade and stir briefly. Add a few cubes of ice, if desired.

VARIATION ——— To make a Diabolo Grenadine, use 2 tablespoons homemade or store-bought grenadine syrup in place of the mint syrup. Add ice, and a squeeze of fresh lemon juice, if desired.

DIABOLO MENTHE FAIT MAISON
Homemade Mint Lemon Soda

Makes 1 serving

¼ cup (60ml) fresh mint syrup (page 272), plus more to taste

2 tablespoons freshly squeezed lemon juice, plus more to taste

About ½ cup (125ml) cold sparkling water

Lemon wheel or wedge, or mint sprig, for garnish

Here's my version of a Diabolo Menthe using homemade mint syrup. The mint syrup can be prepared in advance, and the drink, which won't be as vividly colored as the version that uses store-bought mint syrup, can be put together when the mood strikes.

———

Stir together the mint syrup and lemon juice in a glass. Pour in the sparkling water and stir briefly, then add ice. Taste, and add additional mint syrup or lemon juice, if desired. Garnish with the lemon wheel or mint sprig.

WHERE'S THE ICE?

Visitors to France are often surprised to find that drinks they're used to having served over ice, such as sparkling water, soda, and even iced tea, come without it. If drinks do have ice, there will be just one—maybe two—cubes languishing in the glass, not piled up to the rim.

One reason for the scarcity of *glaçons* is that cafés only have room for very small ice-makers, making ice cubes a rather precious commodity. Another is that business owners like to keep their electric bills down, and ice machines use a lot of energy. But the reason I hear most often for the lack of ice is that very cold drinks can cause a host of unspecified maladies, from "they make your mouth too cold" to "your stomach will freeze" (I'm no doctor, but I think that's impossible).

Drinks like the Diabolo Menthe Classique (page 39) and sparkling lemonade are rarely served with ice. If you do get ice in your drink, rest assured that there won't be enough to require a trip to the emergency room.

So how surprised was I to discover, when I remodeled my kitchen, that my new refrigerator had an ice maker—after ten *glaçon*-free years in France! It took me a while to get used to having ice again, but my Parisian partner took to it right away, and now puts ice in everything he can. Perhaps the ice situation will change in the future. And if it does, the country may have to brace for an outbreak of, well . . . who knows? But for now we're taking our chances and enjoying our drinks well chilled.

BLANC LIMÉ
Lemon-Flavored Wine

Makes 1 serving

3 ounces (90ml)
dry white wine

1 to 2 ounces (30 to
60ml) homemade
Limonade (page 36)
or store-bought lemon
or lemon-lime soda

Lemon wheel,
for garnish

Parisians don't believe in "defiling" wine, which I discovered after receiving disapproving looks in Paris for plopping a few ice cubes in my rosé. I learned to do this in Nice, and have even witnessed Corsicans putting ice in their *vin rouge* in the summer. "It's too hot here *not* to . . ." they told me, before dropping another cube in their glasses of red.

Popular in the southwest of France, *blanc limé* is a glass of white wine topped with sparkling lemonade. As in other drinks that call for sparkling lemonade, lemon or lemon-lime soda is a common substitute in France. Consider the insistence on keeping ice out of wine, but allowing a splash of soda into the glass, another French paradox.

Since personal tastes vary, I recommend that you start with 1 ounce (30ml) of *limonade* per glass, and add more to taste. It's often served very cold, without ice, but you can add a cube or two, if you dare.

Pour the wine and limonade into a wine glass. Stir briefly, add a cube or two of ice, and garnish with the lemon wheel.

BEER

It's easy to imagine everyone in France sitting in cafés sipping wine. But plenty of Frenchmen and women opt for *une bière*. The majority of beer sold in French cafés are *pressions*, full-size draft beers, or half-size *demi-pressions*. The beer in France is quite good, although people don't debate the merits of beer as they do wine. They just drink it. Most people are fine with a *pression* of whatever's on tap, which comes served in whatever type of glass best complements that style of beer.

Draft beer is frequently ordered by color. *Blonde* is the lightest, brewed from barley. *Blanche* is another popular light-flavored beer, brewed with a high percentage of wheat and frequently served with a lemon wheel floating on top. *Ambrée* is more full-bodied than the previous two; its name refers to the reddish hue it takes on due to the color of the malt used, whose flavor also comes through in the finished beer. *Brune* is the darkest of them all, with a rich, malty, almost licoricelike taste, served with a creamy head of foam floating on top.

IPA beers, which are hoppy and bitter, have become popular with young people who are taking a more acute interest in craft beers. Also popular is *bière de garde*, a strong beer typical of brewers from the north of France (close to Belgium), which get their inspiration from home-brewed bottles. There's no absolute definition for this kind of beer, which gives makers more latitude to bottle up whatever they think resembles "homemade," but *bières de garde* are notable for their large brown bottles and caps held in place by wire stoppers. In keeping with

their home-grown roots, some aren't filtered, and they appeal to the French, who are proud of their agricultural traditions.

Mix-ins are common in draft beer served in cafés, and can include fruit or mint syrup, lemon soda, or a shot of a dark *amer*, such as Amer Picon (see page 98), a bitter apéritif distilled from oranges and other botanicals, to make a Picon Bière (page 48). If you're not used to drinking beer with lemonade or *amer* added, you'll find it turns a simple glass of draft beer into something much more interesting and refreshing.

As popular as draft beers are, there are more than a thousand craft breweries in France, and the beer bars popping up in French cities feature artisanal beer on tap, as well as a fine selection of French (and other) handcrafted beers by the bottle, with local favorites invariably included in the lineup.

DECK & DONOHUE BREWERY

Beer doesn't automatically spring to mind when one thinks of a French drink, but if you pass by any café in any city or village in the afternoon (and sometimes earlier), you'll see just as many glasses of draft beer as there are glasses of wine, and often more. The "eat local" movement that swept through other countries didn't get as much notice in France because the French have been eating that way for most of their lives. That also applies to the wine they drink, as people tend to consume wines from their region, with a mix of familiarity and pride. But with the exception of the north of France and Alsace, beer didn't have the same cachet.

Thomas Donohue, a warm Frenchman who was a dedicated home brewer, decided to change all that by turning his hobby into a craft beer business. He teamed up with an American friend from college, Mike Deck, and Deck & Donohue began brewing in 2013. At the time, much of the beer served in France came from large corporations, partly because beer was consumed in draft form in cafés, and small brewers didn't have the capacity to fill and distribute beer kegs. But Thomas and Mike weren't deterred. When I asked Thomas if it was difficult to navigate the notorious French bureaucracy to open a brewery, he shrugged and said that unlike distilling, there are few barriers to brewing and they were able to open without any problems.

Mike eventually returned to the States, and Thomas kept on brewing at the *brasserie* in Montreuil, a scruffy *commune* on the outskirts of Paris that's become popular due to its proximity to the city and its lower rents. (They've since moved to a larger space in Bonneuil.) Thomas says that making beer is more like cooking than making wine, as it involves mixing ingredients and heating them to certain temperatures. Unlike wine, beer doesn't rely on *terroir* (regionality) for its flavors. Still, Deck & Donohue is resolutely French and uses mostly French malt and hops from Alsace, which prove to be just the right blend for their now iconic beer.

Before hops were used for making beer in France, lavender, heather, thyme, and other aromatics went into beer, and Thomas occasionally brews up a batch with a variety of uncommon ingredients as a base. In the spring, he uses *bergamots* (sweet lemons) to flavor beer, and in the fall, he adds pumpkin. (Although like most French cooks, he stays away from pumpkin-spiced anything.) When he stops by Ten Belles, a bakery in Paris that uses heirloom grains for their rustic loaves, he snags any leftover rye bread ends to make *kvass*, a beverage popular in Eastern Europe and Russia made by letting bread ferment with grains. *Was ist Kvass?* is my favorite of their brews.

Freshness is key here, and Thomas wants his beers to be enjoyed within four months of bottling, so you'll have to come to France to have one. Once you taste one, though, you'll be glad you made the trip. While his beers are served at a variety of bars and cafés in France, you can find the full range at Le Saint-Sébastian, a restaurant in Paris owned by his wife, Danielle.

PANACHÉ

Lemon-Flavored Beer

Makes 1 serving

½ cup (125ml) cold beer, such as a pilsner or pale lager

½ to 1 cup (125 to 250ml) homemade Limonade (page 36), lemon soda, or lemon-lime soda

In France, beer is often used as a base for a number of café drinks. If mixing beer with *limonade* (sparkling lemonade) or lemon soda sounds odd to you, then you haven't had a Panaché. It may become your favorite drink of summer.

A typical Panaché is equal amounts of beer—a light one, such as *bière blonde*, a pale lager, or a pilsner—mixed with *limonade* or lemon or lemon-lime soda. The classic 1:1 ratio is fine, but I find that adding two parts *limonade* (or soda) to beer makes an extra-refreshing, and less-intoxicating, drink.

———————

Pour the beer and limonade into a beer glass, using the higher amount of sparkling lemonade for a lighter drink, or the lesser amount if you want the beer to be more prominent. Stir briefly. Add ice if you wish.

MONACO

Lemon Pomegranate–Flavored Beer

Makes 1 serving

1½ tablespoons store-bought or homemade grenadine syrup (page 274)

¾ cup (180ml) cold beer, such as a pilsner or pale lager

⅓ cup (80ml) homemade Limonade (page 36)

While *ambrée* beer is naturally reddish, the vividly red-colored beers that stand out on the tables of sidewalk cafés in France are usually Monacos, a drink that's sometimes referred to as a Tango Panaché, as the ingredients "dance" together in the glass. (Pictured, opposite.)

———————

Pour the grenadine into a beer glass. Add the beer and limonade, and stir briefly.

VARIATION ——— To use store-bought lemon or lemon-lime soda instead of homemade *limonade*, combine 1 tablespoon grenadine, ½ cup (125ml) soda, and 2 teaspoons freshly squeezed lemon juice with the beer as above.

TANGO

Pomegranate-Flavored Beer

Makes 1 serving

2½ to 3 tablespoons store-bought or homemade grenadine syrup (page 274)

1 cup (250ml) cold beer, such as a pilsner or pale lager, plus more to taste

A café barman told me that to make a proper Tango, the beer must be "saturated" with grenadine. If you find it to be too much, add more beer.

———————

Pour the grenadine into a beer glass. Add the beer and stir briefly.

PICON BIÈRE

Beer with Picon

Makes 1 serving

1½ ounces (45ml) Amer Picon

1 cup (250ml) cold beer, such as a pilsner or pale lager

Every café in France has a bottle of Amer Picon, or a similar *amer*, at the bar to add to beer. A mix of botanicals that includes bitter gentian root, quinine, caramel, and orange, Amer Picon isn't considered an extraordinary ingredient in France, but elsewhere, it has achieved cult status because it's not readily available. Sipping a Picon Bière while watching the world go by is a good enough reason to plan a visit to France. And if you bring back a bottle of Amer Picon for your favorite local bartender, they should thank you with a round of free drinks, like a Brooklyn (page 187), since it's an essential ingredient in the cocktail. (If you can't get your hands on a bottle of Amer Picon, check out some of the alternatives on page 99.)

———————

Pour the Amer Picon into a beer glass. Add the beer and stir briefly.

VARIATIONS ——— To make a Cercueil (Coffin), add a dash of store-bought or homemade grenadine syrup (page 274).

To make a Picon Cider, substitute chilled hard apple cider for the beer.

To make a Picon Club, combine 2 tablespoons Amer Picon with ½ cup (125ml) chilled dry white wine.

KIR

White Wine with Black Currant Liqueur

Makes 1 serving

2 teaspoons crème
de cassis

½ cup (125ml) chilled
dry white wine

When it comes to French apéritifs, the Kir is the gateway drink for
many of us. While theoretically, the drinks that follow could be
placed in the Apéritifs chapter (page 55), Kir and its variations are
such iconic café drinks that I decided to put them here.

The clever combination of brisk white wine and black currant
liqueur is named after Félix Kir, who was the mayor of Dijon, the
capital of Burgundy. He heavily promoted the local liqueur, crème
de cassis, which brought the economy of the region back to life
after World War II. The *blanc-cassé* ("broken" white wine), as it
was previously called, was renamed the Kir, and the drink became
a worldwide legend. Aligoté is the classic white wine to use in a
Kir, but any crisp, dry white will work.

Pour the crème de cassis into a wine glass. Add the wine and
stir briefly.

KIR ROYAL

Champagne with Black Currant Liqueur

Makes 1 serving

2 to 3 teaspoons
crème de cassis

Champagne, crémant,
or another dry
sparkling wine

The Kir gets royal status when champagne is used instead of white
wine. If you decide to go with another sparkling wine, I recommend
a crémant de Bourgogne, to keep the drink connected to its
Burgundian roots.

Pour the crème de cassis into a champagne flute. Fill the glass with
champagne and stir briefly.

VARIATION —— To make an Elderflower Royal, substitute
elderflower liqueur or syrup for the crème de cassis. I use homemade
Elderflower Cordial (page 127), but you could also use a store-
bought elderflower liqueur or syrup, such as St-Germain, Giffard, or
Védrenne, for the same effect. Add 1 tablespoon elderflower cordial,
liqueur, or syrup to a flute of champagne or dry sparkling wine.

THE COLORS OF KIR

There are various versions of Kirs (and Kir Royals) in France that use other fruit-flavored syrups, such as Kir Mûre made with *crème de mûres* (blackberry syrup), Kir Ardéchois made with *crème de chataigne* (chestnut syrup), Kir Framboise made with raspberry syrup, Kir Lorrain made with *crème de Mirabelles* (a liqueur made from tiny yellow plums), and Kir Pêche made with peach syrup or RinQuinQuin (page 102), a rosy apéritif from Provence that's flavored with peaches and peach leaves.

I like my Kir on the *légèr* (light) side, so I tend to add a little less crème de cassis than others do. Sweetness and intensity can vary by brand, so add what tastes best to you. A lesser-known apéritif is Kir's cousin, the Communard, which substitutes red wine for the white wine. When the red wine comes from Burgundy, where much of the wine is made from Pinot Noir grapes, it's called a Cardinal.

LA BICYCLETTE

Makes 1 serving

1 ounce (30ml) crème de cassis

2 ounces (60ml) dry vermouth

3 ounces (90ml) champagne, crémant, or another dry sparkling wine

Lemon twist, for garnish

All crèmes de cassis are not created equal. The famed *crème de cassis de Dijon* is held in such high esteem that there's a detailed, four-page document of conditions that must be met for it to be labeled as such. (Crème de cassis is made elsewhere in France, but to be called *crème de cassis de Dijon*, it must be made in Dijon.) Lejay is the original maker of *crème de cassis de Dijon*, and one of only four producers remaining today.

True *crème de cassis de Dijon* must also be made from two types of black currants, including the choice Noir de Bourgogne variety, which is especially rich in flavor, color, and aroma. It's particularly appealing in this drink, La Bicyclette. Legend has it that the apéritif was invented on the Île de Ré, a sunny island off the Atlantic coast of France, a popular vacation spot, where people use bikes to navigate around town and to the beaches.

This light apéritif is adapted from a recipe from Lejay. Its base of black currant liqueur is tempered with dry vermouth and topped off with a festive froth of champagne or sparkling wine. It makes for a lovely ride indeed.

In a large wine glass or footed goblet, mix the crème de cassis and vermouth. Add the champagne and a small handful of ice. Stir briefly, then garnish with the lemon twist.

PLAYING WITH PASTIS

It wasn't until I was deep into a game of *pétanque* (which had become rather contentious, as any game of *boules* tends to get) that I appreciated the true value of pastis. Romain and I spent many weekends in the countryside with his family, and I always chose Romain's father, who was born in Marseille, as my *pétanque* partner. My strategy paid off and, in spite of my being a newcomer to the sport, we usually won. While playing, it's obligatory to have rounds of pastis to fortify your game and cheer you on, or soften the blow in case you lose.

Pastis is the generic name for the anise-based drink, although it's also called *un petit jaune*, a reference to the drink's yellow color when water is added, which causes the anise seed oils in the pastis to go from clear to cloudy.

In cafés, pastis is served in a glass with a pitcher or carafe of cool water alongside. The traditional proportion is one part pastis to five parts water to begin with, then you dilute it with more water as you pass the time. The water not only weakens the pastis so you don't get too blotto but also has another appeal: It allows you to remain in the same café seat for hours, as you nurse that one single glass.

Its popularity boomed when, in 1936, the French were granted paid vacations and many headed to the sunny South of France. While there, people developed a taste for pastis, which they continued to drink when they returned home to keep the spirit and flavor of *le sud* alive. It became trendy to drink pastis everywhere in France, and many regional apéritifs fell out of favor, with some disappearing entirely. According to the

Pernod Ricard website, pastis is currently the eleventh best-selling spirit in the world.

Glasses of pastis are sometimes tinted with colorful syrups. For a Tomate, 2 teaspoons of grenadine are added to the glass. Use almond-flavored orgeat syrup, and it becomes a Mauresque (Moorish). A Bleu is made with blue mint syrup, a Rourou contains a dash of strawberry syrup, and an Indien uses lemon syrup. To make a Perroquet (parrot), mint syrup is added, which turns the drink a splashy green. A Feuille Morte (dead leaf) has both mint and grenadine syrup added, which turns it as brown as a fallen frond. To make your own pastis at home, see page 164.

2 APÉRITIFS

My favorite time of day is when *l'heure de l'apéro* begins.

Not only is the apéritif hour a leisurely period that marks the end of the day, when you can unwind with a drink and a little snack before dinner, it's also the "grace period" when the French get a little leeway before arriving late to a dinner party. This is also when hosts get a few extra (and welcome) minutes to put the finishing touches on the evening. It's not rude to be late for dinner in France . . . in fact, it's considered impolite to show up on time.

Although drinking habits in France have shifted over the years, the ritual of the apéritif remains popular, and I'm fascinated by the diversity of French apéritifs. Many of them began their lives as *vin toniques* or *apéritif toniques*—health tonics to cure whatever ailed you. And with some apéritifs originally containing as much as 65 percent alcohol, it's no wonder people felt better after taking a spoonful (or two)! That said, I've also included recipes for some of my favorite low-alcohol apéritifs, which align with the slow, leisurely way the French like to drink.

The word *apéritif* comes from the Latin *aperire*, or "to open." Bitter flavors are said to stimulate one's appetite before a meal, and to calm your stomach afterward if you ate too much, so many apéritifs lean toward the bitter side. Lillet (see page 78) and vermouth (see page 95) are milder in flavor than gentian-based apéritifs, like Suze and Salers (page 86), which are much more forcefully flavored. Quinine-infused apéritifs, such as Bonal (page 92) and Cap Corse (page 106), are drinkable enough to enjoy on their own, while others, such as Amer Picon (page 98), are added to either wine or beer. Pommeau, a blend of apple juice and calvados,

and Pineau des Charentes, grape juice or must blended with cognac, are refreshingly fruity regional specialties that deserve to be better known outside of France.

Some predinner apéritifs enjoyed in France, however, aren't French at all. White port is a popular light apéritif served before a meal. And single-malt Scotch whisky, whose heavily peated flavor contrasts with the subtlety of flavor normally favored by French palates, is also common. Pierre-Olivier Rousseaux of Dolin (see page 182) told me that interest in American whiskey developed after the two world wars, when the French wanted to show their appreciation. The fondness for whiskey could also be attributed to the French who fraternized with American soldiers, but others say favorable trade tariffs after the wars made drinking imported whiskey especially appealing. That interest in whiskey eventually spread to an appreciation of Irish and Scotch whiskys, and now the French are the number one consumers of whiskey in the world, per capita, with whiskey accounting for nearly 40 percent of all spirit sales in France.

Quentin Chapuis of the Fédération Française de l'Apéritif (see page 91) explained over a drink and a bite to eat at his unofficially designated apéritif bar that, historically, France didn't have a national apéritif because every region has its own spirit or libation based on its particular *terroir*. Interested in learning more about them, I visited distilleries and *caves* (cellars) around France to see how some of the most popular apéritifs are created. I discovered how herbs from the nearby forests were infused to make fortified wine in the French Alps. I sampled spirits made from grape must and gentian roots as they were trickling out of a copper still in

Burgundy (see page 132). And I marveled at barrels of wine left in the open Mediterranean air to intentionally oxidize before it became vermouth (see page 95). I learned a lot from my visits, but the biggest takeaway is my increased appreciation for what's in every bottle I open, after seeing for myself what went into making it. French apéritifs represent a piece of their history, in addition to being expressions of the specific places where they're made. Each bottle contains years, and sometimes centuries, of knowledge, skill, and *savoir-faire*, as well as a clear sense of cultural pride. And I'll toast to that.

AMERICANO

Makes 1 serving

1½ ounces (45ml)
Campari or another
red bitter apéritif

1½ ounces (45ml)
sweet vermouth

1 ounce (30ml)
sparkling water,
plus more to taste

Orange twist,
for garnish

People are sometimes curious to know how French people treat me, assuming that they're not nice to me because I'm from the United States. France and America have deep roots together: Thomas Jefferson helped General Lafayette write the *Déclaration des droits de l'homme et du citoyen* (the French Bill of Rights), and Lafayette fought alongside the American colonists to gain our independence from Britain. Like any long-term relationship, we occasionally have our differences, but we survive our ups and downs and remain allies.

The Americano mirrors our countries' friendship and highlights their differences. An equanimous hint of sweetness in the vermouth tempers any mild bouts of bitterness, and a pour of unbiased bubbles pleases all parties involved.

In a short tumbler or rocks glass, mix the Campari and sweet vermouth. Add the sparkling water (you can add more, depending on how mild you want the drink), stir briefly, then add a small handful of ice. Garnish with the orange twist.

NOT LOST IN TRANSLATION

Translating ideas from English to French or French to English doesn't always work the way people intend it to. (These challenges are especially clear when I see eyebrow-raising signs in Paris for places like the Hor Hotel, or a meal delivery service called Eat Your Box.) But one thing the French do get right is happy hour, which usually isn't just one hour but several, hence all the signs for "Happy Hours" (in English) around town. Because the French do actually drink for hours, starting with a glass of wine or beer, or an apéritif after work, followed by dinner, which never begins before 8 p.m. and is accompanied by wine. Afterward, there's an *infusion* or *tisane* (see page 21), *un café*, or an after-dinner digestif—although many people just pull the cork on another bottle of wine to accompany the conversation, which lasts late into the night. These rituals may explain why apéritifs are more popular in France than cocktails. Tristan Simon, a bartender from Dijon, told me that French people spend a lot of time drinking because they're very social, which is why dinner parties don't end until late in the evening. I'll have to agree: When I go to a dinner party, even on a weeknight, it's rare to find myself in bed before midnight. And they drink for quality, not quantity, which allows them to drink longer. While the French enjoy drinking, they tend to do so in *modération*, so they can prolong the pleasure. That's another thing they get right!

GRAPEFRUIT ROSÉ

Makes 1 serving

1 raspberry, fresh or thawed frozen (optional)

½ cup (125ml) rosé wine

2 teaspoons freshly squeezed lime juice

2 teaspoons grapefruit syrup (page 276) or spiced tangerine syrup (page 275)

When I moved to France, Parisians wouldn't touch rosé. Whenever I offered a glass of rosé, people looked at me as if I were handing them a glass of gasoline. Now, some fifteen-plus years later, French supermarket shelves are crammed with cases of rosé, and one in every three bottles of wine sold in France is a rosé (I probably account for a lot of them). Because I always have plenty of rosé on hand, I've found other uses for it. In this uncomplicated, refreshing rosé-based apéritif, tart lime juice and a *soupçon* of citrus syrup balance the wine. If you want to skip the syrup, add a scant teaspoon of honey or agave nectar in its place. Sometimes I muddle a raspberry in the bottom of the shaker, which adds a little extra fruit flavor and augments the rosy color.

If using, muddle the raspberry in the bottom of a cocktail shaker. Add the rosé, lime juice, and grapefruit syrup to the shaker. Fill the shaker with ice and shake until well chilled. Strain into a chilled coupe or wine glass.

TWINKLE

Makes 1 serving

1 ounce (30ml) vodka

½ ounce (15ml) Elderflower Cordial (page 127) or liqueur

½ cup (125ml) champagne, crémant, or another dry sparkling wine

Thin lemon twist, for garnish

When a friend, who's a well-respected *viticulteur* (winemaker), told me he likes to add a dash of vodka to champagne, I thought he was nuts. (And worried that he might be kicked out of the country.) But then I tried it, and discovered he was right. Adding a small amount of elderflower cordial as well makes the drink even more appealing.

Add the vodka and elderflower cordial to a cocktail shaker. Fill halfway with ice and shake until well chilled. Strain into a chilled champagne flute or coupe glass and top with the champagne. Garnish with the lemon twist.

ADDING SOME SPARKLE

Champagne, of course, is always the best choice. Or is it? They say that champagne is sparkling wine, but not all sparkling wines are champagne—which is true. You'll get no argument from me that champagne is the most festive wine of them all.

To be called champagne, the sparkling wine must come from Champagne and be made using grapes grown in the region, primarily Pinot Noir, Pinot Meunier, and Chardonnay, which go through a process of pressing, blending, and double-fermenting, the first happening a few weeks after the juice is pressed, and the second occurring while the wine is in the bottle. That part of the process is called *méthode champenoise*; during the second fermentation, the yeast deposits sink to the neck of the bottles, which are held in racks, upside down. The bottles are opened, the yeast released, and a small *dosage* of sugar is added to give the wine a touch of sweetness before it's capped with a cork and a wire cage to firmly keep those precious bubbles in place. (There are a few *zéro dosage* champagnes on the market that are very, very dry. But as someone who likes dry champagne, I find they can be almost too dry.)

In France, a number of regions produce crémant, a sparkling wine that's also fermented twice, but isn't bound by the same rules as champagne and can be made from different varieties of grapes. Crémants are made in Alsace, Burgundy, Bordeaux, the Loire, the Savoie, and the Jura. They can't be called champagne, but there are some excellent crémants that give champagne a run for its money. There are also some mediocre ones, so it's worth asking a knowledgeable wine merchant for advice. The upside is that crémants are more attractively priced than champagne, so even if you don't love the one you bought, you aren't so heavily invested in the bottle.

My friend Lauren likes to do a blind tasting at her dinner parties in Paris, where she serves champagne and crémant side by side, to see if people can tell the difference. Many are unable to identify which is the real champagne. Her guests, myself included, aren't professional wine tasters, so if you are one, you might notice the difference. But if you aren't (or even if you are), feel free to pop open a bottle of crémant when the mood for bubbly strikes.

Spain and Italy produce cava and prosecco, respectable sparklers that can vary in quality and sweetness. Prosecco leans toward the fruity side and works particularly well in a spritz-style drink, while cava tends to be less sweet, although this can vary by brand. A number of very good sparkling wines are produced in the United States and England, some by French champagne producers.

In most of my drink recipes, I give several options, as I'm conscious of your budget. In some instances, however, I'm specific when I think champagne will make a noticeable difference in the final result, such as in the Grapefruit Twist (opposite page) and the classic Champagne Cocktail (page 65). If you want to use an alternative to champagne, find one that's dry. Most wine shops carry inexpensive sparkling wines, and a good *caviste* (wine salesperson) should be able to point you in the right direction. But if you want to spring for champagne, you won't get any complaints from me.

FRENCH 75

Makes 1 serving

2 ounces (60ml) gin

1 ounce (30ml) freshly squeezed lemon juice

1 teaspoon simple syrup (page 270)

½ cup (125ml) champagne, crémant, or another dry sparkling wine

Thin lemon twist, for garnish

License plates in France feature a number specific to the region where the car is registered. If you're a passenger in a car with a French person behind the wheel, you'll likely get an earful about drivers from regions outside of theirs.

Paris is number 75, and plates with the number 92 especially vex Parisians because the drivers, who come from a nearby suburb that's quite affluent, tend to drive more prudently, stop for red lights, and slow down for pedestrians.

I don't think this numbering system is why this classic cocktail is called a French 75, but when I'm a passenger in a car with 75 on its license plate, I usually need a drink when we finally come to a stop.

Add the gin, lemon juice, and simple syrup to a cocktail shaker. Fill halfway with ice and shake until well chilled. Strain into a chilled champagne flute or coupe glass. Top with champagne, and garnish with the lemon twist.

GRAPEFRUIT TWIST

Makes 1 serving

1½ ounces (45ml) cognac

1 ounce (30ml) freshly squeezed grapefruit juice

1 teaspoon store-bought or homemade grenadine syrup (page 247)

2 ounces (60ml) champagne

1 dash Angostura aromatic bitters

Thin lemon twist, for garnish

Some drinks that call for sparkling wine work just fine with crémant (see opposite page). But real champagne has an arguably more refined character, and I suggest you open a bottle and use it for this drink. You'll have some left over, but I'm sure you won't have any trouble figuring out what to do with it.

Add the cognac, grapefruit juice, and grenadine to a cocktail shaker. Fill with ice and shake until well chilled. Strain into a chilled champagne flute or coupe glass. Add the champagne and Angostura bitters and stir briefly. Garnish with the lemon twist.

CHAMPAGNE COCKTAIL

Makes 1 serving

1 sugar cube

2 or 3 dashes Angostura aromatic bitters

Champagne

Originally invented as a remedy for stomach troubles, Angostura aromatic bitters have become an essential ingredient in a number of cocktails. The rust-colored bitters are scented with a mix of spices that include clove and cardamom, which have a particular affinity with champagne; a few dashes in a glass of bubbly, along with a little sweetness, add a surprising amount of pizzazz.

Angostura bitters are also notable for their ill-fitting label, which the founder's sons are responsible for. One designed the bottle, and the other designed the label for a competition, without consulting each other. Even though they didn't win, one of the judges told them to keep the label as is, which they wisely did, and it's become a design icon. It's also a warning of how important it is to work together, which the three ingredients in this classic cocktail do so well.

Drop the sugar cube into a chilled champagne flute and saturate it with the Angostura bitters. Fill the glass with champagne and stir briefly.

LEBOVITZ ISLE

Makes 1 serving

1½ ounces (45ml) unsweetened pineapple juice

3 ounces (90ml) champagne, crémant, or other dry sparkling wine

Pineapple spear or a slice of your favorite tropical fruit, and a fresh mint sprig, for garnish

I never thought I'd have a drink named after me. Back in the mid-1990s, a few of us early food bloggers went on a trip together to the Bahamas. None of us had met before, except through our online personas. One was Matt Armendariz, a vibrantly tattooed art director from Los Angeles whose blog photos were so good that it's no surprise he's now a very sought-after food photographer.

In addition to knowing how to hold a camera, Matt is no slouch when it comes to holding a drink either. One breezy island evening, I was taking a break from our usual round of mai tais, yet still in the mood for something tropical, but slightly less boozy. So I asked the bartender for a glass of sparkling wine with pineapple juice. I got some funny looks, but I shared a few sips with my new friends, and by the end of the week, the Lebovitz Isle (named by Matt) was born.

Mix the pineapple juice and champagne together in a chilled champagne flute. Garnish with the pineapple spear and mint sprig.

TANGERINE SPRITZ

Makes 1 serving

2 ounces (60ml)
freshly squeezed
tangerine juice

¾ ounce (22ml) red
bitter apéritif, such as
Dolin, Bruto Americano,
or Campari

About 2 ounces (60ml)
prosecco or another
dry sparkling wine

Half an orange wheel
or a tangerine wedge,
for garnish

I wrote about the spritz on my blog several years before *le Spritz* took over the tables of seemingly every café in France, but I still can't say that I saw it coming. I had taken a trip to Trieste, Italy, near Venice, to learn how to make espresso. In the evening, while doing my best to unwind after a day of drinking a few dozen shots of very strong coffee, I noticed that everyone was sipping from large goblets filled with orange liquid. In my mixed Italian, I asked for "one of those orange drinks, *per favore*," and after my first taste, I was immediately taken with the spritz, too.

I still drink them, although now I reach for a red French bitter, such as Dolin, to provide the bitterness. Dolin is less aggressive than some of the Italian red bitter apéritifs, whose intensity can mask any subtle botanical flavors. I've also become smitten with Bruto Americano, made by St. George Spirits in California, which is naturally colored and keeps the flavors of the roots and spices in the forefront.

Mix the tangerine juice and red bitter apéritif in a stemmed goblet. Fill the glass three-quarters full of ice, then pour in the prosecco. Stir briefly, then garnish with the orange wheel half.

GETTING TO KNOW FRENCH APÉRITIFS

I considered titling this "What's in All Those Bottles Behind the Bar?" or "What Are All Those People Drinking in French Cafés?" since I used to wonder about them, too. I could also call it "How to Make French People Nostalgic," because almost every French person I told that I was writing about French apéritifs recounted a memory of Dubonnet or Suze, either by breaking into song or repeating a clever advertising slogan they remembered from their past. Others recalled a painted sign on the side of a building in their village or advertising in the métro stations. The most memorable of those were the ads for Dubonnet, which featured an angular triptych of a lone gentleman, skeptically eyeing, then drinking, then refilling his glass, accompanied by text that read "Dubo, Dubon, Dubonnet," which translates to "Dubious (Dubo), Good (Dubon)," and then "Dubonnet."

Most French apéritifs start with a base of wine, which is infused with herbs, spices, barks, flowers, citrus peels, roots, and, in some cases, even cocoa beans. The wine is fortified with a dose of stronger alcohol, which helps it keep longer. Still, most apéritifs have a relatively low percentage of alcohol, between 15 and 19 percent, so they fit into the French style of drinking: enjoying it enough to be social, but not enough to make you *beurré*, or drunk.

The bitterness in some of them is what makes them ideal apéritifs, something "to open" the appetite. Another well-known ad, from the 1930s, is a poster for Bonal Gentiane-Quina that's a line drawing of a well-fed man leaning back and gulping from a bottle, as stars float from the bottle, down to his throat, then into his stomach. A large key has been inserted into his belly, with a caption that reads "*Ouvre l'appétit.*"

Others, like Byrrh, were even marketed for parents to give to their children. One ad showed a mother pouring Byrrh into glasses that are happily being gulped down by her kids. Another shows a baby in a high chair lifting a bottle of Byrrh and pouring it into a wine glass.

Many French apéritifs began their lives as distinctly regional drinks, but during recent trips to the United States, I've been surprised to see how many formerly elusive French spirits (ones that I have a hard time finding in France) have become available due to the flourishing interest in cocktails, and French spirits, worldwide. Well-stocked liquor stores have expanded their selection of apéritifs to meet demand. And I've listed a few places that carry a very comprehensive selection online (see Resources, page 283), if you need help finding them. Once you get your hands on a bottle or two, you'll find several ideas about how to use them in this chapter and in chapter 4, Cocktails. But any of them can be enjoyed on their own, with a few cubes of ice and perhaps a dash of sparkling or tonic water, finished with a twist of lemon or orange, for an easy and light way to open your *appétit.*

BYRRH

This curiously named apéritif doesn't contain *bière*, as its name might suggest, but at one point, Byrrh was so popular that it commanded half of the world's apéritif market. In anticipation of Byrrh remaining a global leader, the largest oak wine vat in the world was installed in the Byrrh cellars to hold the base for the apéritif.

Byrrh was the invention of two brothers, Simon and Pallade Violet, fabric-sellers in a small French town close to the Spanish border. Looking for something that would bring in additional revenue, they developed a quinine-based health tonic with a base of Spanish wine. It became a hit with locals, but as its popularity grew, local pharmacists didn't appreciate the competition, and the brothers were forced to stop making health claims. Nevertheless, Byrrh's popularity continued to climb, and to keep up with demand, the company installed its own private railroad track so grapes could be delivered directly to their facility.

A contest launched in 1903 further fueled the success of Byrrh, making it an international sensation, and proved the genius of the Violet brothers. The competition offered a financial incentive for artists to create posters for the apéritif. Nearly two thousand entries arrived, ranging from curvilinear Art Nouveau figures extolling the virtues of the *tonique* and *hygiénique* drink, to more forward-thinking designs with angular, strikingly cubist graphics encouraging everyone, from overworked housewives to *les enfants* (yes, kids!), to drink Byrrh. And drink they did: In the 1930s, more than thirty million bottles were sold annually.

While Byrrh doesn't hold the commanding lead in the apéritif market it once did, it's made a comeback thanks to the reissue of Byrrh Grand Quinquina, a re-creation of the original 1873 recipe.

After taking two trains, a local bus, then sprinting the final distance so I didn't miss the last tour, I arrived at the Byrrh production facility in Thuir, not far from the city of Perpignan. Nowadays, apéritifs such as Suze and Dubonnet are made in the same facility, but only Byrrh is open to visitors. In spite of my best efforts, I did not manage to visit the part of the winery that was designed by Gustave Eiffel, but I did get to wander around oak casks with a guide and see their fantastic collection of Byrrh posters. There were also displays of vintage copper stills and bottling equipment, as well as historical figures speaking to us as holograms and explaining the history and process of making Byrrh. At the end, a real person, our guide, offered a tasting before I headed home. Getting lost in the small forest surrounding the buildings where Byrrh is made, I almost missed my bus, which would have made me miss the two trains I had to take afterward to get home. But it might have been worth it, as I could have stayed for one of the cocktail classes they offer at *les caves Byrrh*. So I'll have to go back.

Byrrh makes a very pleasant before-dinner drink at home, over ice with a twist of orange. It also works well in place of sweet red vermouth in other whiskey-based drinks. Since I didn't get to take the cocktail class, I came up with a few Byrrh-based drinks of my own.

ROB BYRROY

Makes 1 serving

2 ounces (60ml)
blended Scotch whisky

1 ounce (30ml) Byrrh
Grand Quinquina

2 dashes orange bitters

Candied amarena cherry
(page 277) or maraschino
cherry, for garnish, plus
¼ to ½ teaspoon of the
cherry syrup from the jar

Use a blended Scotch for this refreshing take on the Rob Roy;
a single-malt would overwhelm the lush, winelike qualities
of the Byrrh.

Add the whisky, Byrrh, orange bitters, and cherry syrup to
a cocktail mixing glass. Fill with ice and stir until well chilled.
Strain into a chilled coupe glass. Garnish with the cherry.

BY'GONE

Makes 1 serving

1 ounce (30ml)
rye whiskey

1 ounce (30ml) Byrrh
Grand Quinquina

1 ounce (30ml)
dry vermouth

Candied amarena
cherry (page 277) or
maraschino cherry,
for garnish

The French are fond of adding apostrophes to English words and
phrases, in addition to sometimes doing so in French (see page 11).
As someone who struggles with French grammar, it's hard to
criticize, but when I see signs for a Sushi'bar or Jazz'club, I wonder
why they've been inserted where they are. You might quibble with
my name for this drink, a mix of grapey Byrrh in tandem with spicy
rye whiskey, fortified with a backup of dry vermouth, but in the
spirit of the French, I took the liberty of inserting an apostrophe
in the title. I hope you don't min'd.

Add the whiskey, Byrrh, and dry vermouth to a cocktail mixing
glass. Fill with ice and stir until well chilled. Strain into a chilled
coupe glass. Garnish with the cherry.

LA DÉCOUVERTE

Makes 1 serving

1½ ounces (45ml) rye or bourbon whiskey

1½ ounces (45ml) Byrrh Grand Quinquina

2 dashes orange bitters or your favorite cocktail bitters

Half an orange wheel, for garnish

My *découverte* (discovery) of rye whiskey was in, of all places, France (see page 184). Although it's popular in North America, spicy rye whiskey still remains elusive in France. When I ask for *whisky de seigle* at a liquor store, most clerks don't even know it exists and I have to head to a specialty spirits merchant (see Bonnes Adresses à Paris, page 279) to get a bottle. This to-the-point cocktail puts the spirited rye on equal footing with the fruity Byrrh. If you prefer bourbon, or if that's what's available, feel free to use it instead. (Pictured, opposite. Recipe for Fontina and Seed Crisps, page 249.)

Add the rye, Byrrh, and bitters to a cocktail mixing glass. Fill with ice and stir until well chilled. Strain into a short tumbler or footed glass. Add 1 large ice cube or a small handful of ice. Garnish with the orange wheel half.

SAINT/SINNER

Makes 1 serving

1½ ounces (45ml) Byrrh Grand Quinquina

1 ounce (30ml) cognac

¼ ounce (8ml) kirsch or another fruit-flavored eau-de-vie

This two-faced cocktail comes from *The Artistry of Mixing Drinks* by Frank Meier, the head bartender at the Ritz Paris from 1921 to 1947, who some say did double-duty as a spy for the resistance against the Nazis during World War II. The cocktail was simply called Byrrh, and was unearthed by spirits writer Jason Wilson. The instructions are equally straightforward. When I Googled the drink, the word *Byrrh* was autocorrected to "beer," and the spirits website I clicked on asked if making a beer-and-cognac-based drink made you a "saint or sinner?" I haven't tried this with beer, but I'm pretty sure mixing it up with Byrrh and just a dash of fruit-flavored kirsch will keep you on the saintly side.

Add the Byrrh, cognac, and kirsch to a cocktail shaker. Fill with ice and shake until well chilled. Strain into a chilled coupe glass.

DUBONNET

Dubonnet was the invention of a Parisian chemist, who developed the quinine-based apéritif in 1846 to fight malaria. At the time, the French government offered incentives to those who could make bitter quinine more palatable to French foreign legion soldiers serving in North Africa. Like Byrrh (see page 70), Dubonnet became popular back home, where it was enjoyed as an apéritif.

Nowadays Dubonnet is best known in France for its catchy advertising slogans and faded signs painted on the sides of buildings, which you still might come across in villages while driving through the French countryside. But across the channel, it's said to be Queen Elizabeth II's libation of choice, mixed with gin, before lunch. And in a note from the queen's mother, which fetched close to $22,000 at auction, she stated her intention to bring "two *small* bottles of Dubonnet and gin . . . in case it is needed" to an outing. Affection for the apéritif seems to run in the family. And I can't say I blame her for bringing her own. I had a lot of trouble tracking down a bottle in Paris, but eventually found one at Les Caves du Roy (see page 281). It was on the highest shelf, proving demand has diminished over the years.

Dubonnet enjoyed some popularity during its time in America, then began a similar decline there as well. As tastes changed over the years, the makers tweaked the formula and in an attempt to keep it *au courant*, a 1972 television ad had Tom Selleck pouring a glass for Farrah Fawcett, while she remarked that "some guys still think it's a drink for little old ladies." But Farrah's endorsement wasn't enough, and eventually it faded away in the United States, too.

Thankfully, Heaven Hill, a Kentucky distillery known for its whiskeys, recently reformulated Dubonnet to be closer to the original, using a light Muscat wine as a base, which lets the quinine come forward. They've also added black currants and tea to the mix, reinforcing the tannins, as well as green coffee beans, cinnamon, and chamomile.

Both the French and American versions of Dubonnet are nonchallenging apéritifs, agreeable served over ice, with or without a splash of sparkling water. Although it's now made by a whiskey-maker, Dubonnet works especially well with gin in cocktails. And even if you're not a queen, sipping on a Reine Rouge (page 76) just might make you feel like one.

REINE ROUGE

Makes 1 serving

2 ounces (60ml)
Dubonnet rouge

1 ounce (30ml)
London dry gin

Lemon twist,
for garnish

This drink, said to be a favorite of *la reine d'angleterre*, more affectionately known as the Queen Mum, demands lots of ice. So don't skimp!

Add the Dubonnet and gin to a short tumbler. Fill the glass three-quarters full with ice and stir briefly. Garnish with the lemon twist.

VARIATION —— For an "up" version of this drink, add the Dubonnet and gin to a cocktail mixing glass. Fill with ice and stir until well chilled. Strain into a chilled coupe glass.

L'AUBERGE

Makes 1 serving

1½ ounces (45ml)
Dubonnet rouge

¾ ounce (22ml) kirsch

2 ounces (60ml)
cold sparkling water

Candied amarena
cherry (page 277) and
an orange or lemon
twist, for garnish

I discovered this drink in *The Auberge of the Flowering Hearth* by Roy Andries de Groot (see page 198), the story of a charming *auberge* (inn) nestled in the French Alps, where two women created magical meals for guests. Like most dinners in France, their menus began with an apéritif, then continued long into the night. One such apéritif was a glass of Dubonnet with an equal amount of kirsch.

I refashioned the drink because I don't know how anyone could have made it through one of their multicourse dinners, which included a different wine pairing with each course, after downing all of that kirsch. If you want to relive the good old days, you're welcome to double the amount of kirsch, but if you want to make it through a meal, I'd stick to the proportions here.

Mix the Dubonnet and kirsch together in a short tumbler or rocks glass. Add the sparkling water and a small handful of ice. Garnish with the cherry and citrus twist.

SOMETHING GOOD

Makes 1 serving

2 ounces (60ml) gin

½ ounce (15ml) Grand Marnier or Cointreau

½ ounce (15ml) Dubonnet rouge

One of the things that makes France such a great place for food shopping is that there are specialty stores for everything: cheese, meat, bread, pastries, and fruits and vegetables. It pays to be on good terms with everyone who works in them, so that they'll rifle through the basket for the crispest baguette, and again so you don't get home to find a mushy tomato hiding in the bottom of your bag.

But anyone who's lived in France for any amount of time knows the most important person in your life is your pharmacist. Everyone in France is on rather intimate terms with theirs. Mine has asked me to remove my shirt in his pharmacy, in front of everyone, to check out a rash on my back. He's also confided in me which of the "male enhancement products" that he carries really work. (Even though I've never asked.)

Du bon in French refers to "something good," and is also part of Joseph Dubonnet's name, the Parisian pharmacist and wine merchant who invented Dubonnet. I like the idea of him combining his two talents to make a fortified wine, but I'm not keen on taking any clothes off at my local spirits shop, so I'll stick with this cocktail . . . keeping my medical counsel and mixology separate.

Add the gin, Grand Marnier, and Dubonnet to a cocktail mixing glass. Fill with ice and stir until well chilled. Strain into a chilled coupe glass.

LILLET

Lillet was the first French apéritif that I fell for. I had never had an aromatised wine before and was caught off guard by how sophisticated what I was drinking tasted. That shouldn't have come as a surprise; the same Sémillon grapes used for making Sauternes, considered one of the best (and most expensive) wines in the world, are used to make Lillet.

Yet there's nothing aloof about this appealing mix of sweet and sour oranges, spices, and quinine bark infused in wine, bolstered with just the right amount of fruit brandy to reinforce the citrus flavor. White and red Lillet are mellowed in oak barrels for up to one year, but the rosé version (introduced in 2011) gets bottled right away, retaining its youthful vigor. A special Lillet *réserve* is aged in smaller oak barrels for longer, which makes the flavors a little less pronounced and more homogenous, but my allegiance remains with the original.

Because Lillet is so popular in the States, Americans are always surprised that few people in France know it. Lillet is considered a local apéritif, consumed mostly in and around Bordeaux, where it originated.

Shortly after I arrived in Paris, I was served a glass of milk (*le lait*, pronounced *leh-lay*) in a café when I attempted to order a glass of Lillet (pronounced *lee-lay*). More recently, I was delighted to see it on a café menu in the Marais, but when the waiter came out, the Lillet was presented in a tiny glass, at room temperature, served as a shot. But you'd be hard-pressed to find a café in Bordeaux, a city that gets blistering hot in the summer, where a majority of locals weren't sitting in the shade, sipping Lillet from large goblets, with a handful of much-appreciated *glaçons* keeping everything cool.

Lillet's popularity in the United States is a result of a decision by the founding family to focus on the U.S. market after the Second World War. Their interests were helped along by the Vesper (opposite page), a favorite cocktail of James Bond. The original version was created when the apéritif was called Kina Lillet, named after the quinine (*kina*) used to flavor it. But as tastes changed, Lillet was revamped in 1985, to focus on the citrus. For those who want a glimpse of the past, Tempus Fugit produces Kina L'Aéro d'Or, a quinine-based apéritif with notes of tart orange marmalade, wormwood (the woody-tasting herb used for making absinthe), and quince. I like both, and you can use Kina L'Aéro d'Or in place of Lillet in recipes, if you wish.

Serve Lillet chilled (*please!*), either without ice or with an ice cube or two, and with a slice of fresh orange.

VESPER

Makes 1 serving

3 ounces (90ml) gin

1 ounce (30ml) vodka

½ ounce (15ml) Lillet blanc or Tempus Fugit Kina L'Aéro d'Or

Lemon twist, for garnish

The Vesper was introduced in 1967 by James Bond in the film *Casino Royale*, which prompted Daniel Craig to order one in the 2006 update of the film. In the reboot, Mr. Craig not only was kind enough to emerge from the ocean wearing a square-cut Speedo-type swimsuit, but was also a sport and ordered a round of Vespers for everyone sitting around the card table with him at the casino. Frankly, I don't know how Mr. Bond kept his poker face (or those abs) while drinking these. But since I don't gamble, and my Speedo-wearing days are over, I treat myself to one every now and then.

Add the gin, vodka, and Lillet to a cocktail mixing glass. Fill with ice and stir until well chilled. (Or you can be like Mr. Bond and shake the drink in a cocktail shaker with ice until well chilled. I'm not tangling with him.) Strain into a chilled coupe glass. Garnish with the lemon twist.

L&T

Makes 1 serving

1½ ounces (45ml) Lillet blanc

3 ounces (90ml) cold tonic water

Half an orange wheel or a slice of cucumber, for garnish

This light summer refresher is easy to pour, and even easier to drink. For best results, use a good brand of tonic water. While tonic water is the classic accompaniment to gin, you'll discover it's an excellent *copain* (friend) with Lillet, too.

Pour the Lillet and tonic water into a large goblet or tumbler. Add a handful of ice cubes and stir briefly. Garnish with the orange wheel half.

LILLET REVIVER

Makes 1 serving

1 ounce (30ml) gin

1 ounce (30ml) Grand
Marnier, Cointreau, or
triple sec

1 ounce (30ml)
Lillet blanc

1 ounce (30ml) freshly
squeezed lemon juice

About ½ teaspoon
Pastis (page 164) or
absinthe

Lemon or orange twist,
for garnish

This drink is also known as a Corpse Reviver No. 2, but I dub it the
Lillet Reviver because it's a good reminder that Lillet isn't just an
apéritif, but also an excellent cocktail ingredient. Keeping a bottle
on hand provides additional motivation for shaking up this classic.

Add the gin, Grand Marnier, Lillet, and lemon juice to a cocktail
shaker. Fill with ice and shake until well chilled. Swirl the pastis
around in a chilled coupe glass and pour out the excess. Strain the
drink into the glass. Garnish with the citrus twist.

CITY OF LIGHT

Makes 1 serving

Half a lemon wheel,
half an orange wheel,
and 2 thin slices of
cucumber, for garnish

1½ ounces (45ml)
dry vermouth

1 ounce (30ml) Lillet
blanc or Vin d'Orange
(page 147)

1 ounce (30ml)
Cointreau

1 ounce (30ml) dry
prosecco or crémant

This cocktail was conceived by Christiaan Röllich, the head bartender
at Lucques restaurant in Los Angeles, who came up with it when the
restaurant hosted a dinner while I was on tour for my book *My Paris
Kitchen*. I packed three events into one hectic day, and I can't tell you
how relieved I was when someone pressed one of these into my hand
as soon as I arrived and said, "Here, drink this."

Christiaan makes his own orange cordial but recommends
Cointreau as a replacement, and Dolin for the vermouth. He also
uses dry prosecco, which you're welcome to try, but if you want
to keep it strictly French, sparkling crémant is another way to go.
(Pictured, opposite.)

Lay the garnishes in the bottom of a footed goblet or large wine
glass. Add the vermouth, Lillet, and Cointreau. Fill the glass two-
thirds full with ice, stir briefly, and top off with the prosecco.

PINEAU DES CHARENTES

More than other French apéritifs, this uniquely regional specialty is an expression of a very specific *terroir*. (See "Other Regional French Apéritifs" on page 85 for examples of similar regional apéritifs.) Pineau des Charentes is made in the Cognac region and comes in red, white, and rosé varieties. It's a blend of local grape juice and cognac that has been aged in oak casks for twelve to eighteen months. (Some versions, called *vieux* and *très vieux*, are aged for five and ten years, respectively.) The flavor relies on a confluence of factors: the variety of grapes used, the soil in which they're grown, the weather, and the *savoir-faire* (know-how) of the people making it. All of these elements affect the final flavor of Pineau des Charentes, an apéritif that leans toward the fruitier side.

Legend has it that the first batch of Pineau des Charentes was made by a winemaker who, in 1589, inadvertently added grape juice to a batch of brandy. Upset by his mistake, he put the oak cask aside; when he needed the barrel a few years later, he opened it up and found the contents to be much better than expected.

Served chilled, either with an ice cube or without, Pineau des Charentes has the same characteristics as a good wine, with a polished grape flavor, a slightly oaky finish, and the bonus of a dash of cognac. It goes down very nicely before any meal.

PINA-PINEAU

Makes 1 serving

2 ounces (60ml) Pineau des Charentes blanc

¾ ounce (22ml) dark rum

2 ounces (60ml) unsweetened pineapple juice

1½ teaspoons freshly squeezed lime juice

8 fresh cilantro leaves, coarsely chopped, plus a few extra for garnish

1 teaspoon rich demerara syrup (page 271)

Sparkling water or dry sparkling wine, for topping (optional)

I thought a Pineau Colada sounded like a fun idea, as the caramel notes of the cognac-based apéritif play well with tropical fruits and dark rum, but, sadly, that name was already taken by a version that used store-bought strawberry syrup. That didn't sound nearly as good as this version I came up with, which I make with homemade demerara syrup. If you decide to finish it with a little sparkling water or wine, increase the amount of rum to 1 ounce (30ml).

Add the Pineau des Charentes, rum, pineapple juice, lime juice, chopped cilantro, and demerara syrup to a cocktail shaker. Fill with ice and shake until well chilled. Strain into a chilled coupe glass. Add a handful of ice and top with a pour of sparkling water, if desired. Garnish with a few cilantro leaves.

APPLE OF MY ŒIL

Makes 1 serving

2¾ ounces (80ml) Pineau des Charentes blanc

1¾ ounces (50ml) cognac

1½ ounces (45ml) unsweetened apple juice

1 teaspoon rich demerara syrup (page 271)

Splash of sparkling apple cider or dry sparkling wine

Tiny pinch of ground cinnamon

There's a misconception that the French don't like cinnamon. They enjoy the flavor but don't add it to recipes by the tablespoon, as Americans do. In France, cinnamon is used as an accent or seasoning, not meant to overwhelm the other ingredients but to enhance them. Like in this cocktail, which calls for the tiniest pinch possible, just enough to heighten the grape and apple flavors.

Add the Pineau des Charentes, cognac, apple juice, and demerara syrup to a cocktail shaker. Fill with ice and shake until well chilled. Strain into a chilled coupe glass. Add the sparkling apple cider and top with the cinnamon.

OTHER REGIONAL FRENCH APÉRITIFS

Similar to Pineau des Charentes, Floc de Gascogne is a blend of Armagnac and grape juice that's also aged in oak, but made in Gascony. In French, *floc* means "splash," but in the Gascon language, it means "bouquet," an apt description of the apéritif's juicy, fruity aroma.

Pommeau de Normandie has a refreshing tart apple flavor and comes from Normandy, a region known for its apples and a highly regarded apple brandy called calvados. It's made by blending two parts apple juice with about one part calvados, then aged for at least a year; the finer ones can be aged for twenty years or longer. Normandy is also famous for its luxuriously unctuous cheeses, such as Camembert, Livarot, and Pont l'Évêque, and Pommeau is often paired with these cheeses after dinner.

Macvin du Jura is the least-known bottle in the bunch. It's produced in the Jura, a region known for excellent white wines that, unfortunately, aren't often seen on wine lists because some have a slightly oxidized flavor, reminiscent of sherry, that people may not expect. To make Macvin du Jura, the juice of late-harvest grapes is mixed with a locally made *marc* (grape brandy). Because the grapes are left to wither on the vine longer than traditional wine grapes, the sugars concentrate, increasing the juice's sweetness. If you're looking for something a little unusual and you can get your hands on a bottle, give Macvin a try. It's a true treat to sip chilled, while nibbling on a slab of Comté, a local mountain cheese made in the same region, or a wedge of tangy blue cheese.

Once opened, most apéritif wines will keep for up to three weeks in the refrigerator. Although they will still be drinkable after a few weeks, the flavors will start to diminish as time goes by.

SUZE AND SALERS

Mention Suze to any French person and you'll almost certainly get the response: *"Ah, la Suze . . . ma grand-mère avait toujours une bouteille dans son placard"* (". . . my grandmother always had a bottle in her cupboard"). Recently, though, the gentian-based apéritif has come out of the cupboard and is back in the spotlight.

French apéritifs Suze and Salers have a bruising bitterness that can challenge the taste buds. The bite comes from gentian root, a common ingredient in many apéritifs, but it's squarely in the forefront in these two. The roots are harvested in the mountains by *gentionaires*. (Yes, there's a specific word for people in France who harvest gentian root.) To uproot the plants, the *gentionaires* use two-pronged iron "devil's forks" weighing between 20 and 40 pounds (about 10 to 20kg) to pry the stubborn, gnarled roots from the soil. The yellow- or blue-blossomed plants are harvested after they've been growing for at least ten years, but many are harvested later, when they're between twenty and fifty years old.

A sunny yellow apéritif with 15 percent alcohol, Suze is sweet enough to balance the bitterness of the gentian, but not so sweet that it's obliterated. It has a minerally roughness and a hint of citrus, and unlike other apéritifs, the main botanical (in this case, gentian root) is infused in alcohol rather than wine, so its taste is clear and precise. This apéritif doesn't mess around.

While Suze has long been a favorite of French grandmothers (and me), modern bartenders have picked up on this apéritif in a big way, taming its bite with spirits such as yellow Chartreuse, Cointreau, or gin. Suze Saveur d'Autrefois is meant to replicate the original apéritif. It's a little higher in alcohol (20 percent) and aged in wood casks for one and a half years. It's drier, with more grassy notes than regular Suze.

Salers claims to be the oldest gentian distillation in France, and it falls decidedly on the less-sweet side, with no coloring added. It also comes in different strengths: 16 percent, 20 percent, and 25 percent alcohol. The latter, which may require a little searching to find, has added spices, citrus peels, and vanilla, and is a surprisingly well-rounded apéritif to sip on its own.

The craft cocktail movement has increased the visibility and availability of Suze and Salers both inside and outside of France. On their own, gentian-based apéritifs are usually diluted with water or ice, or both; you can also add a wedge or wheel of citrus to highlight the fruitiness. Like pastis (see page 52), these are extremely pleasant to sip in warm weather, whether you're a French grandmother or not.

SEAT OF YOUR PANTS

Makes 1 serving

1 ounce (30ml)
crème de cassis

3 ounces (90ml) Suze

Lemon twist, for garnish

Fond de Culotte, which translates to "seat of your pants," is a truly *autrefois* (old-fashioned) café drink in France. Two parts Suze tamed with one part crème de cassis, it's also referred to as a *Suze-cassis*, or *suzecass*. An advertising phrase that once promoted the Fond de Culotte was *"Il ne s'use qu'assis!"* When spoken, *s'use qu'assis* sounds like you're saying *"Suze-cassis,"* but the phrase refers to wearing down the seat of your pants (or maybe not), presumably because you're sitting around drinking Suze. At least this is how a French friend explained it, which, after multiple tries, still confounds me.

This drink is an easy-to-understand introduction to Suze. However, you may want to have a backup pair of trousers nearby while you drink it, in case it does what they say it's going to do.

Mix the crème de cassis and Suze together in a small tumbler. Add 2 or 3 cubes of ice. Garnish with the lemon twist.

TRIPLE MÉNACE

Makes 1 serving

1½ ounces (45ml) gin

1 ounce (30ml)
Lillet blanc

½ ounce (15ml) Suze

Orange or lemon twist,
for garnish

This drink is a triple threat (*ménace*), combining three of my favorite spirits: gin, Lillet, and Suze.

Add the gin, Lillet, and Suze to a cocktail mixing glass. Fill with ice and stir until well chilled. Strain into a tumbler or a rocks glass. Add 1 large ice cube or a small handful of ice. Garnish with the citrus twist.

SUZE & TONIC

Makes 1 serving

1 ounce (30ml) Suze

3 ounces (90ml) cold tonic water

2 lime wedges, or 1 lemon wedge and 1 lime wedge, for garnish

This Gallic take on the gin and tonic swaps in Suze for more thirst-quenching briskness. I enjoy mine with French tonic water, but feel free to use your favorite brand to add sparkle to the drink.

Mix the Suze and tonic water together in a tumbler or Collins glass. Add a handful of ice. Gently squeeze the juice of the lime (and lemon, if using) wedges into the glass, add the rinds, and stir briefly.

VARIATION —— To make a Gentian Fizz, a tropical take on the Suze & Tonic, combine an additional 1 ounce (30ml) Suze and 2 ounces (60ml) unsweetened pineapple juice with the tonic water. Add the ice as above, and garnish with a thin spear of fresh pineapple and a lime wheel.

SUZE IN PARADISE

Makes 1 serving

1½ ounces (45ml) Suze

½ ounce (15ml) crème de framboise or crème de cassis

3 ounces (90ml) freshly squeezed pink grapefruit juice

3 to 4 ounces (90 to 120ml) cold tonic water

Grapefruit, orange, or lemon twist

Tucked in a corner on the rue Paradis is the "headquarters" of the Fédération Française de l'Apéritif (FFA), presided over by cofounder Quentin Chapuis. This *apéro* bar features food and drinks, everything proudly (and officially) made in France. To prove that point, two long rows of Suze bottles crowd shelves stocked with everything from French whiskey to Macvin du Jura (see page 85). This fizzy drink is their version of a spritz, sticking to their mission, with French spirits as its base.

And because apéritifs always taste better when there's something to snack on, there are also jars of red pepper–spiked Basque pâté, socca chips from Nice (be careful with these; once you open the bag, you'll have a hard time not finishing them all), and even dried *insectes pour l'apéritif*. These beetle larvae seasoned with garlic and *fines herbes* may, indeed, be tasty (they are French, after all . . .), but I'll stick with the FFA's well-curated selection of French charcuterie and cheeses, *merci*.

Mix the Suze, crème de framboise, and grapefruit juice in a large footed goblet or wine glass. Add the tonic water and fill the glass with ice. Stir briefly, and garnish with the citrus twist.

VARIATION ——— To make a less-bitter, orange-based Spritz Paradis, combine 1 ounce (30ml) Suze, ¾ ounce (22ml) crème de framboise, and 1¾ ounces (50ml) freshly squeezed orange juice with the tonic water and proceed as above.

BONAL

Bonal was created by Hyppolite Bonal, who had been sent as a young orphan to live with the monks at the Grand Chartreuse monastery in the French Alps, which also happened to be where Chartreuse was being distilled (see page 198). It was a fortuitous start for the young man.

Bonal ended up studying medicine and became the monastery doctor. To treat his brethren, he gathered the same local roots and wild plants the monks were using to make Chartreuse and created a fortified wine that would eventually be called Bonal Gentiane-Quina. Bonal's apéritif contained both gentian and quinine, which are considered helpful for one's digestion. In a country where eating and digestive health are topics of frequent discussion, it's no surprise the fame of his drink grew after it was made available to the public. In addition to being marketed as an aid to digestion, it was also billed as "*L'ami des sportifs*" (the friend of athletes), with posters showing a rugby player catching a winning pass or a boxer delivering the final blow to his opponent, both presumably fueled by Bonal.

Bonal is now made in nearby Chambéry at the Dolin distillery (see page 182), where its tradition is kept alive. It is ruddier in color, and flavor, than apéritifs like Byrrh and Dubonnet, with a taste reminiscent of dried fruits, and additional earthiness from roots and bark. I enjoy it in a short tumbler with a few ice cubes as an apéritif, and sometimes spike it with a splash of hard apple cider. Adding Bonal in place of sweet red vermouth in your favorite cocktail recipe, especially those with whiskey, will give it some extra heartiness. And although the owner of the distillery told me they can't get away with advertising Bonal as a "key" to good health as they once did, I can tell you that serving the following Bonal-based drinks would be the key to a good *apéro* hour.

BLACKBERRY AIGRE-DOUX

Makes 1 serving

2 ounces (60ml) Bonal

1 ounce (30ml) blackberry shrub (page 276)

½ ounce (15ml) store-bought or homemade grenadine syrup (page 247)

Sparkling water

Orange or lemon wheel and fresh blackberries, for garnish

Vinegar is an important ingredient in French cooking, and it's starting to make an appearance in the French cocktail canon as well. There isn't a word in French to describe a shrub—yet. The closest I can get is *aigre-doux*, a reference to something that tastes sweet and tangy at the same time. It's a fitting description of this bracing berry-based apéritif.

Mix the Bonal, blackberry shrub, and grenadine in a short tumbler or Collins glass. Fill the glass three-quarters full of ice, stir briefly, and top with sparkling water. Garnish with the citrus wheel and several blackberries.

BONALGRONI

Makes 1 serving

1 ounce (30ml) London dry gin or Gin de Sapin (page 153)

1 ounce (30ml) Bonal

¾ ounce (22ml) Lillet blanc

4 dashes eucalyptus bitters (optional)

Lemon twist, for garnish

This is a Frenchified take on a Negroni, which some claim is actually a French, or to be more specific, a Corsican drink. In 1980, a newspaper in Corsica claimed that the drink was first mixed by General Pascal Negroni, a Corsican. He either made the drink in Paris, or Senegal (depending on what you read), before going into battle, or to aid his wife's digestion (depending on whom you ask).

The story has raised a few eyebrows and cultural hackles over the years, but this version with Bonal and Lillet puts it squarely in the "Made in France" camp. I adapted the recipe from Hella Bitters, and use a few dashes of their balmy eucalyptus bitters. That inspired me to try this with spruce tip gin, which nicely bolsters the alpine qualities of the Bonal.

Add the gin, Bonal, Lillet, and eucalyptus bitters (if using) to a cocktail mixing glass. Fill with ice and stir until well chilled. Strain into a short tumbler or rocks glass. Add 1 large ice cube or a small handful of ice. Garnish with the lemon twist.

VERMOUTH

Vermouth has a long association with Italy, but the French have their own quite respectable tradition of making vermouth, which should come as no surprise since the Savoy, the birthplace of *vermouth de Chambéry* (see page 182), was once under the auspices of the House of Savoy in Turin, Italy, before it became a part of France. The two most prominent brands of French vermouth are Dolin (see page 182) and Noilly Prat (see page 96), both of which are well-regarded around the globe as premium vermouths. In fact, dry vermouth is also referred to as French vermouth.

The French have been drinking vermouth as an apéritif for years, although you'd be hard-pressed to find bottles of French (dry) vermouth in cafés these days. Sweet red vermouths are more appealing to the French, who enjoy the sweeter, fruitier style of vermouth as an *apéro*, and visitors are surprised when they order *un martini* at a café in France and are served a glass of Martini & Rossi.

Vermouth is an aromatized wine, infused with botanicals such as roots, bark, flowers, herbs, and citrus. It gets its name from one of its ingredients, wormwood; the German word for wormwood is *wermut*, the same plant that provides the flavor in absinthe. Vermouth is a necessary addition to a vast array of cocktails, but if you haven't had vermouth on its own, give it a try. It's an excellent apéritif (especially my homemade version on page 129), and wonderful to sip while idling away an afternoon in a café. Munch on some salted almonds or peanuts while you sip, and you'll have created a very typical French *apéro* hour.

A VISIT TO NOILLY PRAT

I was surprised to find hundreds (or thousands?) of weathered barrels of wine baking in the sun behind the Noilly Prat facility when I arrived. From the entrance, in the unassuming town of Marseillan close to the Mediterranean, it didn't look like the location of one of the world's biggest brands of vermouth. But there they were: rows and rows of battered barrels, left *en plein aire* to re-create the oxidizing effect the elements had on the barrels of wine as they were shipped on boats to Noilly Prat back in the old days.

Noilly Prat was founded by Joseph Noilly, a wine and spirits merchant who gets credit for inventing "French" vermouth, a dry, herbaceous style of vermouth that's different from the fruity, voluptuous Italian vermouths and is frequently used as an ingredient in cocktails. (In the States, dry vermouth is also a pantry staple used to deglaze a skillet or to enrich a sauce.)

The wines used as a base for Noilly Prat vermouths are aged outdoors for up to a year in barrels that were previously used for aging cognac, sherry, or whiskey, and they profit from any residual flavors. Because the barrels are already "broken in," they don't add heavy wooden tannic tastes to the vermouth.

Once the wines are ready, they're brought indoors and infused with a variety of herbs and spices, ranging from chamomile, elderflower, and saffron to vanilla, thistle, and cocoa beans. The maceration of the herbs with the wine lasts about three weeks, and every day the mixtures are hand-stirred with a long metal tool that resembles a scythe in a process called *dodinage*. The room where the vermouth goes through a final marinating in large oak casks is called *le salle des secrets* (the hall of secrets), since the exact formulations are confidential.

Nowhere does French vermouth shine (or matter) more than in a classic, straight-up martini (see opposite page). You want the cocktail to maintain its bracing juniper flavor, but finish with a gentle flourish of herbs that complements, rather than overwhelms, the gin. For the American market, Noilly Prat makes an extra-dry vermouth that is transparent and makes a "neater" martini than their Original dry, which has more pronounced flavors and a slight yellow hue.

But not to worry, they haven't neglected the French market. Noilly Prat makes an amber vermouth flavored with rosebuds, cardamom, and lavender, that leans toward the sweet side, and which they told me is available only at their boutique in Marseillan. (Although I did find it for sale online when I returned home.) The other vermouths are available at the distillery, too, including the Extra Dry, which isn't sold in France; I bought a bottle to slip in my suitcase.

Those who visit the distillery in Marseillan can tour the facility and hit their cocktail bar afterward. The bartender made me a fine Bloody Mary (page 221) with the addition of Noilly Prat vermouth, *bien sûr*, which I sipped as the sun set over the rows of wine casks, listening to the sounds of fishing boats bobbing by the docks and planning my next drink, which would be a martini.

MARTINI

Makes 1 serving

2½ ounces (75ml)
London dry gin

½ ounce (15ml)
dry vermouth

1 dash orange bitters

Lemon twist, for garnish

No drink inspires more controversy than the martini. Some say it's an offshoot of the Martinez cocktail, which is made with red (Italian) vermouth. Others claim that a dry martini means the cocktail is made with dry vermouth, often called French vermouth; it doesn't mean that it contains less vermouth. But what people no longer question is the practice of asking bartenders to "just wave the open vermouth bottle near the glass" rather than actually adding any to the drink.

I know, because I used to be one of those people, but now I concede that a martini needs a certain amount of vermouth to balance the gin. And as much as I love olives, I've also learned that they're better nibbled alongside the drink, rather than in the glass.

Add the gin, vermouth, and bitters to a cocktail mixing glass. Fill with ice and stir until well chilled. Strain into a chilled coupe glass. Garnish with the lemon twist.

POMMES AWAY

Makes 1 serving

1½ ounces (45ml)
calvados

1½ ounces (45ml)
dry vermouth

2½ ounces (75ml)
unsweetened apple
juice, preferably
unfiltered

1 dash spiced bitters
(optional; see headnote)

Slice of dried apple,
for garnish

According to the calendar, the French year begins in January, but in reality, it starts in September, with the *rentrée*. This is similar to the back-to-school period in the U.S., except that people are returning from five- to eleven-week vacations. (No, that second number isn't a typo.) Early one summer, I was invited to a dinner party in Angoulême. Over apéritifs, our host told us that he had finally started his summer vacation. "I just *can't* work once it's June," he said, following this up by saying that he'd start thinking about work . . . sometime in September.

This double-apple drink is for when you've had enough breezy apéritifs and are ready to get back to business with some calvados. If you don't have calvados, try this with cognac, applejack, or good-quality brandy. For a little spice, add a dash of pumpkin bitters from Workhorse Rye, or cinnamon bitters.

Add the calvados, vermouth, apple juice, and bitters (if using) to a cocktail shaker. Fill with ice and shake until chilled. Strain into a stemmed glass. Add a handful of ice. Garnish with the dried apple.

PICON

When I tried to unravel the mystery of Picon *amer*, I didn't plan on taking as deep a dive as I eventually did. There's scant information about modern-day Picon, including the varieties available, and none at all from the manufacturer, whose identity is well cloaked.

Amer Africain, as Picon was originally called, was invented in 1837 by Gaéton Picon, a Frenchman who had distilling experience prior to doing his military service. While stationed in Algeria, Picon contracted malaria and developed the quinine-based tonic to help himself and others fight the disease, adding the flavor of oranges, and sweetening it up to make it more palatable. It was also 78 proof, or 39 percent alcohol, which surely made it more enjoyable for the troops to drink as well.

Soon enough, the beverage began to draw attention outside of Africa. Though Gaéton Picon wasn't interested in entering his drink in any competitions, French government officials entered it anyway, and it was awarded a bronze medal at the 1862 London World's Fair. With that recognition, sales took off, and it became so successful that production was eventually moved to Marseille, where Picon is still made today (as part of the Diageo portfolio of spirits)—although the alcohol percentage has been reduced considerably.

The name of the spirit has changed over the years, from Amer Picon to Picon *amer* to today's versions, Picon Bière, a bitter apéritif meant to be added to beer, and Picon Club, an orange-based apéritif that can be consumed on its own but is often added to white wine. Picon is the best-known *amer* in France; *amer* is the French version of amaro, although French *amers* are far more subdued in bitterness than their Italian and Swiss counterparts. Unlike amaro, Picon Bière isn't consumed on its own; in addition to adding it to beer, it shows up in several classic cocktails, most notably the Brooklyn (page 187). Picon Bière is especially popular in the north of France, where beer is the beverage of choice—no surprise, given the proximity to Belgium.

Picon is not exported to the United States. Over drinks in Paris, Peter Schaf of Tempus Fugit Spirits told me it's because the spirit contains calamus, a flowering plant that's used for medicinal purposes but is banned by the FDA. So it may come as a surprise, then, that a drink called the Picon Punch (page 100) is still very popular in, of all places, Nevada. Invented by Basque Americans when Picon was still available in the United States, Picon Punch is a potent blend of grenadine, brandy, sparkling water, and Picon, and was initially made with the higher-proof version of Amer Picon. Due to the enduring popularity of Picon Punch, a few American-made alternatives to Picon exist. Amer dit Picon, made by Golden Moon Distillery, boasts 78 proof, similar to the original. The Depot, a craft brewery and distillery in Nevada, produces Amer Depot. Torani Amer is another American-made option. (See Resources, page 283, for availability.) The American Picon-style *amers* are somewhat rough around the edges, especially when sipped on their own, but are fine used in cocktails.

In France, one can buy Picon, as well as knockoffs labeled *"amer"* or *"amer bière,"* in any supermarket. And occasionally you'll come across a regional variation, such as the cleverly named Birabelle, an *amer* flavored with tiny yellow Mirabelle plums that's meant to be added to beer. While Picon Bière (as it's currently called in France) isn't available in the United States, Bigallet China-China, a similar bitter made in France, is an excellent substitute, as is French newcomer Sepia Amer, made by Audemus Spirits, which founder Miko Abouaf calls a modern take on the "old spirit" of Picon, with distinct flavors of angelica, oranges, and chicory.

In cocktails, you can also use a less-aggressive Italian amaro, such as Montenegro, CioCiaro, or Ramazzotti. They don't have the same deep orange profile, but adding a dash of orange bitters brings in some orange flavor. Zwack is a Hungarian herbal liqueur that's said to be similar to Picon, although I haven't found a bottle of it in France, but it's worth tracking down . . . if just for the name!

I am holding out hope that, like other French apéritifs, Amer Picon will someday become more widely available outside of France. In the meantime, think of it as another reason to come visit.

FRENCH SECRET

Makes 1 serving

1 ounce (30ml) Amer Picon or another amer (see page 98)

½ ounce (15ml) Cointreau

2 ounces (60ml) cold sparkling water

Orange twist, for garnish

While it's no secret that a good deal of the Amer Picon in France gets used to fortify glasses of beer (see page 48), I'll confide that it also pairs well with Cointreau, an orange-based French triple sec.

———————

Mix the Amer Picon, Cointreau, and sparkling water in a short tumbler or rocks glass. Add a few ice cubes. Garnish with the orange twist.

PICON PUNCH

Makes 1 serving

1½ ounces (45ml) Amer Picon or another amer (page 98)

1 teaspoon store-bought or homemade grenadine syrup (page 247)

2 ounces (60ml) cold sparkling water

½ ounce (15ml) cognac or brandy

Lemon twist, for garnish

Picon is just as popular in France as it is in Nevada (see page 98). To temper the roughness for Americans, I imagine a spoonful of grenadine was added to soften the blow. Later, bartenders also added a pour of cognac, turning this into a proper, and very respectable, cocktail.

———————

Mix the Amer Picon, grenadine, sparkling water, and cognac in a short-stemmed glass (see Note). Add ice cubes, then garnish with the lemon twist.

NOTE

This punch is often served in an Irish coffee glass, a stemmed glass with a curved goblet, such as the "Georgian Irish coffee glass" made by Libbey, which is called a *fizz verre* in French.

DARKER ET STORMIER

Makes 1 serving

2 ounces (60ml) Amer Picon or another amer (see page 98)

1 ounce (30ml) dark rum

½ ounce (15ml) freshly squeezed lemon juice

4 ounces (120ml) cold ginger beer

Lime or lemon wheel, for garnish

Reminiscent of a Dark and Stormy, this version replaces some of the dark rum with the darker, and even more tempestuous, Amer Picon.

Mix the Amer Picon, rum, and lemon juice in a tumbler or Collins glass. Add the ginger beer, then fill the glass with ice. Give the drink a few stirs, then garnish with the citrus wheel.

AMER AVAILABILITY

In the recipes above and elsewhere in this book, the term *Amer Picon* refers to the original apéritif, which you're welcome to use if you can get your hands on a bottle.

Otherwise, my preference is to use Bigallet China-China, which is available in the U.S., or Sepia Amer, if it becomes available outside of France.

RINQUINQUIN

If you're looking for a bottle that captures the spirit of sunny Provence, you won't do better than RinQuinQuin. The name means "invigorating drink" in the Provençal language, and your search for an easygoing apéritif ends here. RinQuinQuin *à la pêche* is a peach-flavored apéritif made by infusing ripe peaches and peach leaves in white wine from the Luberon, and mellowing it in oak casks before bottling. It's on the sweet side, so on its own, RinQuinQuin benefits from a few ice cubes in the glass to cut any cloyiness. Due to its lush flavors, it's a nice after-dinner drink, too, sipped with an almond dessert, such as a frangipane tart baked with berries or stone fruits, or a bowl of lightly sweetened sliced peaches, nectarines, and strawberries.

If you want to make the following drinks and can't find RinQuinQuin, substitute a good-quality crème de pêche or peach schnapps.

RINQUINQUIN RICKEY

Makes 1 serving

1 lime

2 ounces (60ml)
bourbon whiskey

½ ounce (15ml)
RinQuinQuin

Sparkling water

Peach slices, for garnish

This peachy apéritif pairs well with the gently caramelized flavors of bourbon. Lime adds a zesty counterpoint to both. Also feel free to give this a go with a blended scotch in place of the bourbon, which adds a bit of smokiness.

———————

Halve the lime, then slice a wheel from one half and reserve it for garnish. Squeeze the juice from the lime halves into a large tumbler or Collins glass, and drop 1 half into the glass. Add the bourbon and RinQuinQuin, then add ice. Fill the glass almost to the top with sparkling water. Garnish with peach slices and the reserved lime wheel.

CRANBELLE

Makes 1 serving

1 ounce (30ml)
RinQuinQuin

1 ounce (30ml) vodka

2¼ ounces (70ml)
cranberry juice

Peach slice, for garnish

A few raspberries or
strawberry slices,
for garnish

This cocktail was inspired by a recipe that appeared in *Elle à Table*, a French culinary magazine that keeps its finger on the pulse of all things *branchées*, which translates to "plugged-in" or "trendy." While there are quite a few quinoa salads, chia seed *détox* smoothies, and variations on avocado toast in the magazine, the article encouraged French people to drink cocktails that lean toward the bitter side, reasoning that the more of them you drink, the more you'll like them.

This cocktail is made with tart cranberry juice cocktail, which used to be tough to find in France, but is now readily available, perhaps because people took *Elle à Table*'s advice and did, indeed, develope a taste for tartness.

Add the RinQuinQuin, vodka, and cranberry juice to a cocktail shaker. Fill with ice and shake until well chilled. Strain into a short tumbler or rocks glass. Add a handful of ice and garnish with the peach slice and berries.

PEACH SMASH

Makes 1 serving

2 ripe peach slices,
peeled, about
⅓ inch (1cm) thick,
plus 2 peach slices
for garnish

1¼ ounces (40ml)
RinQuinQuin

2 ounces (60ml)
bourbon whiskey

½ teaspoon maraschino
cherry liquid (from
the jar)

Fresh or maraschino
cherry, for garnish

I make this in a shaker to get it really mixed—or smashed—up, but you can also assemble this right in the glass. Make sure to use a very ripe peach.

In a cocktail shaker, muddle the peeled peach slices and RinQuinQuin until the peaches are liquefied. Add the bourbon and cherry liquid. Fill with ice and shake until well chilled.

Open the shaker and strain the mixture through a julep or mesh strainer into a short tumbler or rocks glass. Add a small handful of ice and garnish with the peach slices and cherry.

L'EMBRASSADEUR

Makes 1 serving

2½ ounces (75ml)
RinQuinQuin

1½ ounces (45ml) gin

3 ounces (90ml)
freshly squeezed pink
grapefruit juice

½ ounce (15ml) freshly
squeezed lime juice

1 or 2 dashes
lavender bitters

Sprig of fresh lavender
or rosemary, for garnish

At a flea market in the South of France, I came across a book from the 1970s with a racy cover depicting two brazenly undressed lovers locked in an intimate embrace—while managing to look straight at the camera. When I rejoined my friends at a café (I tend to wander off at flea markets so I can do my scavenging without interruption), I told them about the book I had found, which was called *Les Embrassadeurs*. The title was a take on the word *ambassadeurs*, but because of the protagonists' saucy relationship, they had been dubbed *embrassadeurs*, a liaison of the words *embrassades* (hugs and kisses) and ambassadors.

My friends roared with laughter at the corny name and told me that I absolutely had to go back and buy the book. Of course I did, like a dope, and was quite red-faced when the vendor made a big deal of announcing to everyone within earshot that he had finally found someone to buy the book, drawing stares from everyone, who wanted to see who'd ended up buying it. (Well, that's one village in France I won't be going back to.)

I never did read the book, but when the *grisaille* (gray skies) of Paris in the winter make me long for a trip south where I can be embraced by the warm sun, this liberating libation is the next best thing.

Add the RinQuinQuin, gin, grapefruit juice, lime juice, and lavender bitters to a cocktail shaker. Fill with ice and shake until well chilled. Strain into a chilled coupe glass. Garnish with the lavender.

CAP CORSE

Corsica is famous for more than being the birthplace of Napoléon and its reluctance to being a part of France—a grudge its people have held since it was conquered in the late 1700s. It's also known for its outstanding charcuterie, cheese, and wine. So, of course, I was excited to visit.

While my Parisian partner has no problem driving through the chaotic round-abouts in Paris, the harrowing roads of *la Corse* were another story. I had never seen him so terrified as he was behind the wheel in Corsica. At every curve in the treacherous mountain roads, locals barreled around blind corners, seeming to prefer the lane that was in the path of oncoming traffic. Happily, Corsican rosé and platters of charcuterie were waiting at every destination we visited.

Another happy memory of Corsica is Cap Corse, an apéritif that's been showing up at bars off the island. Bottles of L.N. Mattei Cap Corse note that they are *le seul vrai*, the "only real makers" of Cap Corse. The company is still family owned and produces two versions: white and red. Both have a base of Muscat grapes, which are grown on the island; they are naturally sweet and spicy, and a good backdrop for the other local flavors, which include citron in the white version, and walnut husks, ginger, cocoa, caramel, and Corsican sour oranges in the red.

Both versions are just right for sipping on their own over ice with a twist, although Cap Corse blanc is an intriguing substitute for Lillet blanc (see page 78) in drinks if you're looking for something with a higher quinine profile. I sometimes use Cap Corse rouge in lieu of red vermouth in a Manhattan or a Boulevardier (page 179) for a drier, more bracing cocktail.

CAP CORSE SPRITZ

Makes 1 serving

2 ounces (60ml)
Cap Corse blanc

1½ ounces (45ml)
sparkling water

2 ounces (60ml)
prosecco

2 dashes Angostura
aromatic bitters

Orange wheel,
for garnish

Prosecco is a recent arrival at *cavistes* (wine shops) and grocery stores in France. Prior to the ubiquitous appearance of *le Spritz* on the French café scene, it was a challenge to get your hands on a bottle. (Trust me, I tried.) Now it's everywhere due to the popularity of the Italian import. Because Corsica was once part of Italy, the time seemed right to use a French-made apéritif in a spritz. The quinine in Cap Corse tips this drink further into the *amer* category, which makes it decidedly French (or Corsican, depending on whom you talk to). Don't omit the Angostura bitters, which add a hint of spice and color. (Pictured on page 107, right.)

In a footed goblet, mix the Cap Corse, sparkling water, prosecco, and Angostura bitters. Add a generous handful of ice. Garnish with the orange wheel.

CAP CORSE TONIQUE

Makes 1 serving

2 ounces (60ml)
Cap Corse blanc

4 ounces (120ml)
cold tonic water

Lemon or orange twist
or wedge, for garnish

The quinine-forward flavor of Cap Corse makes a great low-alcohol alternative to a gin and tonic, or as the French call it, *gin tonic*. Time-pressed Parisians often shorten that to *gin toe* (not pronouncing the final "-nic") and leave it at that. So, if you want to feel more French, you're welcome to abbreviate the name of this cocktail to Cap Co To. (Pictured on page 107, left.)

In a tumbler or Collins glass, mix the Cap Corse and tonic water. Fill the glass with ice and garnish with the citrus twist.

OPPOSITE ENDS

Makes 1 serving

1 ounce (30ml)
Cap Corse rouge

1 ounce (30ml) calvados

Splash of apple juice

2 dashes cinnamon
bitters or apple
blossom bitters

1½ to 2 ounces (45 to
60ml) sparkling water

Apple slice or orange
twist, for garnish

Cap Corse and calvados are made on the opposite ends of France, in Corsica and Normandy respectively, but they meet in the middle in this drink, where the caramel-chocolate notes of Cap Corse rouge strike a comfortable balance with the clear apple flavor of calvados. (Pictured on page 107, middle.)

In a short tumbler or rocks glass, mix the Cap Corse and calvados. Add a small handful of ice, the apple juice, and the bitters. Add the sparkling water and stir briefly. Garnish with the apple slice.

MAURIN QUINA

This *oublié* (forgotten) apéritif was brought to my attention by a French friend who shares the same name as this unique spirit from the Auvergne. Monsieur Maurin, who also comes from the same region, insisted I try his namesake drink, which is infused with wild cherries, quinine, cherry brandy, and bitter almonds, a combination of flavors that hits you in the nose before you even take a sip.

Even more famous than its flavor is the Maurin Quina label, which sports a green devil and leads some people to think it's absinthe. (Absinthe is associated with the "green fairy," which you supposedly see when you've drunk too much of it. So far, that hasn't happened with either beverage, one benefit of always drinking responsibly.)

GINGER DEVIL

Makes 1 serving

1 ounce (30ml) Maurin Quina

½ ounce (15ml) Campari

1 ounce (30ml) freshly squeezed lime juice

¾ ounce (22ml) rich fresh ginger syrup (page 275)

Sparkling water

Lime wedge and slice of candied ginger, for garnish

This spiced, tangy Collins recipe was created by Zac Overman, co-owner and bar manager of L'Oursin bar and restaurant in Seattle. The restaurant and bar he presides over is an *homage* to France and French cuisine, presented with a glint of appreciative humor and a cocktail list where you'll find a few unexpected, and lesser known, French spirits. In this drink, several seemingly disparate ingredients come together to taste like the most delicious pink lemonade of your life.

Add the Maurin Quina, Campari, lime juice, and ginger syrup to a cocktail shaker. Fill with ice and shake until well chilled. Strain into a tumbler or Collins glass, top with sparkling water, then fill with ice. Garnish with the lime wedge and candied ginger.

FERNET-VALLET

This Franco-Mexican *amer* is the Mexican counterpart to Fernet-Branca, but it never gained the same notoriety. Scientist Henri Vallet emigrated across the ocean to Mexico when France was trying to colonize the country. The colonization didn't quite go as planned, which may explain the dearth of Mexican food in France. Yet Vallet stayed on and began distilling in the 1860s. His very dark bitter is labeled an "aperitivo-liqueur" in both languages, with not much fanfare save for the flourish of his signature scribbled below the label of authenticity.

With forceful notes of clove, mint, gentian root, and cardamom, Fernet-Vallet is a bracing mouthful. While it's admittedly a tough sell on its own, it works well in a cocktail, such as a Toronto (page 184). It also goes surprisingly well with Coke (see page 113).

FERNET AFFOGATO

Makes 1 serving

1 good-size scoop vanilla or coffee ice cream

1 ounce (30ml) espresso

½ ounce (15ml) Fernet-Vallet or Fernet-Branca

One of my favorite desserts is affogato, a scoop of ice cream *submergé* in strong coffee. My friend Brad Thomas Parsons doubled down on the ice cream, with an extra shot of Fernet-Branca in his book *Amaro*, which focuses on Italian *amers*. I've adjusted the proportions and use Fernet-Vallet in lieu of its Italian counterpart, Fernet-Branca, which he often corrects my pronunciation of since in French, the final "t" in Fernet is silent (pronounced *Fer-nay*), whereas in Italian, the "t" is pronounced. But I think you'll agree this is an excellent reason to keep a bottle of Fernet on hand, no matter how you say it.

Put the scoop of ice cream in a deep ice cream dish or short tumbler. Pour the espresso and Fernet over the ice cream.

COKE AND FERNET

Makes 1 serving

1½ ounces (45ml)
Fernet-Vallet or
Fernet-Branca,
plus more to taste

5 ounces (150ml)
cold Coca-Cola

Lemon wedge,
for garnish

When Coca-Cola began to market Coke to the French in 1950, it wasn't an immediate hit. There's a black-and-white photo that appeared in *Life* magazine during that era of a beret-sporting Frenchman spitting out his mouthful of Coke right at the camera. I'm a little skeptical, though, as I wonder what happened to the rest of the Coca-Cola from the three-quarters-empty bottle on the bar next to him?

Gone are the days when *un Coca* ordered at a café marked you as *Américain*. The French drink quite a bit of *Coca*; diet-conscious Parisians even accompany meals with a Coca Light or Coca Zéro nowadays. I'm not a big soda drinker, save for an Orangina every now and then, but once in a while, I give in and have a Coke with lots of ice, sometimes fortified with a shot of bitters.

Mix the Fernet and Coca-Cola in a tumbler. Taste, and add more Fernet if desired. Add a handful of ice, then garnish with the lemon wedge.

WINE

No drink is more associated with France than wine. Wine is *everywhere*, and while visitors are astounded by the dairy aisle in French supermarkets (which is rather impressive), the wine and spirits selection is even larger. From the wine-laden aisles at the stadium-size *hypermarchés*, to the haphazard shelves of *les épiceries* (corner stores), you'll always find a surprisingly generous and varied selection of wines from every corner of the country. Walk into the humblest of cafés at lunch- or dinnertime, and the tables are already set with wine glasses, with a blackboard listing several *vins de mois* (wines of the month), and a separate menu with additional white, red, rosé, and sparkling wine selections.

I'm not a wine expert, but neither is everybody else in France. While most French people can reel off names like Bordeaux or Burgundy (which you can probably do, too), many don't know that much about what's in the bottle, or even what's on the label. That's not meant to be a swipe at anyone, but just because someone is from a country doesn't mean they're an authority on the food and wine. To most people in France, wine isn't a sacred beverage; it's an everyday drink, something you enjoy with a meal.

Until a few years ago, if you mentioned Pinot Noir or Chardonnay in France, few people would have known what kind of wine you were talking about. But if you said *vin rouge de Bourgogne* (Burgundy) or Chablis, which are made with the two aforementioned grape varieties, respectively, they'd know. French wines are based on *terroir*, and are expressions of a particular climate and soil

of a geographical area. French law dictates what kind of grapes can be grown in each winemaking area, hence their classification by location (*appellation*), rather than by variety of grape. Recently, however, some French winemakers have begun putting the *cépage* (grape variety) on the label. This has not only helped with overseas sales, but it also reflects a generational shift to more globalized drinkers in France, who've become familiar with wines from other countries and recognize a *cépage*, as opposed to an *appellation*.

As much as the French love wine, consumption has dipped in the last few decades, from a high of 53 liters (nearly 71 bottles) per person per year in 2003 to 40 liters (about 53 bottles) nowadays. Some of the decline has to do with a change in laws, which sharply decreased the amount of alcohol you can legally consume before drinking and driving. Another has been the *loi Évin*, a law enacted in 1991 that curtailed wine advertising and put strict limits on how wine can be depicted in the media. Wine can no longer be advertised on television, and it is forbidden to show people enjoying themselves while drinking wine in print ads or on billboards in the métro and transit stations. Wine ads also have to carry a prominent warning about the dangers of drinking.

In addition, encouraged by heavy marketing campaigns from multinational liquor companies, young people have become more excited about mojitos and spritzes, and smaller winemakers don't have the budgets to make lingering over glasses of *vin rouge*

look nearly as exciting or trendy. Or they drink beer, an economical choice for cash-strapped twentysomethings; a *pinte* of beer (sometimes called a *sérieux*, a reference to its "serious" size) costs the same as a glass of wine, but is three times larger.

One wine that has bucked the trend is rosé, which wasn't popular when I arrived in France. No one in Paris would touch it. Only when I went to the South of France could I order a glass of rosé without receiving a look of mild disdain from those around me for indulging in a suspiciously pink glass of wine. Then, suddenly, rosé became all the rage, and now, come June, supermarkets start piling cases of it in the middle of the aisles, not even bothering to put it on shelves. The windows of wine shops become a rainbow of rosé bottles, in every hue of crimson, red, rose, orange, and pink. Even

stodgy winemaking regions, such as Cahors and Burgundy, have begun producing rosé. While I like to think that my persistence was responsible for all of this, all I know is that rosé now outpaces white wine in sales; a report by the International Organization of Vine and Wine and the Provence Wine Council noted that nearly one in every three bottles of wine sold in France is rosé. Some years winemakers have even announced that there might not be enough rosé to meet demand. A headline in *Les Echos* newspaper wondered, *"Y aura-t-il assez de rosé cet été?"* ("Will there be enough rosé this summer?"), alarming readers of a possible shortage. In other words: Stock up!

Vins naturels have also taken off in France, with the *bobo* quarters of Paris

continued

being ground *zéro* for these quirky wines. There are no defined rules for what makes a *vin natural* "natural." Broadly speaking, the wines are in as close to their natural state as possible. There are few or no chemicals used, no industrial yeast, and little to no sulfides added, and they are sometimes unfiltered. Since sulfides inhibit oxidation, the wines can develop flavors that aren't to everyone's taste, but some natural wine fans overlook what would be considered flaws in regular wine in favor of natural wine's other attributes. (Curiously, at many natural wine bars, a majority of the people quaffing the chemical-free wines accompany them with a cigarette.) One of the things I enjoy about natural wines *are* the irregularities and imperfections, which give me a feel for how the wine is made. They taste alive, although I'll admit that I've had some that taste like a work in progress.

Pét-nats, or *pétillants naturels*, are natural sparkling wines that are bottled before the fermentation is finished, a process called *méthode ancestrale*. Some of the wines are cloudy, and it's not unusual to find sediment lingering in the bottom of the bottle. I find these wines a little more interesting than standard natural wines, as any irregularities in the wine are mitigated by the effervescence.

And frankly, any excuse to drink sparkling wine, natural or otherwise, works for me.

In the end, a good wine is one that you like—not what wine people (or I) say you're supposed to like. The only way to learn more about wine, and what you like, is to try as many varieties as possible. Fortunately, in France, there are plenty to choose from. Wine bars abound, and some even specialize in natural wines, so you can try them by the glass, or the bottle, and form your own opinions.

IN FRANCE, THE GLASS IS ALWAYS HALF FULL

The French penchant for *modération* means glasses are never poured full. Part of this approach is practical; pouring wines just to the widest part of the glass allows more oxygen to get in touch with the wine, which helps it breathe. (Water glasses are never filled to the brim either.) The other reason for this practice can be summed up by words I hear frequently: "*C'est plus jolie*"— a wine (or water) glass is prettier when it's only halfway full. But don't worry; if you're in France, you're never far from a bottle of wine, so there's always more to refill your glass with. Just no more than halfway.

3 LIQUEURS & INFUSIONS

The best way to truly understand France is to travel around the country. Paris is the big, bustling capital, but *la France profonde* is where you'll experience a profoundly different slice of French life.

I've woken up alarmingly early to meet cheese makers in the Jura and shared a breakfast of rustic bread topped with sticky (and stinky) cancoillotte, dipping it in our coffee at 6 a.m. (They'd already been working for hours, so to them, it was their midmorning snack.) I've savored fresh oysters in Brittany, on the shores of the frigid waters where they'd been harvested, downing them with a glass of minerally Muscadet. And on my first day of class at pastry school near Versailles, when we sat down for our morning break at 10 a.m. to sample the croissants, brioches, and *pains au chocolat* that had just come out of the oven, our chef instructor brought out a bottle of cold Aligoté wine and poured a round of glasses for us to accompany the pastries. He insisted that it was very agreeable to have a glass at that hour, which surprised me at first, but I had to admit, he was right. (Although it's not a habit I've kept up.)

All of these great food memories involved something to drink alongside. In addition to wine and coffee, there have been apéritifs, beers, whiskeys, eaux-de-vie, ciders, brandies, and other distillations. But what has interested me the most are the local infusions—many of which never leave the region—that were offered before or after a meal, or that I came across at local markets or wine shops.

In the past, infusions, crèmes, liqueurs, and distillations were opportunities to use up a bumper crop of fruit or preserve the harvest. A crock of Confiture de Vieux Garçon (page 143) could provide bachelors with a spirited dessert to last them through the long winter. Wild cherries found their way into Guignolet (page 124), and infusing elderflowers made a fragrant cordial (see page 127) that turned a glass of sparkling water into an explosion of summer flavor. Many are now made commercially. But you don't need an overload of fruit to make an infusion. You can turn a bag of fresh fruits or berries, a bunch of herbs, or a handful of roasted cocoa beans into homemade liqueurs, crèmes, cordials, or aromatized wines.

A few of the ingredients in the recipes that follow might seem unusual, but I include them because they're popular in France and can be tracked down. You may not find green walnuts (see page 163), sour Seville oranges (see page 147), or spruce tips (see page 149) at your local supermarket (don't worry; they're not in French supermarkets either), but if you're fortunate to live where they are

available, you'll be rewarded with several bottles, and seasons, of delicious drinking. See the Resources on page 283 to find some ingredients online.

Before you get started, here are a few tips for making homemade infusions and liqueurs:

- - Start with fresh, unblemished fruit. Fruits or berries with brown spots or deep bruises should be avoided. All fruits, berries, and other ingredients should be washed, cleaned, and dried before using. It's preferable to use organic or unsprayed fruits and berries for infusions. Farmers' markets are the best places to find fruits and other ingredients, but many grocery stores now also carry fruit that hasn't been sprayed.

- - Bottles and jars should be very clean. You can run wide-mouth jars through the dishwasher, or fill heatproof jars and bottles with boiling water, let them stand for five to ten minutes, then drain and let them air-dry afterward.

- - Choose the right base for your infusion. The French use eaux-de-vie (clear distillations of fruit), which come in a wide variety of flavors and prices, as a base for many liqueurs and infusions. Pear William and kirsch are the most commonly available varieties, and they work well with any recipe in this chapter that calls for eau-de-vie. I've listed several American brands in the Resources on page 283. Since eau-de-vie can be expensive, you can also use vodka as a lower-priced alternative.

- I tested inexpensive vodka alongside moderately priced vodka, and the vodka that cost just a few bucks more resulted in a better-tasting infusion. You don't have to buy the most expensive bottle on the shelf, but do choose a brand that you'd stock in your bar. The exceptions are recipes such as the Vin d'Orange on page 147 and Vin de Noix on page 163, in which a small quantity of higher-proof liquor is used primarily to boost the alcohol level. In these cases, you can go with the inexpensive stuff.

- The higher the proof, the better. When using rum, or other alcohols, higher-proof versions are best for extracting flavors. Standard rum is 80 proof (40 percent alcohol by volume, or ABV), but if you use one closer to 100 proof (50 percent ABV), that'll do a better job of pulling out flavors. For the Confiture de Vieux Garçon (page 143), it's obligatory to use rum that's at least 100 proof to prevent the fruit from fermenting.

- I go easy on the sugar. Traditional French recipes for liqueurs and crèmes can be very, very sweet. Since my preference leans toward the less-sweet side for libations, my recipes will result in liqueurs and infusions that are a lot less cloying than what you buy. (If you like things sweeter, see "Crèmes and Liqueurs," opposite page.)

- Use raw granulated sugar when called for. Raw sugars come in various guises, from turbinado to demerara, which have large, coarse crystals that don't dissolve easily. Raw granulated sugar has small crystals and a light amber color and lends a subtle hint of natural toffee flavor, which is what I recommend. Brand names to look for include Florida Crystals and Kirkland (at Costco). You can usually find it in well-stocked supermarkets, natural food stores, or online. If you can't get your hands on raw granulated sugar, regular white granulated sugar can be used.

- Feel free to scale the recipes up or down. All of the recipes can be cut in half, or doubled or tripled. A few recipes make a small amount, while others yield several bottles. I've designed particular recipes this way because, for example, during sour orange season, you'll probably want to take advantage of their availability and make a few bottles of Vin d'Orange (page 147), but the recipe for Crème de Cacao (page 156), which uses cocoa nibs and can be made any time of the year, makes less.

- Store your stash in a cool, dark place. Almost every home and apartment in France, including those in Paris, has an underground *cave* (cellar), which is the perfect place to store homemade infusions. Temperatures can vary, but it's usually somewhere between 50°F and 60°F (10°C and 16°C). This is the approximate temperature range when a recipe directs you to store a maceration or infusion in a "cool, dark place." If you don't have a *cave* or basement, they can be stored in the refrigerator or in a cool, dark spot in your house, away from heaters. I store low-alcohol infusions, like Vin d'Orange (page 147) and Vin de Sureau (page 128), in the refrigerator after they're bottled, to preserve their bright flavors.

•• Drink up! Infusions made with higher-proof alcohol, such as gin or vodka, will keep for at least a year, although I've kept some for several years with no problem. Wine-based infusions will also keep for up to a year, but purists claim they should be drunk within a few months. Some infusions are better after they mellow for a while, which I note at the end of the recipe, but they could certainly be enjoyed sooner, if you just can't wait.

CRÈMES AND LIQUEURS

In France, crèmes and liqueurs are often enjoyed as apéritifs, but sometimes they're consumed as after-dinner drinks, so they can contain a fairly substantial amount of sugar. Technically, crèmes don't contain any cream, but they are sweetened, and must have 250 grams of sugar per liter (1¼ cups per quart). One exception is crème de cassis, which can contain up to 400 grams of sugar per liter (2 cups per quart). Liqueurs are less sweet, and must contain a minimum of 100 grams of sugar per liter (½ cup per quart). Since I'm not bottling up and selling the fruits of my labors, I took some liberties and generally use the term *liqueur* in this book, which makes more sense in English.

If you'd like to add additional sugar to your infusion, feel free to do so, but start out with the amount called for. Once the infusion is finished or nearly finished, you can add more sugar to taste. If so, you'll want to give the infusion a little more time for the sugar to dissolve before drinking it.

GUIGNOLET
Cherry Liqueur

**Makes about
2 quarts (2L)**

2 pounds (900g)
dark sweet cherries,
stemmed and pitted

1½ cups (300g) sugar

6 cups (1.5L) fruity red
wine, such as Merlot,
Gamay, or Pinot Noir

1½ cups (355ml) kirsch
(preferably), another
eau-de-vie, or vodka

Half of 1 whole star
anise, or a cinnamon
stick (optional)

Guignolet is a favorite liqueur in France, where it's sipped as an apéritif. The maceration is traditionally done with *guignes*, a soft and juicy variety of cherry that tends to be prolific. As a result, *guignes* are often used for distillations and infusions that require a lot of fruit.

I keep my guignolet pretty straightforward, and use dark, sweet cherries, which are easier to find; you might find that adding star anise or a cinnamon stick complements the natural spiciness of them. Another option is to crack open a few of the cherry pits and extract the kernels inside, warming them with the cherries to add a slight bitter almond flavor. (Pictured on page 118.)

In a medium nonreactive saucepan, simmer the cherries with the sugar and ½ cup (125ml) of the wine over medium-high heat, covered, stirring occasionally, until the cherries start to soften and exude their juices, about 5 minutes.

Lower the heat and continue to cook the cherries at a very low simmer with the lid ajar (so you can keep an eye on them, as the cherry liquid can foam up), stirring occasionally, until the cherries are completely wilted and have given up their juices, another 8 to 12 minutes. Remove from the heat and let cool to room temperature.

Pour the cherries and their liquid into a clean 2-quart (2L) jar. Add the remaining wine, the kirsch, and the star anise (if using). Cover and let sit in a cool, dark place for 1 week, gently shaking the jar every few days.

Using a mesh strainer lined with cheesecloth, strain the cherry mixture into a bowl, pressing on the cherries with a flexible silicone spatula or kitchen spoon to extract as much liquid as possible. (Save the cherries to spoon over ice cream or yogurt, or to mix into a pie or fruit crisp. If you've included any bitter cherry kernels, remove them before serving.) Transfer the liquid to a large measuring cup or container with a spout for easy pouring, then pour it into clean bottles and tightly cork. Let rest for a few weeks before drinking. Guignolet is best enjoyed within 3 to 4 months.

CHERRY BLANC

Makes 1 serving

¾ cup (175ml) Lillet blanc (or rosé) or Cap Corse blanc

2 tablespoons (30ml) Guignolet (opposite page)

1 tablespoon white wine vinegar or apple cider vinegar

2 ounces (60ml) sparkling water

A few cherries, halved and pitted, a few fresh berries, or a lemon wedge, for garnish

This highly drinkable refresher was inspired by a cocktail my friend Heidi Swanson included in her book *Near & Far*, where she chronicled her travels to France. I swapped some ingredients around, using cherry guignolet as a base for this sweet-tart cocktail, with a pleasant tingle coming from a splash of vinegar. Shaking this up really mixes the ingredients well, but if you don't have a cocktail shaker or a large jar, you can simply stir it up in a glass.

Add the Lillet, guignolet, and vinegar to a cocktail shaker filled with ice. Shake until well chilled, then strain into a tumbler. Add the sparkling water and a handful of ice. Garnish with the cherries.

LE TEMPS DES CERISES

Makes 1 serving

2 ounces (60ml) cognac

¾ ounce (22ml) sweet vermouth

½ to ¾ ounce (15 to 22ml) Guignolet (opposite page)

Fresh, maraschino, or candied amarena cherry (page 277), for garnish

"Le temps des cerises" is the name of a popular French song written in 1866 and is associated with a worker uprising during that period. The song, and the idea of worker struggles, remains a popular theme in France (if you've ever been caught in one of the frequent strikes, you know what I mean), and it's been covered by everyone from Yves Montand to Joan Baez.

I associate this title with springtime cherry pitting, when my own version of "cherry time" happens. If you want the drink to be more cognac-forward, use ½ ounce (15ml) of guignolet.

Add the cognac, vermouth, and guignolet to a cocktail shaker. Fill with ice and shake until well chilled. Strain into a short tumbler or rocks glass. Add 1 large ice cube or a small handful of ice. Garnish with the cherry.

ELDERFLOWER CORDIAL

**Makes about
1 quart (1L)**

4 cups (1L) water

3¼ cups (650g) sugar

3 lemons, thinly sliced

2 cups (60g) fresh
elderflowers (about
25 heads)

1 tablespoon citric acid
(see Note)

NOTE

Citric acid can be
found in pharma-
cies and shops that
sell Indian, North
African, or Arabic
ingredients. It's also
available online and
is sometimes called
sour salt.

You don't come across elderflowers at the markets in Paris, but
one day when I was walking down the Avenue Trudaine, I spotted
a huge elderflower tree in the traffic median! It's illegal to forage in
Paris, so I resisted picking them. But I couldn't resist taking a sniff,
and found the ones that managed to flourish between the several
lanes of diesel-fueled cars and motorcycles differed from the "all
of summer" fragrance the flowers usually have.

A few days later, I was at a friend's house outside of town
for a barbecue and noticed a spindly, flower-laden tree leaning
against their house. "*Ah . . . bon? Les sureaux?*" they said when I
asked if they were, indeed, elderflowers, before I sprinted over to
get a closer look. Once my suspicions were confirmed, they gave
me *carte blanche* (and a few big bags), and told me to pick away.

Elderflowers blossom in May or June. Do not rinse the flowers,
because they're delicate, and you'll wash away some of the flavor.
Any bits of debris or bugs should be gently picked or brushed off.
To remove the flowers from the stems, run your fingers down the
flower heads over a bowl; they'll easily drop off.

Heat the water, sugar, and lemons in a medium nonreactive saucepan,
stirring until the sugar is dissolved. Remove from the heat, add the
elderflowers, and let the mixture cool until tepid. Cover the pot with
a kitchen towel or plastic wrap and let the flowers infuse at room
temperature for 3 to 4 days, stirring the mixture once a day.

In a small saucepan, warm about ¼ cup (60ml) of the elderflower
liquid with the citric acid, stirring until dissolved.

Pour the citric acid solution into the infused elderflower mixture.
Using a mesh strainer lined with cheesecloth, strain the elderflower
mixture into a bowl, pressing on the flowers with a flexible silicone
spatula to extract as much liquid as possible. Transfer the liquid to
a large measuring cup or container with a spout for easy pouring,
then pour it into clean bottles and tightly cork. Elderflower cordial
is best stored in the refrigerator and will keep for at least a year.

VARIATION —— To make a sparkling drink with elderflower
cordial, pour about 1 tablespoon of the cordial into a tumbler. Add
ice and fill with sparkling water or Limonade (page 36). Garnish
with a lemon wedge or wheel.

ELDERFLOWER FRENCH CHAMPAGNE COCKTAIL

Makes 1 serving

1½ ounces (45ml) gin

½ ounce (15ml)
Elderflower Cordial
(page 127)

½ ounce (15ml) freshly
squeezed lemon juice

3 to 4 ounces (90 to
120ml) champagne
or dry sparkling wine,
such as crémant

Lemon twist,
for garnish

Elderflowers have a particular affinity with champagne, and I can't think of a better way to toast your success after bottling your elderflower cordial than to shake up this summery, bubbly take on the classic French 75 (page 63).

––––––––––––

Add the gin, elderflower cordial, and lemon juice to a cocktail shaker. Fill with ice and shake until well chilled. Strain into a chilled champagne flute or coupe glass. Top with the champagne. Garnish with the lemon twist.

VIN DE SUREAU
Elderflower Wine

Makes 1 quart (1L)

1 cup (30g) fresh
elderflowers (about
13 heads)

1 bottle (750ml)
dry white wine

¾ cup (175ml)
eau-de-vie or vodka

¾ cup (150g) sugar

This elderflower-infused wine is a beautiful sight while it's steeping. It's also lovely to use in place of dry vermouth in your favorite cocktails.

––––––––––––

In a clean 1½- to 2-quart (1.5 to 2L) jar, mix the elderflowers, wine, eau-de-vie, and sugar. Cover and shake vigorously, encouraging the sugar to dissolve.

Let the flowers infuse at room temperature for 3 days, shaking the jar a couple of times a day.

Using a mesh strainer lined with cheesecloth, strain the elderflower wine into a bowl, pressing on the elderflowers with a flexible silicone spatula or kitchen spoon to extract as much liquid as possible. Transfer the liquid to a large measuring cup or container with a spout for easy pouring, then pour it into a clean bottle and tightly cork. Refrigerate until ready to serve.

VERMOUTH MAISON
Homemade Vermouth

**Makes about
1 quart (1L)**

6 orange slices, cut
¼ inch (6mm) thick

1 teaspoon sugar,
plus ½ cup (100g)

¾ teaspoon
angelica bark

½ to 1 teaspoon
wormwood

¼ to ½ teaspoon
gentian bark

½ teaspoon
lightly crushed
chamomile flowers

½ teaspoon
coriander seeds

4 cardamom pods,
lightly crushed

3 whole cloves

1 stalk fresh
lemongrass

1 bottle (750ml)
dry white wine

1 cup (250ml)
dry sherry

While many consider vermouth to be an ingredient mixed with other spirits in a cocktail, Europeans sip it on its own, as an apéritif, appreciating the appealing mix of citrus, roots, barks, flowers, and spices that are used to flavor it. Homemade vermouth isn't hard to make; the trick is gathering the flavorings. But thanks to the internet, getting your hands on them can take just a few clicks. On the other hand, if you have an herbalist near you, do stop in. For me, it's an excuse to visit the Herboristerie d'Hippocrate in Paris, where tidy little paper bags of dried peels, roots, and twigs are lined up on old wooden shelves, and the staff is always happy to help.

I've made quite a few batches of vermouth. If you are fortunate to have a small aging barrel, pour in the vermouth and let it mellow for a week or two. (I had a hard time locating an aging barrel until the nice folks at Maison Ferrand distillery obliged me with one of theirs.) Barrel-aging gives the vermouth a more finished flavor.

Feel free to tweak these ingredients to your taste. You could use juniper berries, dried rose petals, star anise, pink peppercorns, or whatever else strikes your fancy. Wormwood gives vermouth its distinctive flavor (the word *vermouth* is derived from *wermut*, the German word for "wormwood," so technically, it should be added), as does gentian, but if you want a milder-flavored vermouth, use the smaller amounts of both.

The ingredients are tricky to measure strictly by weight as most home scales won't register such small quantities, but there's no need to fuss with the details; a little more of this, a little less of that will make your vermouth uniquely yours. Sherry gives the vermouth a slightly nutty flavor, but you can also experiment with vodka or brandy instead.

Preheat the oven to 425°F (220°C). Line a baking sheet with parchment paper. Toss the orange slices with 1 teaspoon of the sugar and arrange them on the prepared baking sheet. Roast the slices until the bottoms are browned, 13 to 15 minutes. Turn the slices over and roast until they're somewhat dried out and browned on both sides, another 12 to 15 minutes. Remove from the oven and let cool.

continued

In a clean jar that holds at least 1 quart (1L), combine the angelica, wormwood, gentian, chamomile, coriander, cardamom, cloves, and orange slices. With a mallet or rolling pin, whack the lemongrass to "bruise" it, which will help it release its flavor. Slice the stalk into three pieces and add them to the jar.

Reserve 1 cup (250ml) of the wine and pour the rest into the jar. Add the sherry.

Spread the remaining ½ cup (100g) sugar in a single layer in a medium skillet. Cook over medium heat, watching it carefully, until the edges start to liquefy. Continue to cook, using a heatproof spatula to move the liquefied sugar toward the center so it melts evenly, but don't overdo stirring it. Once the sugar is liquefied, continue to cook it until it turns a deep amber color, similar to an old penny, which will happen very quickly once the sugar starts to color, so watch it carefully.

Immediately turn off the heat and pour in the reserved 1 cup (250ml) wine, swirling the pan to combine the wine and caramel. Some of the caramel may seize into hard pieces, but they should melt if you keep swirling the caramel. (A little stirring with a heatproof spatula or whisk will help, too.) Don't worry too much if any crunchy, undissolved bits still remain in the caramel; they'll melt after they're added to the vermouth infusion. (If a lot of the caramel is stuck to the bottom of the pan, you can warm the caramel over medium heat and use a heatproof spatula to release any stubborn, stuck-on caramel.)

Let the caramel cool, then add it to the jar. Cover and let steep at room temperature for 3 to 5 days, shaking it every day. I like mine on the stronger side, so I let it macerate for the full 5 days. Taste after 3 days, and if it's to your liking, use a mesh strainer lined with cheesecloth to strain it into a bowl, then transfer the liquid to a container with a spout for easy pouring. (If you want to let it steep longer, leave it for 2 additional days, then strain and bottle it.)

Pour the vermouth into a clean bottle and tightly cork.

The vermouth is ready to drink right away, but it will be better if left to sit for a few days in a cool, dark place to mellow, or in an oak aging barrel (if you have one) for 1 to 2 weeks.

LIQUEUR 44

**Makes about
3½ cups (830ml)**

3½ cups (830ml)
brandy, applejack, or
white rum, or 2 cups
(500ml) vodka plus
1½ cups (355ml) brandy,
applejack, or white rum

6 tablespoons
(75g) sugar

4 whole cloves,
or ½ vanilla bean,
sliced lengthwise

1 large orange

44 coffee beans

Europeans are often vexed by the U.S. measuring system, saying that measuring things in cups and tablespoons isn't precise. But the French have their own culinary peccadillos; traditional recipes sometimes call for *un verre de vin* of milk, or *une cuillère à soupe*, with no mention of the exact size of "a wine glass of milk" or a "soupspoon." I haven't actually measured mine, but I'm pretty sure that every soupspoon in my silverware drawer would hold a different amount of soup or leavening (too much of which could lead to explosive results).

Proving that exact quantities don't always matter, Liqueur 44 is traditionally made with 44 *morceaux* (cubes) of sugar (which I took the liberty of weighing for you), along with 44 coffee beans. It's also traditionally made with eau-de-vie, although I suggest using something more flavorful, like brandy or rum, either on its own or mixed with vodka.

Pour the liquor into a clean 1-quart (1L) jar and add the sugar and cloves.

Make 44 deep slits in the orange with the point of a paring knife. Press 1 coffee bean into each slit. Add the orange to the jar.

Cover the jar and put it in a cool, dark place for 44 days, shaking the jar every couple of days. Using a mesh strainer lined with cheesecloth, strain the liqueur into a bowl. Transfer the liquid to a large measuring cup or container with a spout for easy pouring, then pour into a clean bottle and tightly cork.

Liqueur 44 should be served chilled or in a glass with a few ice cubes, garnished with a strip of orange zest. It's used in the Cinq Cylinder (page 208), and in place of orange-flavored liqueur in other recipes.

ALAMBIC BOURGUIGNON

Our Citroën wound its way through quiet villages with unassuming country houses surrounded by vineyards. It was late fall, and despite their picked-over appearance after the recent grape harvest, the vineyards we passed were known for making some of the most sought-after wines in the world. Mathieu had told us to "look for the cemetery," and once we found it, we also found Matt, which he prefers to be called.

Matt Sabbagh is a *bouilleur ambulant* who travels around Burgundy with a copper still on wheels. Once he arrives at a village, he parks across from the town church (or, in this case, a cemetery), and locals begin bringing him roots, grapes, and other fruits to distill. There are few traveling distillers left in France, and Matt left twenty years of corporate life to get back to his roots, so to speak, and become one of them.

Matt was an international director for Pernod Ricard, launching Pernod absinthe and making Suze (page 86), a once obscure French apéritif, a hit with bartenders around the world. He has lived in Morocco, London, and L.A., but returned to his native France to spend his days heaving fruits and roots into a copper still until a stream of clear distilled liquid starts to trickle out.

The day I visited, Matt was distilling gentian roots for eau-de-vie, and a mucky brown sludge was boiling away in the pots. As he shoveled more gentian roots into one still, a transparent stream of liquid began trickling out of the spout of another. Matt told me the glistening liquid was so strong in alcohol that it has to be diluted before it's bottled. He held a glass under the spigot and offered a taste.

I took the smallest of sips, and the undiluted distillate had the unmistakable bitterness of gentian, which, with the fiery alcohol, was both warming and alarming. I didn't want to put the glass down, but since it was nearly 70 percent alcohol, I stopped after one sip. (Okay, I finished the glass. I didn't want to let any go to waste.)

With his enterprising spirit, he created Alambic Bourguignon to continue the tradition of distilling regional specialties, such as *eau-de-vie de marc*, made from the *marc* (the skin and seeds left over after grapes are pressed for wine), which is turned into Marc

de Bourgogne by aging the clear distillate in oak for at least two years. He's also making Fine de Bourgogne, a distillation that's even more elusive, made from the violet-colored grape lees (the yeasty liquid and sediment left in the bottom of oak barrels after the wine has aged), which is aged in oak for a minimum of three years. Both take on a luminous amber color, which gets deeper and richer the longer they're aged.

These classic French spirits are deeply ingrained in the culture of Burgundy, but they're in danger of falling out of favor as tastes, and generations, change and fewer people drink distillations. But Matt is determined to keep them going and in the public eye. When I saw how hard he was working, I knew he would succeed.

Because he had so much success with gentian-based spirits, he helped Distillerie Grandmont launch Amer Gentiane, a 32 percent ABV apéritif that's flavored with cardamom, angelica, and citrus and is less sweet and more elegant than other gentian-based apéritifs. Matt recommended mixing up Amer Gentiane in a Seat of Your Pants (page 88), an apéritif made with black currant liqueur, another specialty of Burgundy. I was able to score one of the few bottles of Amer Gentiane that remained from their initial batch of 2,400; so far, it is only available locally. I brought it home to give it a try, doing my part to keep his spirit, and spirits, alive.

LIQUEUR DE NOYAU
Apricot Kernel Liqueur

**Makes about
2¼ cups (560ml)**

80 apricot, peach, or
nectarine kernels

2 cups (500ml) kirsch,
vodka, or brandy

½ cup (100g) sugar

½ vanilla bean,
split lengthwise

NOTE

When using apricot
kernels, the ques-
tion of toxicity often
comes up. To be safe,
I avoid consuming
the pits on their own
in large quantities.

When fruits are in season and at their most abundant in the
spring and summer, I load my basket up with as many apricots,
nectarines, and peaches as I can carry home. I also make a point
of using everything I bought, and I mean everything. Within the
hard pits of stone fruits lies a *noyau*, an almondlike kernel that's
strongly scented of bitter almonds. One of the oldest liqueurs in
France, Noyau de Poissy, is made with apricot kernels, and the
distillery produces only 25,000 bottles a year.

Making *liqueur de noyau* at home is easy; the only trick to
making it is extracting the fragrant kernels from the hard pits. The
best way to do this is to place a few pits on one half of an old, and
expendable, kitchen towel. Fold over the other half of the towel
(to keep the kernels and shells from flying all over the place), then
whack away at the pits with a hammer. (Tip: Don't use a wooden
rolling pin or you'll dent it.) I tap lightly, but repeatedly, until I hear
the pits crack. Then I open the towel and extract the kernels.

If you don't feel like cracking your own pits but want to make
cocktails that use the liqueur, a few companies make crème de
noyau, including Tempus Fugit, whose version is excellent. My
homemade version is less sweet than the ones you buy, which is
what I prefer for cocktails. It's also nice sipped in little glasses
after a meal, or splashed over a bowl of fresh peaches, nectarines,
plums, or berries.

Coarsely chop the kernels and put them in a clean 1-quart (1L) jar
with the kirsch, sugar, and vanilla bean. Cover and shake well.

Let rest in a cool, dark place for 2 months, shaking it every few days.

Using a mesh strainer lined with cheesecloth, strain the mixture into
a bowl. Transfer the liquid to a large measuring cup or container with
a spout for easy pouring, then pour it into clean bottles and tightly
cork. Let the liqueur stand for a month before drinking.

DRINKING FRENCH

FAIRBANKS

Makes 1 serving

1½ ounces (45ml)
London dry gin

¾ ounce (22ml)
dry vermouth

2 teaspoons Liqueur de
Noyau (page 134)

2 dashes orange bitters

Orange twist,
for garnish

This straight-up cocktail is a variation on the Martini (page 97), with additional intrigue from the almondy bitterness of the *liqueur de noyau*.

————————————

Add the gin, vermouth, liqueur de noyau, and orange bitters to a cocktail mixing glass. Fill with ice and stir until well chilled. Strain into a chilled coupe glass. Garnish with the orange twist.

L'ÉCUREUIL ROSE
Pink Squirrel

Makes 1 serving

1½ ounces (45ml)
Liqueur de Noyau
(page 134)

1½ ounces (45ml) Crème
de Cacao (page 156)

1½ ounces (45ml) heavy
cream or half-and-half

Candied amarena
cherry (page 277),
maraschino, or fresh
cherry, for garnish

NOTE

Commercial liqueurs
de noyau are often
tinted red, hence the
rose in the name.

One of the hardest French words for nonnative speakers to pronounce is *écureuil* (squirrel), which sounds like *ek-kerr-roy*. I learned from a woman at my boulangerie, who likes to practice her English with me, that the French struggle with the exact same word in English. After she returned from a vacation in the United States, she told me with great fascination about the "scroll" she saw running in a forest. The French are no strangers to scrolls of paperwork, but I didn't think they extended through the woods. It took a moment before I realized that she was talking about "squirrels," which are much less common in France than they are in America.

For those who enjoy a rich cocktail, L'Écureuil Rose (Pink Squirrel) is an easy-to-understand choice. A classic Pink Squirrel is sometimes made with ice cream, but I prefer this one, made with cream or half-and-half.

————————————

Add the liqueur de noyau, crème de cacao, and cream to a cocktail shaker. Fill with ice and shake until well chilled. Strain into a chilled coupe glass. Garnish with the cherry.

POUSSE RAPIÈRE

Makes 2 cups (500ml)

2 cups (500ml)
Armagnac or brandy

½ cup (100g) sugar

¼ cup (60ml) water

15 black peppercorns,
lightly cracked

Zest of 2 oranges,
preferably sour oranges
(but sweet oranges
will do)

Zest of 1 lemon

½ vanilla bean,
split lengthwise

After many years of struggling to keep up with the avalanche of paperwork that comes with having a foot in two countries (especially when one of those countries has a reputation for substantial amounts of paperwork), I finally got an assistant. When she got married in Gascony, the locals insisted that the bubbly used to toast the happy couple be served with a dash of a local liquor called Pousse Rapière. The liquor is meant to be added to a local dry sparkling wine, which coincidentally (. . . or not?) is made by the very same château that makes the Pousse Rapière base. And wouldn't you know it? They even offer them for sale together as a kit.

I was intrigued enough to want to try it, but too frugal to buy it. The base is simple enough to make at home, and takes only a few weeks to infuse. There's no need to wait for a wedding, and indeed, it's a fun drink for toasting any kind of *fête*.

Pour the Armagnac into a clean 1-quart (1L) jar.

In a small saucepan, heat the sugar and water, stirring, until the sugar is dissolved. Remove from the heat and let cool to room temperature.

Add the peppercorns, orange and lemon zests, and vanilla bean to the jar, then pour in the cooled sugar syrup. Close the lid and shake the ingredients together.

Store the jar in a cool, dark place for 2 to 3 weeks, shaking the jar every couple of days.

Using a mesh strainer lined with cheesecloth, strain the liqueur into a bowl. Transfer the liquid to a large measuring cup or container with a spout for easy pouring, then pour into a clean bottle and tightly cork.

To make a Pousse Rapière cocktail, pour ½ ounce (15ml) Pousse Rapière liqueur into a chilled champagne flute or coupe glass. Add 4 ounces (125ml) dry sparkling wine or champagne and gently stir. Traditionally the drink has a light pink color, which this homemade version lacks, so feel free to add a drop or two of Peychaud's bitters to add some color.

VARIATION —— A no-wait Gascon cocktail can be made by pouring 1½ ounces (45ml) Armagnac into a champagne flute, then filling it with champagne or dry sparkling wine.

LIQUEUR DES FRAISES
Strawberry Liqueur

Makes 3 cups (750ml)

3 cups (750ml) vodka

8 ounces (225g) strawberries, quartered

2 tablespoons sugar

NOTE

The strawberries used for infusing that are strained out can be tossed with other fruits and used to make a fruit crisp or cobbler.

A sign of springtime is when the much-heralded Gariguette strawberries arrive at the markets in France. These slightly elongated berries get most of the attention, and they're often laid out like jewels in picture-perfect rows that people ooh and aah over. Other varieties, like Mara des Bois, arrive with less fanfare, but are just as delicious. (Actually, I like them better.) They're so fragrant, I can find them just by following my nose. Fortunately, good strawberries can be found at farmers' markets everywhere. Choose the darkest, deepest red ones for the most vibrant-colored strawberry liqueur.

Being an inveterate scavenger at *brocantes* (flea markets), I've amassed quite a collection of vintage wine and cocktail glasses that I use every day. However, I also find cordial-size footed ones that are just too pretty to pass up. They don't get used very often, but are perfect for sipping this crimson liqueur.

Pour the vodka into a clean 1-quart (1L) jar. Add the strawberries and the sugar.

Cover and let infuse in a cool, dark place for 5 to 7 days, shaking the jar gently once a day. Using a mesh strainer lined with cheesecloth, strain the liqueur into a bowl.

Transfer the liquid to a large measuring cup or container with a spout for easy pouring, then pour it into a clean bottle and tightly cork. Store the liqueur in the refrigerator or freezer until ready to use. If serving this straight up, it's best serve chilled in small glasses.

STRAWBERRY SPIKED LIMONADE

Makes 1 serving

2 ripe, medium-size strawberries

1½ ounces (45ml) Liqueur des Fraises (page 139)

4 ounces (120ml) sparkling Limonade (page 36), good-quality store-bought sparkling lemonade, or lemon soda (see Note)

Sliced strawberries, lemon wheel, and a sprig of fresh mint or tarragon, for garnish

NOTE

If using store-bought sparkling lemonade, add 1 to 2 teaspoons freshly squeezed lemon juice to ramp up the lemon flavor (optional).

This easy-going cooler gets a boost from strawberry vodka. It's perfect in the summer but equally welcome during the winter.

In a tumbler or rocks glass, muddle the strawberries with ½ ounce (15ml) of the liqueur des fraises until the strawberries are liquefied. Add the remaining 1 ounce (30ml) liqueur des fraises and the limonade. Taste, and if using store-bought lemonade, add lemon juice, if desired.

Add a handful of ice to the glass and garnish with the strawberries, lemon wheel, and sprig of mint.

RHUBARB CORDIAL

Makes 3 cups (750ml)

1 pound (450g) rhubarb, trimmed and cut into ½-inch (1.5cm) pieces

3½ cups (830ml) gin, plus more if necessary

3 wide strips orange zest

½ cup (100g) sugar

3 tablespoons (45ml) Grand Marnier, Cointreau, or triple sec

NOTE

You can use the leftover rhubarb to make a compote by adding additional sugar, to taste, and cooking it in a saucepan over medium heat, stirring, until the rhubarb pieces have broken down into a thick, chunky puree. Add a dash of vanilla extract at the end of cooking, or add a vanilla bean, split lengthwise, at the start of cooking, if you wish.

Anyone raising objections to rhubarb won't have a case when they see this rose-hued cordial, a term often used to describe an infused liqueur, and taste how well it goes with gin. Use the reddest rhubarb you can find for the rosiest color.

The rhubarb cordial should be served chilled in small glasses or mixed in a favorite cocktail in place of gin. It can also be served in small tumblers with a few ice cubes, a twist of orange or tangerine peel, and a splash of sparkling water or tonic water as an apéritif.

Put the rhubarb, gin, orange zest, and sugar in a clean 2-quart (2L) jar. Cover and shake to encourage the sugar to dissolve.

Store in a cool, dark place, shaking it every few days. After a few days, if some of the rhubarb is still floating above the level of the liquid, add another pour of gin, enough so the rhubarb is covered.

Let stand for 1 month, continuing to shake the jar every few days.

Using a mesh strainer lined with cheesecloth, strain the liqueur into a bowl. Add the Grand Marnier. Transfer the liquid to a large measuring cup or container with a spout for easy pouring, then pour it into clean bottles and tightly cork. Store the cordial in the refrigerator for 1 to 3 months before drinking.

SPRING SMASH

Makes 1 serving

2 medium strawberries, thinly sliced, plus a few for garnish

1¾ ounces (50ml) Rhubarb Cordial (page 141)

1 ounce (30ml) sweet vermouth

1 ounce (30ml) gin

1 teaspoon (5ml) freshly squeezed lime juice

Orange wheel, for garnish

Everyone is relieved when stalks of rhubarb, sometimes tied in bundles, start showing up at the markets. It's the first sign that spring is here, or at least that it's on its way. Then, strawberries come along, which fortunately—and naturally—have an *affinité* for rhubarb, as they do in this invigorating, and fruity mash-up to toast the season.

———————

Muddle the sliced strawberries in the bottom of a cocktail shaker. Add the rhubarb cordial, vermouth, gin, and lime juice. Fill the shaker with ice and shake until well chilled. Open the cocktail shaker and strain through a julep strainer or mesh strainer into a chilled coupe glass.

Garnish with the strawberries and orange wheel.

RHUBERRY COLLINS

Makes 1 serving

2 fresh or thawed frozen raspberries, plus a few fresh raspberries for garnish

½ teaspoon freshly squeezed lemon juice

¾ teaspoon sugar

2 ounces (60ml) Rhubarb Cordial (page 141)

1 ounce (30ml) gin

Strawberries often get preferential treatment alongside rhubarb, but the more intensely flavored raspberries deserve a chance to be in the mix, too. In this fruit-forward libation, they're happy to share the spotlight.

———————

Muddle the raspberries in a cocktail shaker with the lemon juice and sugar. Add the rhubarb cordial and gin. Fill the cocktail shaker with ice and shake until well chilled. Remove the lid of the shaker and strain through a mesh strainer or julep strainer into a chilled coupe glass. Garnish with the raspberries.

CONFITURE DE VIEUX GARÇON (BACHELOR'S JAM)

The name of this "jam" is a misnomer. It isn't a *confiture* in the traditional sense but rather refers to preserved fruit that *un vieux garçon* (an older bachelor) would start in the spring and add to all summer long, ending up with a dessert to sustain him through the following winter and beyond. Without a spouse, presumably these gents would go without dessert if left to their own devices. (With all the pâtisseries in France, you'd hardly think that was possible. . . .)

There's no one single recipe for *confiture de vieux garçon*; you simply use what fruit is available and in season. After a few trials and errors, I found the *confiture* to be easy to make, but it requires some attention to details. Following the seasons in France, you would start with strawberries in the spring, then move on to cherries. A few weeks later, apricots, plums, peaches, and nectarines would be added as each comes into season. Raspberries or red currants could be included as well. Some people add pineapple, kiwifruit, and grapes, but I like to stick to summer fruits, which make the *confiture* an extra-special treat during the winter.

Choose fruits and berries without blemishes or dark spots. Strawberries should be hulled; I usually add them whole. Cherries should be stemmed, and I like to pit them, as I find it more luxurious when I can pop the whole thing in my mouth. Apricots can be halved or quartered, depending on their size. I generally quarter plums unless they're small, then I halve them. Peaches and nectarines can be cut into quarters or sixths. You're welcome to peel the peaches, but I don't.

Most importantly, you want to use rum that's at least 100 proof (50 percent ABV). Using lower-proof rum can lead to fermented fruit. If that's not available, you can mix 151 proof rum with 80 proof rum in 1:1 proportions to approximate.

Start by finding a crock with an opening wide enough to insert a small plate or plastic lid to weigh down the fruits and keep them fully submerged in the rum. (Tip: You can sometimes find jars designed specifically for making *confiture de vieux garçon*, which are usually referred to as *rumtopf* jars.) If you can't find the right size crock, you can use a large, wide-mouth jar and then submerge the fruits by weighing them down with a sturdy ziptop (food safe) plastic bag that's been partially filled with water and then emptied of extra air before sealing. If you do this, you'll have to jiggle the bag around a little to make sure no fruit bobs up around the sides. (One drawback to this method is possible leaks. French ziptop bags aren't as sturdy as their U.S. counterparts. Make sure the bag is well-sealed and the sealed end is on top, so if it opens, it doesn't drain into the fruit-and-rum mix.)

1. Begin by cleaning your wide-mouth crock or jar well with soap and very hot water. Let it air-dry.

2. Prepare the first layer of fruit by rinsing and patting it dry, then preparing as noted above. Combine the fruit in a bowl with half its weight in sugar. For example, for 1 pound (450g) of hulled strawberries,

continued

use 8 ounces (225g) of sugar. I prefer raw granulated sugar, but regular sugar would be fine, too. Toss together and let the mixture stand until the sugar is mostly dissolved, adding a splash of rum to encourage the sugar to melt if the fruit isn't juicy. Add the fruit and sugar, along with any liquid the fruit exudes, to the crock.

3. If you want to add another layer (or layers) of fruit now, combine them as above and add each layer. When you have layered all of your fruit, pour enough high-proof rum over the fruit so it's covered by at least a few inches.

4. Prepare to cover the fruit with whatever weight you're using. If you're using a plate or a plastic lid, cover the fruit with plastic wrap first, pressing it against the top of the fruit and partway up the insides of the crock so the fruit is completely covered; lay the plate or plastic lid on top so the fruit stays submerged. Check around the edges of the plate, and if any fruit is bobbing up around it, partially fill a plastic ziptop bag with water and lay it over the plate to form a seal that keeps the fruit from bobbing up around the edges.

5. Cover the crock or jar with a loose-fitting lid, piece of cheesecloth, or kitchen towel to keep bugs out. The fruit inside needs air, and if it's sealed too tightly, the contents can ferment, and the jar may explode.

6. Store the crock in a cool, dark place while you wait for the next fruit to come into season. Check the crock during the first few days to make sure the fruit is covered and not turning brown. If you see any bubbles, give the fruit a few very gentle stirs to make sure everything is submerged and melding properly.

7. When the next fruit comes into season, prepare it as in Step 3, mixing it with half its weight in sugar, letting it stand until the sugar is mostly dissolved, then adding it to the crock with enough rum to keep the fruits well covered. If you're adding raspberries or currants, add them whole without tossing them in sugar; I like the way they look with the other fruits and don't want them to get broken up. Cover and weigh down the fruits as before. Continue to check the crock for several days to make sure the fruit is submerged and not fermenting. If you see bubbles, give the fruits another gentle stir, and perhaps another pour of rum, which inhibits fermenting.

8. Continue with other fruits as they come into season. After a while, the fruits will have absorbed enough rum, and changed color as a result, and don't need to be checked as often. I check mine every few weeks or so to make sure everything is going smoothly. I have a hard time resisting a small sample when I do, but it's best to wait for at least 2 months so the fruit is fully imbibed, before enjoying.

I haven't lived that long, but folks say *confiture de vieux garçon* will keep indefinitely. I know people who have kept theirs going for years, adding more fruit, sugar, and rum as the seasons pass, to top off the pot and replenish what they've used. Serve the fruits with yogurt or fresh cheese, with vanilla ice cream, or over *le cheesecake*, a favorite dessert in France.

SIDONI'S PUNCH

Makes 1 quart (1L)

1 bottle (750ml) dark rum

¾ cup (150g) raw granulated sugar or granulated sugar

1 small lime, halved

1 vanilla bean, split lengthwise

1 cinnamon stick

3 slices fresh ginger (unpeeled)

It's not easy making friends when you arrive in a new country. I was very fortunate to meet Frédéric Chambeau not long after I landed in France . . . and I was even more fortunate when I found out that he owned a chocolate shop. Score!

Frédéric and his sister, Catherine, are the fifth-generation owners of Fouquet, where, in addition to making their own chocolates and candies, they produce vinegar, jams, and candied fruit, as well as a variety of liqueurs. When I go into Fouquet, my focus is usually on the boxes of dark, bittersweet chocolates and the colorful *pâtes de fruits* (fruit jellies) on the shelves. But one day, I took my eyes off them long enough to notice several bottles of rum punch amongst the bottles of eaux-de-vie. When I asked Frédéric about them, he paused for a moment, as though his mind was reaching for something, until a warm smile spread across his face. The punch had been made for the shop by a clerk who'd once worked there. Her name was Sidoni, and she had come from Martinique; he couldn't recall the exact year, but her daughter had been his *nounou* (babysitter) when he was young, and he had very fond memories of them.

Then Frédéric led me down to the cool *cave* underneath the shop to show me the bottles of *le punch*, which they still make, lined up on wooden shelves. First he opened one that had been aging for six months; then he held up one, which he said was much better, that had been aging for nine months. When he let me smell the two, I knew he was right; the younger one had a nicely spiced rum fragrance, but the second had a visibly deeper amber color, and when I tasted them both, the one aged longer had distinctly more complex caramel notes. I made a mental note right then and there to put Martinique on my list of places to visit.

In this recipe, I hewed pretty close to Sidoni's original, but I couldn't help adding a few slices of fresh ginger to the mix. You could certainly double the recipe, and six (or better, nine) months later when you taste it, you'll be glad you did. This is best made with raw granulated sugar (see page 122), which adds a little toffee note to the punch. Enjoy this punch well chilled, in small glasses.

Put the rum, sugar, lime, vanilla bean, cinnamon stick, and ginger in a clean 2-quart (2L) jar. Shake and set in a cool, dark place for 6 to 9 months (or longer), shaking it every so often as it sits.

VIN D'ORANGE
Orange Wine

**Makes about
2 quarts (2L)**

2 bottles (1.5L total)
dry white or rosé wine

1 cup (250ml) vodka

¾ cup (150g) sugar

3 sour oranges (also
called Seville oranges)

1 orange

1 lemon

1 cinnamon stick

Orange or lemon twist,
for garnish

Vin d'orange is a popular apéritif in Provence, using bitter oranges, which are cultivated in the winter. The *orange amer* season is fleeting, though, and they're hard to come by at the markets in Paris. (I suspect *les Provençaux* are keeping them all for themselves.) When I see the elusive orange *agrumes* (citrus) whose insides are bursting with sharp, puckery orange flavor, I snag 'em and put up a batch of this apéritif wine so it's ready for spring.

In France, you would use a *vin ordinaire* as a base; the apéritif is going to be fully flavored by the oranges, so there's no need to spring for a pricey Montrachet or Pouilly-Fuissé. An unfussy Sauvignon, Chenin Blanc, or similar dry white, or a rosé, will work well. You could get away with using an inexpensive boxed white wine, which I often use.

Pour the wine, vodka, and sugar into a large, clean jar that will hold at least 2½ to 3 quarts (2.5 to 3L). (You can also divide the vin d'orange between two large glass jars, if you don't have one large enough to macerate all of the fruit in the same jar.)

Cut each orange and the lemon into eight pieces. (Don't worry about removing any seeds.) Add them to the jar along with the cinnamon stick. Cover and shake the jar to encourage the sugar to dissolve.

Let rest in a cool, dark place for 1 month, shaking it every few days.

Using a mesh strainer lined with cheesecloth, strain the wine into a bowl. Transfer the wine to a large measuring cup or container with a spout for easy pouring, then pour it into clean bottles and tightly cork.

Store in the refrigerator or in a cool, dark place until ready to drink.

Serve in a glass with ice, garnished with the orange twist.

VIN DE SAPIN
Spruce Wine

Makes 3 cups (750ml)

2 cups (115g) pine or spruce tips

3 cups (750ml) dry white wine

6 tablespoons (75g) sugar

¾ cup plus 2 tablespoons (205ml) eau-de-vie or vodka

Romain Meder is one of the most fascinating chefs in France. He runs a Michelin three-star restaurant, but doesn't do fanciful or acrobatic presentations that look too precious to eat. That's fine with me because I prefer his approach to cooking, which starts with searching out the very best producers in France, and then letting their products star on the plate, rather than burying them under heavy sauces or swoops and swirls. He's more comfortable serving heirloom grains and vegetables from the gardens at Versailles, and if I ever find out where in Brittany he gets that salted butter they put on the table, I'm moving there.

After dining at the Alain Ducasse restaurant in the stately Hôtel Plaza Athénée where Chef Meder works, they let me visit the kitchen. A brigade of cooks was wielding heavy copper pots, hard at work over the stoves, and others were meticulously boning fish and slicing vegetables with a respect you don't see often in kitchens. Sensing my keener-than-usual interest, Chef Meder led me to a room behind the two rows of stoves, where there were two floor-to-ceiling cupboards. He opened the doors, and inside of each was a wonderland of various jars, filled with everything from bright orange Charentais melon wedges bobbing in liquor to vinegar being infused with bunches of hay and kefirs fermenting with celery from the famed gardens of Louis XIV. Most French chefs of this caliber are more fixated on caviar, foie gras, and foam, rather than fermenting vegetables, which includes putting up jars of kimchi. For some reason, the idea of serving kimchi at a Michelin three-star French restaurant both amused and delighted me.

Chef Meder brought out spoons, and my palate went to places it had never been before. I was most fond of the *vin de sapin*, an apéritif wine infused with pine tree buds. He plucked out a frond and gave it to me to taste: It had an alpine, resiny flavor, and he handed me the recipe so I could give it a go at home. Chef Meder's recipe uses *bourgeons de sapin*, blue spruce tips (see the Resources, page 283). If you want to pick your own, make sure the pine buds are edible. Either have them identified at your local cooperative extension or ask an experienced gardener. Similar-looking yew trees are a common landscaping plant, but shouldn't be consumed.

continued

This aromatized wine is a lovely apéritif on its own, and it can also replace dry vermouth in a favorite cocktail recipe, including a Martini (page 97).

———————

Mix together the pine tips, wine, sugar, and eau-de-vie in a clean 1- to 1½-quart (1 to 1.5L) jar. Shake vigorously. Let stand in a cool, dark place for 1 month, shaking every few days.

Using a mesh strainer lined with cheesecloth, strain the mixture into a bowl, pressing on the pine tips with a flexible silicone spatula or kitchen spoon to extract as much liquid as possible.

Transfer the liquid to a large measuring cup or container with a spout for easy pouring, then pour it into clean bottles and tightly cork.

Store in the refrigerator until ready to drink.

KEEP THE TIP

Makes 1 serving

1½ ounces (45ml) Vin de Sapin (page 149)

1½ ounces (45ml) dry sherry

2 dashes Angostura aromatic bitters

1 dash orange bitters

Lemon twist, for garnish

Small splash good-quality lemon soda or dry sparkling wine, such as crémant

People are often confused on how to tip (or even if they should) in France. The French word for "tip" is *pourboire*, a word that comes from *à boire* (to drink) and translates to "for a drink," presumably because whatever money you leave is what the server would use to buy a drink after their shift.

In restaurants and cafés, it's become more common to leave a *pourboire*, usually some of the change you get back after paying for your drink, or a few euros after a meal. This feels awkward for visitors used to adding on an extra 20 percent (or more) as a tip, as is customarily done in the States. Some travelers can't resist doing the same when they're in France, which is why waiters are happy to work in places frequented by visitors.

This recipe is a riff on a Bamboo cocktail, substituting spruce tip wine for the dry vermouth, a tip I got from a bartender friend after he tasted it. To make it more festive, I add a small splash of sparkling lemon soda. Here's another tip: If you've got an open bottle of sparkling wine, that would be nice *à boire*, too.

Add the vin de sapin, sherry, and Angostura and orange bitters to a cocktail mixing glass. Fill with ice and stir until well chilled. Strain into a chilled coupe glass.

Hold the lemon twist over the top of the drink and twist it to release the oils from the peel into the drink. Drop the lemon twist into the glass, and top with the lemon soda.

GIN DE SAPIN
Spruce Tip Gin

**Makes about
3½ cups (830ml)**

2 cups (115g)
spruce tips

3½ cups (830ml)
London dry gin

⅓ cup (65g) sugar

When I told a friend with a large garden that I was looking for spruce tips to make Vin de Sapin (page 149), she said, "*Ah bon? J'ai beaucoup!*" And *voilà*, a few days later, she handed me a generous bag of green fronds. I knew the resiny flavor of the pine tips would go well with the juniper in gin, and I use this as the base for a sleek Sapatini (recipe follows), but if you're the vodka-martini type, substitute vodka in this recipe. You can also use this to mix up an herbaceous Bonalgroni (page 94).

Mix together the spruce tips, gin, and sugar in a clean 1- to 1½-quart (1 to 1.5L) jar. Shake vigorously. Let stand in a cool, dark place for 5 to 7 days, shaking every few days.

Using a mesh strainer lined with cheesecloth, strain the mixture into a bowl, pressing on the spruce tips with a flexible silicone spatula or spoon to extract as much liquid as possible. Reserve a few spruce tips in some of the liquid in the refrigerator if you want to use them for garnishing drinks.

Transfer the liquid to a large container with a spout for easy pouring, then pour it into a clean bottle and tightly cork. Store in a cool, dark place until ready to drink.

SAPATINI

Makes 1 serving

2 ounces (60ml) Gin de
Sapin (above)

½ ounce (15ml) dry
vermouth

Spruce tip, fresh or
reserved from making
Gin de Sapin, or lemon
twist, for garnish

The martini has always been a stalwart of the cocktail world, but it's been through a lot in recent years: infiltrated with bacon, pumpkin spice, and even cake batter. I like martinis, and I like cake, but to me, ne'er the two shall meet.

Spruce tips, however, pair beautifully with dry vermouth for a riff on the classic. I like to use Dolin vermouth, made in the French Alps, which gives this cocktail a double-dose of alpine allure. (Pictured, opposite.)

Add the gin de sapin and vermouth to a cocktail mixing glass. Fill halfway with ice and stir for 30 seconds, or until well chilled. Strain into a chilled coupe glass. Garnish with the spruce tip.

RHUM ARRANGÉ
"Arranged" Rum

**Makes about
1 quart (1L)**

1 quart (1L) white rum

½ cup (100g) raw
granulated sugar
or granulated sugar

½ pineapple, peeled
and cut into 2-inch
(5cm) pieces (include
the core)

1 mango, peeled
and cut into 1-inch
(2.5cm) pieces

1 fresh coconut,
cracked, meat cut into
1-inch (2.5cm) pieces
(no need to peel)

3 slices fresh ginger
(no need to peel)

1 vanilla bean,
split lengthwise

The French love rum, and even *les supermarchés* have an impressive array of bottles from islands like Martinique and Guadeloupe, where the French take their vacations. If you look closely, though, you'll see that some of the rums are a whopping 70 percent alcohol. I couldn't figure out who would drink them until I asked a clerk at Christian de Montaguère, a specialty rum seller in Paris (see page 280). He told me that people like these high-alcohol rums (known as overproof rums) because they remind them of their vacations. No wonder those islands are such popular destinations! Overproof rums are also better for making *rhum arrangé*, an infusion of tropical fruits, because the higher alcohol pulls more flavor from the fruits than a lower-proof rum does.

Here is the basic recipe I use with a standard-proof rum, but you can infuse all sorts of things in *rhum arrangé*, from vanilla beans and macadamia nuts to bananas, passion fruit, and fresh ginger. So feel free to mix up your own combination. Skip the fresh coconut and add some kiwifruit slices, or split open a few passion fruits and add the pulp and seeds. If mangoes aren't available, orange slices can fill in for them. Spices like cinnamon sticks and allspice berries can be added as well; use enough to accent the fruits, but not enough to overwhelm. And if you are able to find a higher-proof rum, no one will mind if you use it.

Pour the rum into a clean 2-quart (2L) jar. Add the sugar, then the pineapple chunks, mango and coconut pieces, ginger, and vanilla bean.

Close the top and shake vigorously to encourage the sugar to dissolve.

Store the jar in a cool, dark place for at least 3 months, shaking it every once in a while; it'll be better if you let it sit for 6 to 9 months. While you can strain and bottle it, most people keep the fruit in the jar, marinating in the rum, and serve it from there. It's best served chilled, in small glasses, or it can be used in cocktails in place of white or dark rum.

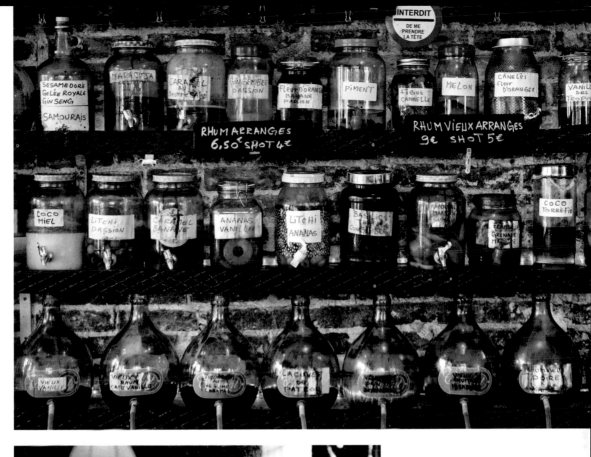

CRÈME DE CACAO
Chocolate Liqueur

**Makes about
1½ cups (355ml)**

1¾ cups (430ml) vodka

¾ cup (75g) roasted
cocoa nibs

¾ cup (150g) turbinado
or raw crystal sugar

¼ cup (60ml) water

1 teaspoon pure
vanilla extract

NOTE

To reuse the cocoa
nibs, spread them on
a baking sheet lined
with parchment paper
or a silicone baking
mat and dry them in
a 350°F (175°C) oven,
stirring a few times,
until they're no longer
damp, about 15 min-
utes. Cool, then break
up the nibs with your
hands. Store in an
airtight container to
add to chocolate chip
cookie dough or sprin-
kle over ice cream.

I was surprised to see a recipe for crème de cacao in *Je Sais Cuisiner* (*I Know How to Cook*), the French equivalent of *The Joy of Cooking*, published in 1932. It called for whole cocoa beans and a formidable amount of sugar, which was considered a luxury until Napoléon ordered sugar beets to be planted in France, making it affordable, and available, to all.

Since then, the French have embraced sugar, and ads once claimed it to be *bonne pour la santé*, or "good for your health." One *Mangez du sucre* ad depicted a sluggish secretary sitting next to a colleague, who was hopped up on sugar, typing away like a crazed maniac. Another urged coffee drinkers to put *three* lumps of sugar in their cups, "two lumps for the taste . . . and one for energy." But who can complain? These ads are probably the reason we have so many great pastry shops in France today.

The French were also ahead of their time by using cocoa beans in recipes before the rest of the world caught on. Nowadays, roasted cocoa nibs are easy to find, thanks to the explosion of bean-to-bar chocolate makers. Infusing nibs in vodka makes an all-natural chocolate liqueur that is a pleasure to sip with dessert, well chilled, and makes an appropriate base for cocktails that call for crème de cacao, such as the Cognac Alexander (page 159).

Mix the vodka and cocoa nibs in a clean 1½-pint (750ml) jar. Let stand for 1 week in a cool, dark place, shaking the jar every few days.

Heat the sugar and water in a small saucepan over medium-high heat, stirring until the sugar is dissolved. Remove from the heat and let cool.

Using a mesh strainer lined with cheesecloth, strain the cocoa nib–infused vodka into a bowl. Stir in the cooled sugar syrup and the vanilla. Transfer the liquid to a large measuring cup or container with a spout for easy pouring, then pour the crème de cacao into a clean bottle and tightly cork. Store in the refrigerator.

CHOCOLATE MARTINI

Makes 1 serving

1 ounce (30ml)
Crème de Cacao
(opposite page)

1 ounce (30ml) vodka

½ ounce (15ml) Fernet-Vallet or Fernet-Branca

A few fresh raspberries or a strawberry, skewered, for garnish

I'm not a big fan of dessert-style martinis, but unlike other chocolate-based cocktails, this one remains decidedly on the sophisticated side courtesy of a dash of Fernet-Vallet.

———————

Add the crème de cacao, vodka, and Fernet-Vallet to a cocktail shaker. Fill with ice and shake until well chilled. Strain into a chilled coupe glass. Garnish with the berries.

21ST CENTURY

Makes 1 serving

1½ ounces (45ml)
dark rum

¾ ounce (22ml)
Crème de Cacao
(opposite page)

¾ ounce (22ml)
Lillet blanc

½ ounce (15ml) freshly squeezed lemon juice

1 or 2 dashes
chocolate bitters

½ teaspoon Fernet-Vallet, Fernet-Branca, or another amaro (optional)

This riff on the classic 20th Century cocktail named after a *chemin de fer* (railroad line) swaps out gin for rum and takes a chocolate-friendly turn with crème de cacao and a dash of chocolate bitters. This isn't a sweet cocktail by any means, and as I do with the Chocolate Martini (above), I sometimes take this in a darker direction by adding ½ teaspoon Fernet-Vallet (or its Italian cousin, Fernet-Branca) or another bitter *amer* (or amaro) to the mix.

———————

Add the rum, crème de cacao, Lillet, lemon juice, chocolate bitters, and Fernet-Vallet (if desired) to a cocktail shaker. Fill with ice and shake until well chilled. Strain into a chilled coupe.

CHOCOLAT À L'ANCIENNE
Chocolate Old-Fashioned

Makes 1 serving

1½ ounces (45ml)
Crème de Cacao
(page 156)

2 dashes
chocolate bitters

2 ounces (60ml)
bourbon whiskey

Candied amarena
cherry (page 277) or
maraschino cherry,
for garnish

In this riff on the standard old-fashioned (*à l'ancienne*), the oaky
fire of bourbon is tempered by a double dose of chocolate. It's a fine
drink, and a new-fashioned way to enjoy chocolate . . . by the glass.
(Pictured, opposite.)

Mix the crème de cacao and chocolate bitters together in a short
tumbler or rocks glass. Add the bourbon, stir, then add 1 large ice
cube or a few small ice cubes. Garnish with the cherry.

COGNAC ALEXANDER

Makes 1 serving

1½ ounces (45ml)
cognac

1 ounce (30ml) Crème
de Cacao (page 156)

1 ounce (30ml) heavy
cream or half-and-half

Pinch of finely ground
espresso, for garnish

If your vision of a Brandy Alexander is firmly fixed in the 1980s,
it's time to rethink the drink. Regular brandy is hard to find in
France because cognac is king. To be fair, when cognac is so readily
available, why drink anything else? But you're welcome to use
another good brandy here. The classic is dusted with nutmeg, but
I find that wisps of espresso powder highlight the chocolate flavor
and are more to my liking.

Add the cognac, crème de cacao, and cream to a cocktail shaker.
Fill with ice and shake until well chilled. Strain into a chilled coupe
glass. Dust the surface with the ground espresso.

LIQUEUR D'ESTRAGON
Tarragon Liqueur

**Makes about
1½ cups (355ml)**

1¼ cups (310ml)
eau-de-vie or vodka

1 cup (15g) loosely
packed fresh tarragon
leaves

¼ teaspoon caraway
seeds, lightly crushed

1 wide strip
orange zest

6 tablespoons
(75g) sugar

3 tablespoons
(45ml) water

Tarragon is an overlooked ingredient elsewhere, but the French use it frequently. If it's not part of your usual *aide-mémoire* (shopping list), one sniff of a bunch will remind you of how good it is—and how much you've missed it. Its delicate anise flavor complements a green salad tossed in a simple vinaigrette and enlivens a plate of sliced tomatoes drizzled with olive oil. It's also one of the few herbs that go well with fruit, especially citrus. If you're a gardener and fortunate enough to have an abundance of tarragon, this recipe can easily be doubled. It's enjoyable sipped on its own, ice-cold in cordial glasses, but it also brightens up orange-based cocktails, such as The Sunny Side (opposite page).

Pour the eau-de-vie into a clean jar that holds at least 1 pint (500ml). Add the tarragon, caraway seeds, and orange zest. Cover and shake the jar.

Store the liqueur in a cool, dark place for 1 month, shaking the jar every few days.

Using a mesh strainer lined with cheesecloth, strain the liqueur into a bowl. Gather the edges of the cheesecloth and *gently* squeeze to extract more flavor from the tarragon leaves.

In a small saucepan, heat the sugar and water over medium-high heat, stirring, until the sugar is dissolved. Let cool to room temperature, then add it to the liqueur. Transfer the liqueur to a large measuring cup or container with a spout for easy pouring, then pour it into a clean jar or bottle and cork tightly.

THE SUNNY SIDE

Makes 1 serving

2 ounces (60ml)
Tarragon Liqueur
(opposite page)

1 ounce (30ml) freshly
squeezed tangerine or
orange juice

1½ ounces (45ml) Grand
Marnier, Cointreau, or
triple sec

2 teaspoons (10ml)
spiced tangerine syrup
(page 275)

Sprig of fresh tarragon
and tangerine or orange
wheel, for garnish

This combination of orange and tarragon reminds me of the sunny South of France, which is just what I need to brighten things up in the Paris winter. Tangerine juice is my preference, but you can also mix it up with orange juice.

Add the tarragon liqueur, tangerine juice, Grand Marnier, and spiced tangerine syrup to a cocktail shaker. Fill with ice and shake until well chilled. Strain into a chilled champagne flute or coupe glass. Garnish with the tarragon sprig and citrus wheel.

TNT

Makes 1 serving

1½ ounces (45ml)
freshly squeezed
grapefruit juice

1 ounce (30ml) Tarragon
Liqueur (opposite page)

1 ounce (30ml) gin

½ teaspoon simple
syrup (page 270)

2 ounces (60ml) cold
tonic water

1 lime wedge

When I arrived in France, I was surprised to see posters plastered on the walls of métro stations extolling the virtues of American grapefruits. The ads presented them as an exotic specialty ingredient, while in the States, we tend to think of them as, well . . . grapefruits. This made me take a fresh look at them, and like the French, I now consider them to be the delicacy that they truly are.

In addition to grapefruits, the French are great fans of acronyms, which tame some of the wordy terms used to describe everything, including baking ingredients like *tant pour tant* (shortened to TPT), a mix of equal parts almond flour and powdered sugar. I dubbed this drink the TNT, rather than Tarragon and Tonic, as I'd rather spend my time drinking one than spelling it out.

Add the grapefruit juice, tarragon liqueur, gin, and simple syrup to a cocktail shaker. Fill with ice and shake until well chilled. Strain into a chilled coupe glass and top with the tonic water, or pour into a short tumbler or rocks glass and top with tonic.

Squeeze the lime wedge over the glass, then drop it into the drink.

VIN DE NOIX
Walnut Wine

**Makes about
4 quarts (4L)**

3 quarts (3L) red wine

3 cups (750ml) vodka

3¾ cups (750g) sugar

1 cinnamon stick,
broken

Zest of 1 orange

4 whole cloves

1 vanilla bean, split
lengthwise

24 green walnuts,
halved (see headnote)

NOTE

If you can't get green
walnuts where you live,
check the Resources
(page 283).

There is no shortage of rules in France; they even extend to
beverages, from what type of grapes can be planted in what wine
region to when you can drink your post-dinner coffee, which is *after*
dessert, never with it. The rule that applies to making *vin de noix*
is that you must pick the green walnuts on the 24th of June. I don't
know what happens if you pick them on another day—wait . . . I
actually do know. After proudly posting a photo online of my bounty
from an afternoon picking green walnuts a few days after June 24,
I was harvest-shamed.

Most of us aren't lucky enough to have the luxury of determining
the best day to pick walnuts. So, do as I do, and use the date as a
guideline; green walnuts are best when the centers are still soft and
a hard shell hasn't yet formed underneath the green husks. Once
the shell starts to form, the walnuts will be harder to cut in half,
but they're still okay to use. Some words of advice: Do not hold
the walnuts in place while you try to halve them, as the knife blade
can slip. I dig the blade into the outer husk, then whack against a
cutting board so it splits in half, keeping my other hand safely out
of harm's way.

A French chef once told me to use absolutely the cheapest wine
you can find when making apéritif *vins* such as this, even boxed wine,
but I advise you not to share that online, either.

Find a very large jar, about 2 gallons (7.5L); it needs to be large enough
to hold everything, including the walnuts. (Or divide the ingredients
amongst several jars.) Mix together the wine, vodka, sugar, cinnamon,
orange zest, cloves, vanilla bean, and green walnuts in the jar.

Let the walnuts macerate in a cool, dark place for at least 40 days and
up to 3 months, to give them a deeper flavor.

Using a mesh strainer lined with cheesecloth, strain the liquid into
a bowl. Transfer the liquid to a large measuring cup or container with a
spout for easy pouring, then pour it into clean bottles and tightly cork.

Let the vin de noix stand for at least 1 month before drinking it,
although it will continue to mellow for several months and will taste
even better after 1 year. Vin de noix makes a lovely after-dinner
digestive, served in small glasses, chilled or at room temperature.

PASTIS
Anise Apéritif

Makes 2 cups (500ml)

2 cups (500ml) vodka

5 whole star anise

1 teaspoon green anise seeds

¾ teaspoon caraway seeds

One 6-inch (15cm) licorice root

¼ cup (50g) sugar

2 tablespoons water

No spirit is more associated with France than pastis (see page 52). Originally made in Marseille, pastis is popular across France, and you'd be hard-pressed to find a bar or café anywhere in the country where the anise-and-licorice-flavored spirit isn't served.

Pastis was created after absinthe was banned in 1915, as distillers looked for another drink to quench the thirst that people had developed for the anise-based drink. Absinthe contains wormwood, a scruffy herb that got its name because it was said to remove worms. Absinthe was also used by French troops stationed in North Africa in the 1840s who fell ill after drinking the water; it was added to the water to help purify it. Its high alcohol content also made absinthe a popular libation with the soldiers, and when they returned home, they brought an affinity for the anise-flavored spirit with them. Absinthe quickly caught on, not only because it was exotic, but also because the 70 percent alcohol made it more potent and a better buzz (and a much better deal) than wine. When the French wine industry was hit by phylloxera, a pest that decimated grape crops, wine prices skyrocketed, and people moved *en masse* toward the cheaper alternative.

Soon (with prodding from the struggling wine industry), absinthe began to be blamed for all sorts of societal ills. People claimed it caused hallucinations, insanity, and even a desire to commit murder, and a ban on absinthe was enacted. *Absinthisme*, as the undesirable side effects were called, was likely caused by copper acetate, methanol, and other toxic compounds that were used to make the cheap absinthes that had flooded the market, not by absinthe itself. (Or, more specifically, not the thujone in wormwood, which was blamed.)

In response to the ban, Paul Ricard came up with a similar-tasting liquor with a more reasonable alcohol level of 40 percent, minus any wormwood. Ricard, who was also an artist, painted his own signs to advertise the drink, which he wisely dubbed *"Le vrai pastis de Marseille"* so people in other parts of France would feel a little roguish when they drank it. Its popularity took off. Eventually, after some wrangling, Ricard got authorization to raise the alcohol level to 45 percent, so the pastis would stand up better to dilution with water, as it's commonly enjoyed.

Around the same time, distiller Henri-Louis Pernod, who had previously made absinthe, decided to make a beverage with a similar profile. The eponymously named Pernod wasn't called pastis, since its primary flavoring agent was (and still is) star anise, not licorice. (Pastis 51 is Pernod's version of pastis, introduced in 1951.) Paul Ricard and Henri-Louis Pernod remained rivals for many years, but eventually the two companies merged in 1974, and Pernod Ricard evolved to become the multinational beverage powerhouse that it is today, continuing to produce both brands.

Pastis means "mixture" in the Provençal language, and making it at home requires little effort once you gather the ingredients. It must contain licorice, and the first time I made it, I had all the spices and flavorings I needed, except licorice root. Combing the aisles of my local natural food stores turned up nothing, nor did visits to the various Middle Eastern spice markets I frequent. While I pondered where to find licorice roots in Paris, I went to my pharmacy to get a prescription renewed (and catch up on the neighborhood gossip). While waiting, I looked at the shelf of anti-smoking aids behind the counter, and there they were: small bundles of sticklike licorice roots tied together. The pharmacist informed me that people chew the roots to get over their tobacco cravings, and while I don't smoke, I was happy to leave with a handful of licorice roots, my prescription, and my fill of neighborhood gossip, and I went home to make my first batch of pastis.

Pour the vodka into a clean jar that holds at least 1 quart (1L).

Coarsely crack the star anise pods with a mortar and pestle, or in a sturdy ziptop bag with a rolling pin or hammer. Place them in a dry skillet along with the anise and caraway seeds, and toast over medium-high heat, stirring, until fragrant and lightly toasted, which will take a minute or so.

Transfer the toasted spices to the mortar and pestle and crush them into smaller pieces, about the size of grains of rice. (If using a ziptop bag, let them cool, then crush them in the bag.)

continued

Add the spices to the vodka. Place the licorice root in the mortar and pestle, or the ziptop bag, and bash it a few times, which will help it release its flavors when you infuse it.

Add the licorice root to the jar, cover, and shake vigorously. Let stand for 5 to 7 days in a cool, dark place, shaking it every few days.

Using a mesh strainer lined with a few layers of cheesecloth, strain the vodka mixture into a medium bowl.

Heat the sugar and water in a small saucepan over medium-high heat, stirring, until the sugar is dissolved. Remove from the heat and stir in ¼ cup (60ml) of the vodka mixture. Let cool to room temperature, then add the sweetened vodka mixture to the liquid in the bowl. Transfer the pastis to a large measuring cup or container with a spout for easy pouring, then pour it into a clean bottle and tightly cork.

Homemade pastis can be served in the same ratio as traditional pastis: one part pastis diluted with five parts cold water. (Note that it won't turn cloudy when you add water, as traditional pastis does.) Serve with a small pitcher of cold water to add more as you drink the pastis. A cube of ice, or two, is optional.

PLUMS IN EAU-DE-VIE

Makes 2 pounds (about 1kg) plums

2 pounds (about 1kg) prune plums (called quetsche, or Italian prune plums)

¾ cup (150g) raw granulated sugar or granulated sugar

⅓ cup (80ml) water

1 cinnamon stick

1 vanilla bean, split lengthwise

4 cups (1L) eau-de-vie or vodka, plus more if necessary

There's nothing I like better than stumbling upon a stack of vintage French cookbooks when scouring a flea market. My favorites are those that focus on the gastronomy of a particular region of France.

One day I came across a used copy of *Ma Cuisine d'Été* (*My Summer Food*) by chef Michel Oliver. Published in 1984, the book is Chef Oliver's joyful ode to the cooking of the South of France, with an abundance of seafood recipes and vegetable dishes that don't skimp on tomatoes (or garlic). It also boasted heavily stylized dessert photographs that are a hallmark of French cookbooks from that era; think rosettes of whipped cream topping everything, and plenty of kiwifruits, which were in fashion at the time.

In France, there aren't the big, round, tart purple plums that one gets in the States, but the tiny, golden Mirabelles and dewy-green Reine Claudes are some of the most desirable fruits in the world. *Les quetsches* (called prune plums elsewhere) arrive late in the summer. They are deeply flavored and hold their shape, making them great for infusing in eau-de-vie, as I do with this recipe inspired by Chef Oliver.

Bring a pot of lightly salted water to a boil. Poke each plum four times with the tip of a paring knife. Turn off the heat and drop the plums into the hot water. Let stand for 1 minute, then drain the plums. Pat them dry with a kitchen towel.

In a small saucepan, heat the sugar and water over medium-high heat, stirring, until the sugar dissolves. Set aside.

Put the plums in a clean 2-quart (2L) jar. Add the cinnamon stick and vanilla bean. Pour the eau-de-vie over the plums, then add the sugar syrup. If the plums aren't completely covered by liquid, add additional eau-de-vie until they are.

Cover the jar and store in a cool, dark place for at least 2 months, although they're much better after 6 months. They'll keep for several years in the jar and get better and better. The liqueur-infused plums can be served spooned right from the jar into small bowls or wine glasses with some of their syrup.

PRUNES IN ARMAGNAC

**Makes about
1 pound (450g)
prunes**

2 wide strips
orange zest

1 vanilla bean, split
lengthwise

1 pound (450g)
unpitted prunes
(about 25 prunes)

1¼ cups (300ml) water

⅔ cup (130g) sugar

1 cup (250ml)
Armagnac

They say that when you're done with cognac, you're ready for Armagnac. I like both, but for different reasons. Cognac is more refined because it's distilled twice, whereas Armagnac is distilled only once. This preserves its rugged character, making it more assertive than its more illustrious cousin. Armagnac has a remarkable affinity with prunes, which are produced in the same region, Gascony, where they're called *pruneaux d'Agen*, which are considered a delicacy in France. (The dried fruits survived a marketing effort in America to be rebranded as "dried plums" in an attempt to disassociate them from their stodgy reputation.)

Gascony is also the home of foie gras and duck confit. Prunes may not be as alluring as a *terrine de foie gras* or crisp-skinned duck, but whether you live here or there, after these prunes (or dried plums) have steeped in Armagnac for a few weeks—or better yet, several months—you might find yourself dipping into the jar a lot more often than you expect, as I do.

Put the orange zest, vanilla bean, and prunes in a clean heatproof 1½-quart (1.5L) jar.

In a small saucepan, bring the water and sugar to a boil over medium-high heat, stirring to dissolve the sugar. Remove from the heat.

Pour the hot syrup over the prunes in the jar. Cover, and allow to cool to room temperature. Add the Armagnac, cover, and let rest in a cool, dark place for at least 2 weeks, shaking the jar every few days.

The prunes will be good after 2 weeks, but they'll get better if left to sit for several months. (They'll keep for at least a year, and in Gascony, some people steep them for years.) They're delicious eaten right from the jar, or served in small bowls or wine glasses with some of the syrup (which makes for delicious sipping, too). The prunes are also the appropriate garnish for the Le Gascon cocktail (page 179).

WINEMAKER'S RAISINS

**Makes about
2 cups (280g)
raisins**

2 cups (290g) golden raisins

1 cinnamon stick

1 vanilla bean, split lengthwise

½ cup (125ml) water

¾ cup (150g) sugar

1¼ cups (310ml) eau-de-vie or grappa

On a visit to a winemaking region near Lake Geneva, after a fondue dinner, I was served a few scoops of vanilla ice cream smothered with boozy raisins. I later learned from a *vigneron* (winemaker) that the raisins are part of a dessert called *coupe vigneron*, or winemaker's raisins. After I scraped the bowl clean, making sure to eat every single raisin, I went back to my room and searched online to find out exactly what was in them. One recipe for preparing the liquor-soaked raisins claimed that they are *idéale pour nettoyer votre foie* (ideal for cleaning your liver). I'm not sure if liquor is the ideal beverage for cleaning your liver, but I know from experience that these raisins are a welcome dessert after a rich meal. They're traditionally made with *eau-de-vie de lis*, a clear distillation of lees, the yeasty deposits from grapes left over after wine is made, which is similar to grappa. The raisins are especially good spooned over vanilla ice cream with some of their richly flavored liquid, but are even better with pear sorbet.

Put the raisins, cinnamon stick, and vanilla bean in a heatproof 1½-pint (750ml) jar.

In a small saucepan, heat the water and sugar over medium-high heat, stirring, until the sugar dissolves. Let cool for 5 minutes, then pour it over the raisins.

Let cool to room temperature, then add the eau-de-vie. Cover the jar and let sit in a cool, dark place for at least 3 months, shaking the jar every so often. The raisins will still be rather strong after 3 months, but if you let them sit longer, the alcohol will soften nicely, taking on more of the natural sweetness of the raisins. These will keep for at least 2 years.

4 COCKTAILS

One evening while sitting at a bar in Paris, I watched as the bartender put together my drink. He picked up a bottle, measured out a dose of the liquor, then poured it into a mixing glass. Then he measured out another ingredient into the jigger and added that to the mixing glass as well. He added a spoonful of lemon juice, seasoned the cocktail with a few dashes of bitters, stirred it all up with a spoon, and strained the mixture into a glass. As I took my first sip of the drink, it occurred to me that he had done exactly what I do when I bake: He made something entirely different from ingredients that were sharp and sweet, fruity and bitter, which came together in a way where everything was perfectly in balance.

That prompted me to start making cocktails myself; I was intrigued and excited by the possible combinations available by adding liquor to a mixing glass or shaker, bolstering it with other spirits, fruit juice, or bitters, and enjoying how the results tasted when sipped from the glass. I was already well-versed in blending and baking French butter and chocolate, and found that with French spirits, I could create something that tastes even better than the sum of its ingredients, the same as when I bake a cake or a tart.

■ ■ ■

When asked to name a French drink, people think of wine or pastis, but cocktails don't instinctively come to mind. But in truth, many of the most sought-after cocktail ingredients are French, including cognac, Armagnac, Chartreuse, Lillet, eau-de-vie, and calvados, as well as champagne, Suze, Grand Marnier, elderflower liqueur, dry vermouth, Salers, and Cointreau, not to mention pastis, crème

de menthe, crème de cacao, and crème de cassis, among many, many others.

A number of drinks that are part of the classic cocktail canon and still enjoyed today were invented in France during Prohibition, when Americans fled to other countries to have a drink. (True, there were other places they could have gone to, but who doesn't want to come to Paris?) On transatlantic voyages, once the boats were exactly twelve miles from shore and out of the jurisdiction of the U.S. government, the onboard bars opened for business, and the liquor started flowing.

The most famous bar in Paris at that time was Harry's New York Bar. Originally located in New York, Harry's was taken apart and reassembled in Paris, opening for business on Thanksgiving Day, 1911. It became a refuge for cocktail-craving Americans, and it's still at the same address today: 5 rue Daunou. In its newspaper ads, the bar advised people to pronounce the address as *Sank Roo Doe Noo* so taxi drivers could get visiting Americans—who might not speak the language—to the right destination.

Not everyone in France was as excited as *les Américains* about cocktails, however. In her book, *Je Sais Cuisiner* (*I Know How to Cook*), published in 1930 and still considered the bible of French cooking, home economist Ginette Mathiot sharply explained that she wouldn't include any recipes for cocktails, as those *mélanges* of liquors were "*extrêmement toxique.*" (She did include recipes for home-made wine, liqueurs, and digestives, however.)

Eventually Prohibition was repealed, and France lost its luster as a destination for cocktails. In subsequent years, the best chance you had of getting a cocktail made from scratch was to head to an upscale hotel bar or café that catered to foreigners.

You paid handsomely for the privilege, and the cocktails were rarely as good as one hoped. In 1994, though, the Ritz Paris embarked on a mission to improve its cocktail program and hired British bartender Colin Peter Field to overhaul the bar. Field, who achieved international recognition and has consistently been named one of the best bartenders in the world, lobbied the French government to include an M.O.F. (Meilleur Ouvrier de France) diploma at the Sorbonne for bartenders. The designation has long been bestowed on bakers, chocolatiers, and chefs for being the best in their field, and it meant the profession was going to be taken just as seriously as other facets of French gastronomy.

A little over a decade later, the craft cocktail movement arrived in Paris. Inspired by a global cocktail renaissance, a trio of partners opened the Experimental Cocktail Club in 2007, creating their own lexicon of French cocktails, using French *spiritueux oubliées* (forgotten spirits). The French quickly made up for lost time, and soon cocktail bars were proliferating. French liquor brands took notice, updating bottle and labels designs and ramping up production, getting their bottles back on liquor store shelves and into the hands of bartenders, who were creating new drinks as well as revisiting the classics.

A subsequent wave of cocktail bars spread across the French capital, prompted by the opening, and success, of Candelaria, a world-class cocktail bar tucked behind an unmarked white door in the back of a taqueria. "A taqueria . . . *in Paris?!*" people wondered. But any doubts were quickly dispelled. Founded by a three-person team with a bit of Brooklyn cred, the bar and the taqueria in the Marais went viral, as did the Guêpe Verte (page 204), a spicy concoction that's become a modern Paris classic.

Today Paris boasts one of the most vibrant cocktail scenes in the world. From Dirty Dick, a retro tiki bar where drinks are served in pineapples and seashells (whose owner kept the name of the "hostess" bar that had previously been in that location) to Le Syndicat, which resolutely stocks only French spirits, there's something for everybody, in every arrondissement. But the movement has also spread outside of Paris, to include Symbiose, a speakeasy known for its uber-creative cocktails in the heart of the wine-centric city of Bordeaux, and Monsieur Moutarde in Dijon, where the bartenders can't resist sneaking a dab of the local specialty into a cocktail every now and then (and serving it in a mustard crock). France is now at the top of its cocktail game, and it's a place I'm delighted to play in.

■   ■   ■

I'm a big fan of classics, like the Scofflaw (page 186), Boulevardier (page 179), and Hemingway Daiquiri (page 224), but I'm inspired and influenced by the spirits and liqueurs of France to create my own cocktails, too. I've culled recipes from my favorite bartenders in Paris, as well as bartenders outside of the country who share my reverence for French-made spirits.

On the following pages are some notes and tips about the ingredients, tools and equipment, and techniques you will need to make the cocktail recipes in this chapter.

ON INGREDIENTS

▪▪ I know how frustrating it is to spend a lot of money on a bottle of liquor when a recipe calls for just a quarter ounce of it, so I have kept your (and my) budget in mind and avoid calling for obscure ingredients. Some spirits, like calvados or cognac, can be expensive—even in France—but a little goes a long way and a bottle will last for years, even after it's opened. In the few instances when I do call for something that seems unusual, even if it's just a very small quantity (such as the absinthe in Le Piqueur on page 186 and in the D-Day Swizzle on page 215), it's because that dash really does make a difference.

▪▪ I tend not to mention specific brands of liquor because you likely have your own favorites. If you don't, ask the staff at your local liquor shop for guidance. In some instances, I specify London dry gin; it has a pronounced juniper flavor and is drier than other gins, which I prefer in certain cocktails.

▪▪ If you want to spring for only one type of cocktail bitters, a bottle of orange bitters is a good, all-purpose choice; it's easily obtainable at liquor stores. As with liquor, I don't want you to have to spend a lot of time or money on elusive ingredients, so I frequently call for orange bitters in my cocktail recipes. I also use Angostura aromatic bitters,

which you can find in any well-stocked supermarket. There are many brands, and flavors, of cocktail bitters, and you're welcome to use another favorite in place of the ones I recommend. In a few cases where I mention a specific cocktail bitter, once you taste it in a drink, I think you'll be glad you added it to your collection.

- ▪ ▪ The two best-known French orange liqueurs are Grand Marnier and Cointreau. Grand Marnier is made with a brandy base, infused with bitter oranges, and aged in oak. Cointreau is made from both sweet and bitter oranges and is transparent. In most recipes, I give the option of using either one, since I don't want you to *not* make a cocktail if you have one but not the other. However, for the Sidecar (page 190), Cointreau, with its neutral-colored base, is specified. Low-priced triple secs can be found, but it's challenging to find one that has the bright, true orange flavor of Grand Marnier or Cointreau. Pierre Ferrand dry curaçao is an excellent French-made triple sec that can be used in recipes that call for either of the orange liqueurs listed above.

- ▪ ▪ Amer Picon (see page 98) is a bitter French *amer* that you likely won't find in the United States. I tussled with myself over including the few recipes in this book that call for it, such as the Brooklyn (page 187), but it was impossible to write a book on French drinks and not include them. But don't worry; I offer good substitutes that are available outside of France (see page 99), or leave a little room to pack a bottle of Amer Picon in your suitcase the next time you visit France.

- ▪ ▪ When a recipe calls for lemon, lemon-lime, or grapefruit soda, it's worth seeking out a "premium" brand, meaning one that has a high proportion of real fruit juice and isn't overly sweet. A good one that's widely available is San Pellegrino, although you're welcome to use another favorite.

ON TOOLS AND EQUIPMENT

- ▪ ▪ You don't need a slew of fancy equipment or techniques to make these cocktails. A cocktail shaker and a mixing glass will do the job for most. If you don't have either one, a large Mason-type jar can be used as a substitute for a shaker or mixing glass, and a chopstick or soupspoon can stand in for a cocktail stirrer.

- ▪ ▪ I use a standard three-piece cocktail shaker (called a cobbler shaker), which has a built-in strainer in the pouring hole under the cap. For some cocktails (or if you're using a two-piece Boston shaker), you'll need to open the shaker so the mixture can be strained through a mesh or julep strainer, since any bits of herbs or berries would clog the built-in strainer of a cobbler shaker.

- ▪ ▪ A cocktail measuring cup is a necessity. I like the Oxo mini angled measuring cup, which is also available as a stainless-steel jigger, although the nonmetal version is a little easier to read.

- ▪ ▪ If you're anything like me, you know that a cocktail *always* tastes better in a proper glass. You can spend a lot of money on fancy glassware, or you can do what I do and hit thrift stores and flea markets. You'll have a hard time finding a complete set of six or eight glasses at a bargain price, but I don't mind. If I find glasses I like, I buy them in sets of two, three, or even individually, and mix and match. Check local flea markets and thrift stores, as well as websites like eBay and Etsy.

ON TECHNIQUES

▪ ▪ Shaking a cocktail not only chills it but also emulsifies the ingredients (most notably in cocktails with fruit juice) and dilutes the mixture just enough to "loosen it up." To shake a cocktail, put the ingredients in the shaker, then fill the shaker three-quarters full with ice. Cover securely, and shake vigorously, holding the shaker parallel (horizontal) to the ground. Keep your thumb over the cap while you shake to make sure it stays in place. The drink inside is well chilled when the outside of the shaker feels very cold, 10 to 15 seconds.

▪ ▪ To stir a cocktail, add the ingredients to the mixing glass, then fill the glass with enough ice to cover the ingredients, about half to three-quarters full. Use a stirring spoon to briskly stir the cocktail until it's well chilled, about 30 seconds.

BOULEVARDIER

Makes 1 cocktail

2 ounces (60ml) rye
or bourbon whiskey

1 ounce (30ml)
sweet vermouth

1 ounce (30ml) Campari

Orange twist or
candied amarena
cherry (page 277) or
maraschino cherry,
for garnish

Frequently billed as the "French Negroni," the Boulevardier may be my very favorite cocktail. It was the creation of another American in Paris, Erskine Gwynne, a *bon vivant* who published a magazine called *The Boulevardier* in the 1920s, whose title refers to someone who strolls along the boulevards of the city. Like the Negroni, a classic Boulevardier calls for its three ingredients in equal parts, but I found that doubling up on the whiskey puts it on equal footing flavor-wise with the decidedly bitter Campari. Some people serve Boulevardiers with one large ice cube, Negroni-style, but I prefer mine served in another direction: up.

Add the rye, vermouth, and Campari to a cocktail mixing glass. Add ice and stir until well chilled. Strain into a chilled coupe glass. Garnish with the orange twist.

LE GASCON

Makes 1 cocktail

2 ounces (60ml)
Armagnac

½ ounce (15ml) Grand
Marnier or Cointreau

1 teaspoon freshly
squeezed lemon juice

1 teaspoon freshly
squeezed orange juice

Armagnac-soaked
prune (page 169),
for garnish

There's nothing more French than Armagnac, or prunes—both of which are in bountiful supply in France. They're especially popular in Gascony, in the southwest of France, where vendors sell bottles of the locally made grape brandy from folding card tables at the markets, and bags and baskets of *pruneaux d'Agen*, a type of prune so luscious and sweet that if you closed your eyes, you'd swear you were savoring a bite of chocolate. These two ingredients come together beautifully in Prunes in Armagnac, as well as in this cocktail, which gives you the best of both.

Add the Armagnac, Grand Marnier, lemon juice, and orange juice to a cocktail shaker. Add ice and shake until well chilled. Strain into a chilled coupe glass. Drop in the Armagnac-soaked prune.

MON DIEU

Makes 1 cocktail

2 ounces (60ml)
rye whiskey

1 ounce (30ml)
blackberry shrub
(page 276)

3 ounces (90ml)
sparkling water

Lime or lemon wedge,
and a few blackberries
or raspberries, for
garnish

Rye whiskey isn't well-known in Paris, nor are—*mon dieu!*—drinks with *vinaigre*, a word based on an alliance of two French words, *vin* and *aigre*, which together means "sour wine." But this cocktail, with its persuasive tinge of blackberries in the equation, has sparked more interest in both.

———————

Stir together the rye, blackberry shrub, and sparkling water in a tumbler or rocks glass. Add a handful of ice. Garnish with the citrus wedge and berries.

FRENCH MANHATTAN

Makes 1 cocktail

1½ ounces (45ml)
cognac

1½ ounces (45ml)
sweet vermouth

¼ ounce (8ml) Grand
Marnier or Cointreau

1 dash orange bitters
or Angostura aromatic
bitters

Candied amarena
cherry (page 277) or
maraschino cherry,
for garnish

The French are just as fascinated with America as Americans are with France. Although, as my friend Grégoire told me, "We both admire the lifestyle of each other, but in the end, each of us prefers our way of life." Even if you're a die-hard (American) Manhattan drinker, this French version might change your allegiance. (Pictured, opposite.)

———————

Add the cognac, sweet vermouth, Grand Marnier, and bitters to a cocktail mixing glass. Add ice and stir until well chilled. Strain into a chilled coupe glass. Garnish with the cherry.

DOLIN

To many of us, vermouth was the dusty green bottle that our parents pulled out of the cupboard every few years when they found a chicken recipe in a magazine that called for a quarter-cup of vermouth. The other time was if a guest came by who was a martini drinker. My parents drank whiskey sours they made from a powdered mix. Needless to say, anyone who asked for a martini at our house probably regretted it, regardless of the age of the vermouth.

I followed in their footsteps and kept a bottle on hand for deglazing a pan, never paying attention to the brand, and never taking a taste of it. Everything changed when I visited Turin, the Italian city where modern vermouth was invented. I casually wandered into one of the city's *apertivo* bars one afternoon, in search of a drink, and pointed to what everyone else was sipping from squat glasses with slices of orange in them. Leaning against the marble bar, taking my first sip of the drink, I couldn't quite put my finger on what all the savory and sweet flavors were in the peculiar red wine. After I took another sip of the pleasant herbal apéritif and found out what it was, I thought, "So *this* is vermouth?" Then, I got it.

While a number of vermouths are produced in that region of Italy, France has its own tradition of making vermouth in Chambéry, a town tucked in the French Alps not far from Turin. The term *French vermouth* doesn't refer only to the country where it's made; it's also a style of vermouth: dry, clean, and herbaceous. Some bartenders consider Dolin French vermouth so smooth and elegantly aromatic that it makes a 50/50 martini (equal parts gin and vermouth) possible.

Dolin created the original *vermouth de Chambéry*, which was once an official designation by the French government. At one time there were seven vermouth makers in Chambéry, but the designation is no longer used because most of the other companies have disappeared. Since I often reach for a bottle of Dolin vermouth when mixing up a cocktail, I went to the Savoy to learn the story behind the label.

Dolin was founded by botanist Joseph Chavasse, who, like many botanists of his time, devised plant-based tonics and remedies. The Savoy region wasn't yet part of France, but a dukedom of the House of Savoy. Intrigued by the herbal wine being produced there, Monsieur Chavasse traveled to Turin to learn how to make it. Taken with the drink, he returned to Chambéry and began producing his own version using the local white wine of the Savoy, which would eventually become *vermouth de Chambéry*.

Monsieur Chavasse's daughter, Marie, married Louis Dolin, a lawyer who joined the ranks and also became a *vermouthier*. After her parents passed away, and subsequently her husband, Marie took control of the company. She became an ardent promoter of her family's vermouth, taking it to the Philadelphia Centennial International Exposition in 1876, where it won a gold medal and gained a following in America as a result. To acknowledge its popularity in the States, Dolin produced a special bottle of vermouth for the U.S., the Américano

Honey Moon, which featured the planet Earth on the label with an American flag proudly waving in the center of it.

On a brisk fall morning, with the persistent drizzle of late autumn coming down, I met Pierre-Olivier Rousseaux at the train station in Chambéry; his family is the fifth generation of vermouth makers at Dolin. At the distillery, Pierre-Olivier explained how Prohibition threatened Dolin's alliance with America, and showed me a vintage bottle of a nonalcoholic vermouth they produced for the United States. When I asked if he'd ever tasted it, he said it was something they wanted to keep intact in their archives, amongst an array of other bottles in a glass showcase in his office. The archives include bottles of vermouth that mirror Dolin's history, as well as those of Bonal Gentiane-Quina (page 92), a local apéritif they acquired and now produce. He also pulled several heavy books off the shelves that were the original Dolin recipe ledgers, where the recipes for their vermouth and other spirits were handwritten in highly stylized cursive with a quill pen. They're the same recipes they use today. When I asked if I could take a photo because I was fascinated by the typography, he uncharacteristically agreed (most companies guard their formulations and ingredients as if they are highly classified state secrets). Today, Dolin continues to produce vermouth in Chambéry, which is a mainstay in bars around the world. With only twenty-one employees, they produce three kinds of vermouth—dry, rouge, and blanc—as well as an impressive collection of fruit crèmes, syrups, and herbal liqueurs made from plants harvested in the surrounding Alps.

When we toured the production area, hyssop, gentian, elderflowers, and stinging nettles were marinating in vats, each infusing separately, rather than all together (since their flavors can vary by the season, or the batch), so they're easier to blend and create just the right balance.

Plants from the region also find their way into Suedois Dolin, a bitter digestive formulated by a Swedish doctor in the seventeenth century; it's a distillation of rhubarb roots (which the label says—or warns—are for "cleansing"), gentian, aloe (a stimulant), myrrh (a disinfectant), wormwood, and génépi, a plant also referred to as mountain sage due to its musky flavor. Another curiosity was Chamberyzette, vermouth flavored with wild strawberries, which is enjoyed as an apéritif over ice.

Over a hearty lunch of the local specialty, *ravioles du Royans*, tiny cheese ravioli served under an overflow of gratinéed cheese that oozed over and down the sides of the baking dish (countering the perception that the French practice portion control), Pierre-Olivier was optimistic about the future of Dolin. He is insistent on keeping the quality high, while updating some of the older beverages for modern tastes. He expressed a little concern that they might get *too* popular, making it difficult for their small number of employees to keep up.

I can't say I'm helping much, as I go through more than my share of vermouth in drinks like Mon Nouvel Ami (page 187) and the Scofflaw (page 186), and it puts the "V" in the TGV (page 206). But I'm confident that with Pierre-Olivier at the helm, the standards of *vermouth de Chambéry* will be upheld, no matter how many people discover it.

TORONTO

Makes 1 cocktail

2 ounces (60ml)
rye whiskey

¼ ounce (8ml)
Fernet-Vallet or
Fernet-Branca

¼ ounce (8ml) rich
demerara syrup
(page 271) or simple
syrup (page 270)

2 dashes orange
bitters or Angostura
aromatic bitters

Orange twist, for
garnish (optional)

A sure way to tell whether you've walked into a good restaurant, bistro, or bar in France is if you received *une bonne accueil*, or a proper welcome. When I pulled up a stool at Le Mary Celeste in the Marais for the first time, the bartender politely came out from behind the bar with his hands folded behind him and asked what I would be having to drink.

I admired his solid professionalism, so thought I'd test his mettle, saying, "Could I have something with *whiskey de seigle*?" Rye whiskey isn't so well-known in France, but a few minutes later, he set down on the bar in front of me a slightly frosted coupe glass, holding a shimmering, caramel-colored pool of liquid, filled to the widest point of the glass. I took a tentative taste of the cocktail, which was so strong that it fell into the category of "make sure you're well-planted on your barstool," and said, *"C'est parfait."* Soon, my head was spinning! And not from the drink, but from learning that a small sip of liquid could taste so good. (And be so potent.) I later learned from the bartender, Carlos Madriz, that this cocktail gets its name from Canadian whisky, which was used during Prohibition when American whiskey became unavailable in France.

The original calls for Fernet-Branca, but I swap it out for Fernet-Vallet (page 111), and I use demerara syrup instead of simple syrup, a tip I picked up from *Meehan's Bartender Manual* by Jim Meehan. It gives this Canadian-inspired cocktail an appropriate maplelike richness.

Add the rye, Fernet-Vallet, demerara syrup, and bitters to a cocktail mixing glass. Fill with ice and stir until well chilled. Let stand in the mixing glass for 10 seconds, stir a few more times, then strain into a chilled coupe glass. Garnish with the orange twist, if desired.

LE PIQUEUR

Makes 1 cocktail

1¾ ounces (50ml) cognac

¾ ounce (22ml) white crème de menthe

¼ teaspoon absinthe

Lemon twist

Fresh mint leaf, for garnish

The bartenders at Maison Premiere in Brooklyn are adept at using an intriguing, and sometimes complex, combination of French spirits to create their enticing cocktails. But their version of the Stinger, or as I've dubbed it, Le Piqueur, is deceptively simple. Bar director William Elliott's preference is Gourry de Chadville cognac, an overproof cognac (at 55 percent ABV versus the standard 40 percent) made by the oldest family-run estate in France. Its higher percentage of alcohol makes it stand out when stirred up with crème de menthe, and this has become one of my "house cocktails" at *ma maison*.

Add the cognac, crème de menthe, and absinthe to a cocktail mixing glass. Fill with ice and stir until well chilled. Strain into a chilled coupe glass. Hold the lemon twist over the top of the drink and twist it to release the oil into the drink. Discard the lemon twist. Garnish with the mint.

SCOFFLAW

Makes 1 cocktail

2 ounces (60ml) rye whiskey

1 ounce (30ml) dry vermouth

¾ ounce (22ml) freshly squeezed lemon juice

¾ ounce (22ml) store-bought or homemade grenadine syrup (page 274)

2 dashes orange bitters

In 1919, when the Eighteenth Amendment was ratified in America and booze was officially banned, a wealthy supporter of the law sponsored a contest to come up with a term describing people who flaunted it. Out of twenty-five thousand entries, two entrants independently came up with the word *scofflaw*. They ended up splitting the prize of $200, and a new word—and a new cocktail— was added to our vocabulary.

Add the rye, vermouth, lemon juice, grenadine, and bitters to a cocktail mixing glass. Fill with ice and stir until well chilled. Strain into a chilled coupe glass.

BROOKLYN

Makes 1 cocktail

1½ ounces (45ml)
rye whiskey

1 ounce (30ml)
dry vermouth

¼ ounce (8ml) Amer
Picon or another amer
(see page 98)

¼ ounce (8ml)
maraschino liqueur

1 dash Angostura
aromatic bitters

Orange twist,
for garnish

The French have developed a fondness for Brooklyn, pronounced Brook-*leeen*, with a drawn-out "eee." Seemingly every café and restaurant that's opened in the last few years in Paris (and beyond) features metal-framed windows, bare-filament lightbulbs, tattooed staff, and, of course, social media–tailored cups of café crèmes.

The affinity isn't exactly new. The original Brooklyn cocktail, published in *The Savoy Cocktail Book* in 1930, relies on one of the Frenchest of all ingredients, Amer Picon (see page 98), to reinforce the woody whiskey flavor, along with French vermouth. This recipe comes from Jeff Galli, the former bar director at Frank's in . . . where else? Brooklyn. Jeff is one of the best (and nicest) cocktail makers I've ever met, so when he recommends using Rittenhouse rye and Dolin vermouth—and Bigallet China-China if you can't get Amer Picon—I follow his lead.

Add the rye, vermouth, Amer Picon, maraschino liqueur, and Angostura bitters to a cocktail mixing glass. Fill with ice and stir until well chilled. Strain into a chilled coupe glass. Garnish with the orange twist.

MON NOUVEL AMI

Makes 1 cocktail

1 ounce (30ml)
rye whiskey

½ ounce (15ml) Dolin red
bitter apéritif (see Note)

1 ounce (30ml) dry
vermouth

Lemon or orange twist,
for garnish

Harry MacElhone of Harry's New York Bar in Paris created this cocktail for an *ami*, and dubbed it the Old Pal after his friend. The proportions are similar to the Boulevardier (page 179), but this cocktail is drier, thanks to the French vermouth. I use Dolin red bitter apéritif here; it's a gentler alternative to Campari, and it doesn't overwhelm the other ingredients. As a result, Dolin—and this cocktail—have become *mes nouveaux amis*.

Mix the rye, bitter apéritif, and vermouth in a short tumbler or rocks glass. Add 1 large ice cube or a handful of ice. Garnish with the twist.

NOTE

You can substitute St. George Bruto Americano, Cappelletti, or Campari for the Dolin red bitter apéritif.

LIAISON

Makes 1 cocktail

2 ounces (60ml)
blended Scotch whisky

¼ ounce (8ml)
dry vermouth

¼ ounce (8ml)
Cap Corse rouge or
sweet vermouth

¼ ounce (8ml) Grand
Marnier or Cointreau

Lemon twist,
for garnish

One of the most difficult things for people to discern when learning to speak French are the *liaisons*, when several words are joined together and slurred so they sound like one word. *Les enfants* becomes *layzonfonts*, and *l'age d'or* becomes *lajdoor*. If you're one of those people who struggle to speak French, this high-test cocktail may loosen up your tongue enough to have you speaking like a local.

Add the whisky, dry vermouth, Cap Corse, and Grand Marnier to a cocktail mixing glass. Fill with ice and stir until well chilled. Strain into a chilled coupe glass. Garnish with the lemon twist.

BOURBON-BONAL BREEZE

Makes 1 cocktail

1¾ ounces (50ml)
bourbon whiskey

1 ounce (30ml) freshly
squeezed orange juice
(from regular or blood
oranges)

¾ ounce (22ml) Bonal
Gentiane-Quina

¼ ounce (8ml) simple
syrup (page 270)

4 fresh mint leaves

Mint sprig and orange
twist, for garnish

People in France like to avoid *courants d'aire* (indoor breezes, or drafts), even in the full-on heat of summer. My take is that it goes back to the Middle Ages, when maladies were spread through the air. So windows stay closed in the summer, and fans are frowned upon as well. But this breezy cocktail is hard to resist, no matter what the season. With a refreshing backbone of quinine from the Bonal, and a healthy belt of bourbon, this brightly flavored cocktail is pretty irresistible. But if anyone is still skeptical, using the colorful juices of *oranges sanguines* (blood oranges) will surely make them a fan. (Pictured, opposite.)

Add the bourbon, orange juice, Bonal, simple syrup, and mint leaves to a cocktail shaker. Fill with ice and shake until well chilled. Open the shaker and strain through a mesh strainer or julep strainer into a short tumbler or rocks glass. Add a generous handful of ice. Garnish with the mint spring and orange twist.

WATERLOO

Makes 1 cocktail

2 ounces (60ml)
bourbon whiskey

1¼ ounces (40ml)
Dubonnet rouge

½ ounce (15ml) Grand
Marnier or Cointreau

½ ounce (15ml) freshly
squeezed orange juice

Candied amarena
cherry (page 277) or
maraschino cherry,
for garnish

Here's my riff on a cocktail called the Napoléon. Like the unexpected outcome of Napoléon's last battle, the original cocktail didn't quite turn out as I anticipated, so I came up with this version, backing up the bourbon with fruity Dubonnet and a double blitz of orange, as my victory lap.

Add the bourbon, Dubonnet, Grand Marnier, and orange juice to a cocktail shaker. Fill with ice and shake until well chilled. Strain into a chilled coupe glass. Garnish with the cherry.

SIDECAR

Makes 1 cocktail

1½ ounces (45ml)
cognac

¾ ounce (22ml)
Cointreau

¾ ounce (22ml) freshly
squeezed lemon juice

2 teaspoons simple
syrup (page 270)

Lemon twist,
for garnish

The Sidecar is a classic cocktail made with very French ingredients: cognac, orange liqueur, and *jus de citron*. I've had plenty of Sidecars over the years, but I've never had one at the Ritz Paris, its purported place of origin. (One version they serve uses a very rare cognac from 1854, and apparently costs $1,600.) Until someone invites me to join them for one at the hotel, this version remains my favorite. It's from bartender and spirits writer Jeffrey Morgenthaler, author of *Drinking Distilled*. Jeffrey is a man of strong opinions (even though he's not French), and prefers Cointreau in his Sidecars. He also skips the sugary rim, which I don't miss either. If you want to splurge on extra-fancy cognac, feel free to invite me to join you. If you go with a cognac from 1854, I'm sure Jeffrey wouldn't mind an invite as well.

Add the cognac, Cointreau, lemon juice, and simple syrup to a cocktail shaker. Fill with ice and shake until well chilled. Strain into a chilled coupe glass. Garnish with the lemon twist.

VARIATION —— To add a little zip, replace the simple syrup with 1½ teaspoons rich fresh ginger syrup (page 275).

EVOLVED REVOLVER

Makes 1 cocktail

2 ounces (60ml)
bourbon whiskey

¾ ounce (22ml) coffee
liqueur, such as Kahlúa

½ ounce (15ml)
sweet vermouth

2 dashes coffee bitters
or orange bitters, or
1 dash cardamom bitters

Orange twist,
for garnish

When you live in Paris, you see people come . . . and you see them go. It's hard when friends leave, but there's an upside: They give away things they don't want to pack up and take home. Invariably, there are sets of wine glasses, since you can't have too many of them if you live in France, but I go for the things that people have hauled over from the States, like rolls of heavy-duty aluminum foil, bags of pecans, Sharpies, and Triscuits. (Romain discovered Triscuits in the United States; if they ever start selling them in France, I recommend the company tap him as their spokesperson.) One thing I was happy to take off a friend's hands was a box of half-empty liquor bottles. Included was a Mexican coffee liqueur, whose bullet-shaped bottle and bright orange-and-yellow label looked like something extracted out of a time capsule from my college years. I considered mixing up a few White Russians with some of the lovely crème fraîche from my fromagerie . . . until I remembered the aftermath of drinking them, and decided to take a more mature tack with it.

If you haven't had coffee liqueur in a while, I suggest you pick up a bottle (or wait for someone to move and give you what's left of one) and try this caffeine-fueled combination. It's my take on the Revolver, which I've evolved with a dose of vermouth.

———————

Add the bourbon, coffee liqueur, vermouth, and bitters to a cocktail mixing glass. Fill with ice and stir until well chilled. Strain into a chilled coupe glass. Garnish with the orange twist.

VARIATION —— For an extra jolt, add 1 to 2 teaspoons cooled brewed espresso to the mixing glass before stirring.

VOILÀ!

Makes 1 cocktail

2 ounces (60ml)
bourbon whiskey

1½ ounces (45ml)
freshly squeezed
tangerine juice

1½ teaspoons spiced
tangerine syrup
(page 275) or simple
syrup (page 270)

1 dash Angostura
aromatic bitters

Splash of champagne or
dry sparkling wine, such
as crémant (optional)

Orange wheel,
for garnish

Coming from California, I wasn't quite prepared for winter in Paris. From mid-November through March, the city slips into darkness, with short days (and frosty-cold weather) providing fewer reasons to linger outside. Parisians fall into a collective funk as the unrelenting gray skies just don't seem to want to budge. What keeps everyone upbeat are the piles of sunny clementines and tangerines at the markets.

Market vendors in Paris don't normally hand out samples, but clementines are the exception, and sellers peel them open and offer a taste. Because the French are discerning shoppers, some try one and move on to the next stand, while others like what they taste and fill a bag.

It's impossible not to be happy if you have a bowl of bright orange clementines with shiny green leaves attached to the stems. When I gaze over at the pile of them in my kitchen—my low-tech version of one of those therapeutic "happy" lamps—*voilà*, I'm instantly cheered up. This drink, with a double dose of tangerine, has the same effect.

Add the bourbon, tangerine juice, spiced tangerine syrup, and Angostura bitters to a cocktail shaker. Put a handful of ice in a short tumbler or rocks glass. Fill the cocktail shaker with ice and shake until well chilled. Strain into the glass and top with champagne, if desired. Garnish with the orange wheel.

POMME ROYALE

Makes 1 cocktail

2 ounces (60ml)
calvados

1 ounce (30ml) freshly
squeezed lemon juice

½ ounce (15ml)
Cointreau or
Grand Marnier

½ ounce (15ml) simple
syrup (page 270)

Lemon wedge

Superfine or granulated
sugar

Splash of dry sparkling
wine, such as crémant

Lemon twist,
for garnish

I questioned my comprehension of French when I read about a bottle of liquor called Pomme Prisonnière, which I thought meant "imprisoned apple." But my understanding turned out to be right. With a bit of the French flair for embellishment, it turns out that indeed, an apple was imprisoned in a bottle. But what a prison it is! In Normandy, Christian Drouin produces a bottle of calvados with an apple apprehended by the aromatic brandy.

This recipe comes from Julia Grossman, who ran a French-themed café and bar in New York City, where she kept a bottle of Pomme Prisonnière safely behind the bar. A splash of sparkling wine finishes the drink, giving it *royale* status and a much better send-off than some of the other imprisoned royals got in France.

Add the calvados, lemon juice, Cointreau, and simple syrup to a cocktail shaker. Fill with ice and shake until well chilled.

Make a slash in the lemon wedge and run it around the rim of a chilled coupe glass. Spread some sugar on a small plate and dip the rim of the glass into the sugar. Strain the cocktail into the glass. Top with the sparkling wine and garnish with the lemon twist.

VARIATION —— To give the drink an earthier note, use honey syrup (page 271) in place of the simple syrup.

STAN'S THE MAN

Makes 1 cocktail

1 ounce (30ml) calvados

1 ounce (30ml) Salers or another gentian-based apéritif, such as Suze

¾ ounce (22ml) sweet vermouth

¼ ounce (8ml) liqueur de noix or Vin de Noix (page 163)

Orange twist

Stanislas Jouenne is one of the most well-respected and well-liked bartenders in Paris. So it's no surprise that he's been put in charge of stirring and shaking up drinks at Gallopin, a brasserie hosting one of the oldest cocktail bars in France. The *galopin*, a tankard of beer served in a small silver-handled *chope* that kept the beer cold, was invented there. The *chope* held a small portion of beer, which was meant to be drunk quickly before galloping away on your horse. The term is still used today in France; a *galopin* (with one "l") refers to a beer served in a stemmed wine glass.

Thanks to Stan, as he's affectionately called, the cocktails at Gallopin are better than ever. He stocks his bar exclusively with French spirits and liqueurs, and I'm always craning my neck to see what sorts of curiosities he's uncovered. On one visit, they included a very old bottle of Picon Amer, absinthe dating back to the 1920s, and vintage bottles of Bonal, Byrrh, and Suze.

In this recipe, I use a homemade liqueur de noix; there's a recipe for it on my website, or you can find it at well-stocked liquor stores. To substitute vin de noix, see the variation below.

Add the calvados, Salers, vermouth, and liqueur de noix to a cocktail shaker. Fill with ice and shake until well chilled. Strain into a chilled coupe glass. Hold the orange twist over the top of the drink and twist it to release the oils from the peel into the drink. Discard the orange twist.

VARIATION —— To substitute vin de noix for liqueur de noix, increase the quantity to ½ ounce (15ml) and reduce the vermouth to ½ ounce (15ml).

CHARTREUSE

My love affair with Chartreuse began when, as a young cook, I read *The Auberge of the Flowering Hearth* by Roy Andries de Groot, an evocative story of a mountain inn run by two women who gathered ingredients from the countryside to create extraordinary meals, and drinks, for their guests. It lovingly captures a certain time and place in France, and it made me want to move there—which I eventually did.

The *auberge* (inn) existed in the village of Saint-Pierre-de-Chartreuse, not far from where a small group of Carthusian monks arrived in 1084 seeking a life of solitude and silence, away from the stresses of "modern" life (whatever those were in the 1000s). What they didn't anticipate were the brutal winters. Since they couldn't raise or grow their own food year-round, they had to find a way to make a living, and to eat.

Over the centuries, the monks tried their hands at several different *métiers* (crafts), and eventually found success as ironworkers. Rumor has it the neighbors weren't too pleased with the monks mining for iron in their region and were jealous of their success, but Emmanuel Delafon, the current Président Directeur Générale of Chartreuse told me that their downfall was a law that forbade the cutting down of trees, enacted by Louis XIV to protect the forests, and because he wanted the wood for building military vessels. Because the monks needed wood to make *charbon de bois* (charcoal), their source of energy for iron-making, the ban put an end to their business as ironworkers.

Fortunately, in 1605, French army officer François Hannibal d'Estrées gave the brothers an ancient recipe for an herbal elixir as a gift; the elixir could be made from the plants, roots, and other botanicals growing in the Alps surrounding the monastery. The complex recipe, however, was challenging to unravel, and it took the brothers more than one hundred years to perfect it. Once they succeeded, they decided to name it after the valley where they resided: La Chartreuse.

The monks first offered bottles of the strongly flavored green Chartreuse elixir as a health tonic. (Later in its history, the elixir was sold as a toothpaste, which, at close to 70 percent alcohol, was a good way to get people to clean their teeth.) People took to it so much that in 1764, the monks created a less-concentrated (and lower-alcohol) version to be enjoyed as a beverage, which is still bottled today.

The monks kept their recipe a closely guarded secret, but when the French government issued a decree in 1810 that all liqueur makers must reveal their recipes, they were forced to submit theirs. After reviewing the lengthy list of ingredients, however, the government rejected the recipe for Chartreuse as *trop compliqué* and returned it. The recipe still remains a secret today, and only two of the monks know the ingredients. For security reasons, they don't travel together.

The monks continued to be plagued with problems, however. During the French Revolution, they were expelled from France. Later they returned, only to be expelled again. Then in 1903, the monks built a distillery in

Tarragona, Spain, to make Chartreuse without interruption. During that period, the Chartreuse distillery in France was nationalized and the monks weren't allowed to use the name Chartreuse. So, the made-in-Spain liqueur was dubbed Une Tarragone, with the words *"fabrique par les Pères Charteux"* (made by the Chartreuse monks) written in even larger type than the name of the liqueur on the label, to differentiate it from the inferior version being made back in France by another distiller.

Nearly two decades later, they were able to return to France once and for all, and resumed production of Chartreuse in the mountains. But after several bankruptcies, and a subsequent landslide that wiped out the distillery, the monks moved their production to a more secure location in Voiron, where it still stands today (it's now used as an aging cellar), with a new distillery finished in 2018. The current capacity of the Chartreuse distillery is 2.5 million liters, and their aging cellar is the longest in the world.

Chartreuse caused a splash in the United States due to the popularity of The Last Word (page 201), a cocktail invented during the Prohibition era. It featured the naturally green spirit, likely because it was strong, and delicious, enough to obscure the taste of bathtub gin. (Proof that Chartreuse makes everything better.) In the ensuing years, however, Chartreuse became more of a curiosity, and bottles sat on the sidelines waiting to make their return. When the craft cocktail movement hit, and French spirits were back in the limelight, bartenders began reaching for Chartreuse again. The herbal liqueur gives a cocktail a beguiling sweet-ness without being cloying, and its herbal complexity pairs well with other spirits and liqueurs, especially in French-focused drinks such as The Yellow Cocktail (page 202).

On its own, Chartreuse is best enjoyed chilled, but not over ice. Cooling the drink tames the alcohol, tipping the taste toward the botanicals. When I sip a glass of Chartreuse, it's a challenge to discern exactly what's in it. And that's okay. The mystery is part of its allure.

I'd visited Chartreuse back in the 1990s, and recently returned. After a tour of the cellars and a tasting, I picked up a few bottles to restock my bar, as well as boxes of chocolates, marshmallows, and *pâtes de fruits* (fruit jellies) made by Sandrine Chappaz, a local chocolatier whose confections are infused with the native liqueur.

For fans of Chartreuse, like me, there's the Grand Festival des Fous de Chartreuse, a gathering held once a year in Paris where those who are *fous* (crazy) for Chartreuse spend the day sipping the green and yellow spirit poured from oversize bottles at Caves Bossetti in the Marais (see page 279). Usually you'll find me there on the first Tuesday in October, elbowing my way through the happy crowd, getting my fill. After all of these years, I'm still *fou* for it.

THE CHAMPS-ÉLYSÉES

Makes 1 cocktail

1½ ounces (45ml) cognac

½ ounce (15ml) green or yellow Chartreuse

¼ ounce (8ml) freshly squeezed lemon juice

¼ ounce (8ml) simple syrup (page 270)

Lemon twist, for garnish

Who knew that one day Chartreuse would become the darling of the modern craft cocktail scene? Probably not the brotherhood of monks who arrived in the rugged Grand Chartreuse valley a thousand years ago, whose only goal was to retreat into a private world of silent meditation. They eventually produced a mystical green liqueur that would one day become so famous that a color would be named after it.

I visited the Chartreuse distillery twenty years ago because I was hooked on the liqueur back then. I have to say, even today, the bottle of shimmering green liqueur is still the most prized spirit on my shelf. Although I wish I had stocked up back then, as Chartreuse continues to age in the bottle and only gets better with time. Slyly sweet, yet profoundly herbaceous, Chartreuse goes well with everything from chocolate to cognac. It's a valiant ingredient in a cocktail, strong enough to hold its own against other ingredients.

In this version, I've upped the original amount of cognac to keep it on equal footing, flavor-wise, with the Chartreuse. My preference in this cocktail is green Chartreuse, which is less sweet than yellow Chartreuse, but you can use either one here.

Add the cognac, Chartreuse, lemon juice, and simple syrup to a cocktail shaker. Fill with ice and shake until well chilled. Strain into a chilled coupe glass. Garnish with the lemon twist.

THE LAST WORD

Makes 1 cocktail

¾ ounce (22ml) London dry gin

¾ ounce (22ml) green Chartreuse

¾ ounce (22ml) maraschino liqueur

¾ ounce (22ml) freshly squeezed lime juice

Lime twist, for garnish

Chartreuse returned to the spotlight when American bartender Murray Stenson unearthed a recipe for The Last Word that had been printed in a cocktail manual from 1951. The cocktail's revival was a potent reintroduction to this enduring herbal spirit.

Add the gin, Chartreuse, maraschino liqueur, and lime juice to a cocktail shaker. Fill with ice and shake until well chilled. Strain into a chilled coupe glass. Hold the lime twist over the top of the drink and twist it to release the oils from the peel into the drink. Garnish with the lime twist.

THE YELLOW COCKTAIL

Makes 1 cocktail

¾ ounce (22ml)
London dry gin

¾ ounce (22ml) Suze

¾ ounce (22ml) yellow
Chartreuse

¾ ounce (22ml) freshly
squeezed lemon juice

Lemon twist

My apartment is on the opposite end of the city from Cravan, a slip of a restaurant in the staid 16th arrondissement. But the food and cocktails are so good, it's worth the trip. The building was designed by architect Hector Guimard, who also designed Paris's Art Nouveau métro stations; their curvilinear style was a reaction to people's distaste for the Eiffel Tower, considered a metal monstrosity when it was built. During the summer, Cravan's expansive sidewalk lined with tables and chairs is hard to beat. The man behind Cravan is Franck Audoux, who is also the author of the book *French Moderne*, from which this cocktail is adapted.

Yellow Chartreuse, made with a touch of honey, is sweeter than its green counterpart. It redirects any wrath from the bitter Suze and provides a spice-driven liaison to the tart lemon. The result is a perfectly balanced cocktail. I can't think of a better way to spend a warm evening in Paris than sipping one of these on the terrace at Cravan, but I often shake this cocktail up when I'm having a night in with friends at home.

Add the gin, Suze, Chartreuse, and lemon juice to a cocktail shaker. Fill with ice and shake until well chilled. Strain into a chilled coupe glass. Hold the lemon twist over the top of the drink and twist it to release the oils from the peel into the drink. Discard the lemon twist.

GUÊPE VERTE

Makes 1 cocktail

1½ cups (355ml)
tequila (100% agave
blanco or reposado)

1 jalapeño (½ to
¾ ounce/15 to 20g),
quartered lengthwise,
or bird's-eye chile,
split lengthwise

5 cucumber slices

15 cilantro leaves

1 tablespoon freshly
squeezed lime juice

1 tablespoon
agave nectar

Authentic Mexican food came to Paris in 2011 via the taqueria
and bar Candelaria. The place was so successful that it led the
way for a new wave of cocktail bars in the city. Candelaria is not
only considered to be one of the best bars in Paris, but it also wins
accolades as one of the best cocktail bars in the world. The Guêpe
Verte is its signature drink, an easygoing cocktail with a few leaves
of citrusy cilantro muddled and shaken with chile-spiked tequila
and cooling cucumber.

Jalapeños work well for spicing the tequila, but since those can
be a challenge to find in Paris (and maybe elsewhere), you can use
a single Thai bird's-eye chile instead, which is quite strong. I like
the tequila to be relatively spicy so it holds its own with the other
ingredients, but you can steep it more or less time, to suit your taste.
This recipe makes enough infused tequila for about seven drinks.

Pour the tequila into a jar and add the chile. Cover and shake. Let
stand for 8 hours. Taste, and if the tequila isn't spicy enough for
your taste, let it steep longer, up to overnight. When the tequila is
well infused, remove the chile. Pour the tequila into a bottle or jar,
cover, and chill until ready to use. (It will keep for up to a year.)

To mix the cocktail, muddle 3 of the cucumber slices and the
cilantro leaves with the lime juice in the bottom of a cocktail shaker
until the cucumbers are well broken down.

Add 1¾ ounces (50ml) of the chile-infused tequila and the agave
nectar, fill the shaker with ice, and shake until well chilled. Fill a short
tumbler three-quarters full of ice, remove the lid of the shaker, and
strain the cocktail mixture through a mesh strainer or julep strainer
into the glass. Garnish with the remaining 2 cucumber slices.

TGV

Makes 1 cocktail

2¼ ounces (70ml) blanco or reposado tequila

1½ ounces (45ml) dry vermouth

½ teaspoon store-bought or homemade grenadine syrup, (page 274)

Lime wheel, for garnish

I spent a lot of time trying to figure out why this popular cocktail is named after France's TGV (high-speed train). Then one evening, while measuring out the three ingredients, I noticed they were **T**equila, **G**renadine, and **V**ermouth, and it suddenly became clear.

Stir together the tequila, vermouth, and grenadine in a short tumbler or rocks glass. Fill the glass three-quarters full of ice. Garnish with the lime wheel.

SUZY'S HANKY

Makes 1 cocktail

1½ ounces (45ml) London dry gin

1 ounce (30ml) sweet vermouth

½ ounce (15ml) Suze

½ ounce (15ml) Grand Marnier, Cointreau, or triple sec

Orange twist and sprig of fresh thyme, for garnish

This is my take on a Hanky Panky, which I have revised by backing up the gin and vermouth with Suze (page 86) and a hint of orange, in lieu of the few dashes of Fernet-Branca found in the original. These changes make this a smoother, more well-rounded (and more French) cocktail. A sprig of thyme used as a garnish reinforces the earthy flavor of the gentian liqueur, and the sweet vermouth makes it go down uncommonly easy.

Add the gin, vermouth, Suze, and Grand Marnier to a cocktail mixing glass. Fill with ice and stir until well chilled. Strain into a chilled coupe glass. Hold the orange twist over the top of the drink and twist it to release the oils from the peel into the drink. Drop the orange twist into the glass and garnish with the thyme sprig floating on top.

ZA'ATAR MARTINI

Makes 1 cocktail

1 cup (240ml) vodka

1 to 2 teaspoons za'atar spice blend

1 ounce (30ml) dry vermouth

⅛ teaspoon pastis or another anise-flavored liqueur

1 dash cardamom bitters (optional, but good)

Strip of preserved lemon or a green olive, for garnish

I spent a day with Abu Kassem, owner of Za'atar Zawtar, wandering around his za'atar farm in Lebanon, where fields of the fragrant, thymelike herb grow abundantly. First, I watched Abu mix the fresh herbs with sesame seeds and sumac, which makes the spice blend also known as za'atar, then he took me over to a distilling pot where another batch of the mixture was simmering away to make a medicinal tonic he called za'atar water. Attached to the steel spout off to the side of the pot was a jug filling up with the distilled "water." A bright orange slick of oil floated on top of the jug, and he offered me a taste. Using a dropper, he put a tiny amount of the egg yolk–colored za'atar oil in my hand. The taste was so strong, I recoiled, then the lower part of my face went numb. The flavor, and effect, of that za'atar oil continues to intrigue me to this day. (And not just because I've imagined the possibilities of something you could apply to someone's mouth to paralyze it temporarily.)

When I saw a za'atar martini on the menu at Jefrey's, an intimate cocktail bar in Paris known for its audacious, expertly crafted cocktails, I was reminded of the powerful aroma of that za'atar in Lebanon. I imagined the flavor would be quite good in a martini, and I was right.

A few nights later, I came up with my own recipe. Store-bought za'atar blends vary considerably in strength. It's a pretty dynamic flavor, and I like it in the background—enough to know it's there, but not so much as to overwhelm the drink or paralyze the drinker. This recipe makes enough infused vodka for about four drinks.

Pour the vodka into a jar and add 1 teaspoon za'atar. Cover and shake vigorously. Let infuse for 30 minutes. Taste, and if you'd like it stronger, add an additional ½ to 1 teaspoon za'atar and let it infuse for 15 to 30 minutes more. Strain the vodka through a mesh strainer lined with cheesecloth into a bottle or jar, cover, and chill until ready to use. It will keep for up to 1 year.

To mix up the martini, add 2 ounces (60ml) of the za'atar-infused vodka, the vermouth, pastis, and bitters (if using) to a cocktail mixing glass. Fill with ice and stir until well chilled. Strain into a chilled coupe glass. Garnish with the preserved lemon.

EL DIABLO

Makes 1 cocktail

1½ ounces (45ml) blanco tequila

¾ ounce (22ml) crème de cassis

½ ounce (15ml) freshly squeezed lime juice

3 to 4 ounces (90 to 120ml) ginger beer

Lime wheel, for garnish

A version of this recipe first appeared in the *Bartender's Guide* by Trader Vic in 1947. The crème de cassis was likely considered an exotic ingredient outside of France back in those days. The lushly flavored French black currant syrup works well in this tiki-inflected cocktail that's finished with a pour of zesty ginger beer. Thanks to the cocktail movement, ginger beer is now available at my local *supermarché*. (Although sometimes the cashiers lift up the bottle to get a closer look, not sure what to make of it.) If you want this devilishly named cocktail to be a little less *fort* (strong) on the tequila side, add the larger amount of ginger beer. (Pictured, opposite.)

Mix the tequila, crème de cassis, and lime juice in a tumbler or Collins glass. Add a handful of ice followed by the ginger beer. Stir and garnish with the lime wheel.

CINQ CYLINDER

Makes 1 cocktail

½ ounce (15ml) London dry gin

½ ounce (15ml) Cap Corse rouge, Dubonnet rouge, or Byrrh Grand Quinquina

½ ounce (15ml) Suze

½ ounce (15ml) Liqueur 44 (page 131), Grand Marnier, or Cointreau

¼ ounce (8ml) dry vermouth

This recipe is inspired by the Six Cylinder Cocktail, which was named after a jet engine and was the winner of a cocktail competition held in Paris in 1928. The original cocktail had six ingredients, but I trimmed it to only five, revving up the flavor with some coffee-fueled Liqueur 44.

Add the gin, Cap Corse, Suze, Liqueur 44, and vermouth to a cocktail mixing glass. Fill with ice and stir until well chilled. Strain into a chilled coupe glass.

GINY GERMAIN

Makes 1 cocktail

1 egg white

One 3-inch (8cm) piece
of cucumber, cubed
(no need to peel), plus
1 thin slice for garnish

1½ ounces (45ml)
London dry gin

¾ ounce (22ml) freshly
squeezed lemon or
lime juice

¾ ounce (22ml)
elderflower liqueur

¾ ounce (22ml)
simple syrup (page 270)

NOTE

If you wish, you can
use pasteurized
liquid egg whites.

A few years back, critics began to openly ponder if *la cuisine française* was over. Few people had time for three-hour lunches, and some bistro owners became lax, resorting to shortcuts. In addition, the French were eating lighter fare—fewer braised meats and vegetables smothered in cream sauce, more soups, salads, and even smoothies.

Happily, a younger generation of chefs and restaurant owners came forth, breathing new life into French cuisine, polishing up the old bistros, and featuring French classics with fresh ingredients, offering updated, but nostalgic, takes on their predecessors, such as *œufs mayonnaise* and leeks vinaigrette, as well as natural wines—and cocktails—too.

One was Antoine Goldschmid, who discovered a lovely but neglected café and got to work restoring its magnificent tiled walls, refinishing the floors, and polishing the zinc counter so his restaurant, Poulette, was as beautiful as the food and drinks.

This cocktail is named for its two main ingredients: gin and St-Germain, a well-known brand of elderflower liqueur. Antoine muddles cucumber with egg white, adds the remaining ingredients and the ice, then shakes it very aggressively, giving the egg white as much lift as possible. (Some bartenders do a "dry shake" when mixing drinks with egg whites, shaking the ingredients together before adding the ice, then again afterward, but Antoine told me that with the cucumbers, he doesn't notice a difference.) Although his version uses lemon juice, I sometimes use lime juice, which gives the drink a little extra tartness.

Muddle the egg white with the cucumber cubes in a cocktail shaker until the cucumber pieces are mostly broken down but still chunky. Add the gin, lemon juice, elderflower liqueur, and simple syrup to the shaker. Fill it half full with ice and shake very hard (at least 20 seconds) until well chilled and frothy. Open the shaker and strain the mixture through a mesh strainer into a chilled coupe glass. Garnish with the cucumber slice.

QUATRESSE

Makes 1 cocktail

2 medium fresh sage leaves, plus additional leaves for garnish

2 ounces (60ml) Salers or Suze

1 ounce (30ml) freshly squeezed lemon juice

Scant ½ ounce (10ml) simple syrup (page 270)

Scant ½ teaspoon peated Scotch whisky

Combat may seem like an unusual name for a bar in Paris. Margot Lecarpentier chose the name for her cocktail bar in Belleville because it's adjacent to the Quartier du Combat. The area got its name because there was once an arena there where savage fights between animals, including wolves, bears, boars, and bulls, took place from the late 1700s until the middle of the next century, when the barbaric practice was banned. Margot told me it was also a nod to the battles she had with multiple banks before she convinced one to give a thirty-year-old woman a business loan to open her bar.

I'm glad she succeeded, because Combat is one of my favorite hangouts in the city. Its unintimidating tablelike bar makes you feel as if you're being served by a friend at a dinner party. And one who makes great cocktails, at that. Margot likens her bartending style to dining, and since she's from Normandy, where people love to eat, it all makes perfect sense to me.

This signature cocktail from Combat gets its name from the four ingredients that start with "s": sage, which adds a savory note; single-malt scotch for smokiness; simple syrup for a touch of sweetness; and gentian-based Salers or Suze to stimulate your taste buds. Margot likes to use Laphroaig scotch, although another peated scotch, single malt or blended, would work.

Tear the 2 sage leaves into two or three pieces each and put them in a cocktail shaker. Add the Salers, lemon juice, simple syrup, and scotch to the shaker. Fill with ice and shake until well chilled.

Open the shaker and strain into a chilled tumbler or rocks glass. Fill the glass with ice, topping it off with shaved ice, if available. Garnish with a few sage leaves.

D-DAY SWIZZLE

Makes 1 cocktail

1 to 1½ ounces (30 to 45ml) elderflower liqueur

1 teaspoon apple cider vinegar

½ teaspoon green Chartreuse

¼ teaspoon absinthe, or up to ½ teaspoon pastis

4 ounces (120ml) hard apple cider

Fresh or dried apple or pear slices, for garnish

Red House is often described as a dive bar, which it certainly is— in the American sense of the word. There's *zéro* pretention, and owner Joseph "Joe" Boley greets his regular customers with a grin and disarming demeanor that explains the bar's popularity with the young French locals who stop by after work. The *portefeuille* (wallet)-friendly pitchers of beer and *le flipper* (pinball machine) are equally popular as well. I'm always entertained watching Joe, with his slicked-back hair and untucked T-shirt, mix drinks and banter with customers.

This cocktail mixes sparkling apple cider and elderflower liqueur with a dash of apple cider vinegar, plus a touch of Chartreuse and absinthe. Since hard apple ciders can vary in sweetness, start with the smaller amount of elderflower liqueur, then add more if desired. When I asked Joe if this could be made with nonalcoholic apple cider, he told me "alcohol is always better." So there you have it.

In a footed goblet or large wine glass, mix 1 ounce (30ml) elderflower liqueur with the vinegar, Chartreuse, and absinthe. Add a generous handful of ice to the glass, then pour in the hard cider. Taste, and add additional elderflower liqueur if desired. Garnish with the fruit slices.

LA MARGUERITE

Makes 1 cocktail

1½ ounces (45ml)
Lillet blanc

1 ounce (30ml) blanco
or reposado tequila

¾ ounce (22ml) freshly
squeezed orange juice

Half an orange or lime
wheel, for garnish

While margaritas aren't exactly French, Lillet definitely is, and the
Bordeaux-based orange-infused apéritif dials down the drink, hewing
it close to an apéritif, but with enough tequila to keep its connection
to the Mexican cocktail. I don't normally salt the rim of the glass for
this one, but if you'd like to do that, rub the rim with a lime or orange
wedge and dip it lightly in a plate of flaky fleur de sel or another
delicate sea salt.

_____

Add the Lillet, tequila, and orange juice to a cocktail shaker. Fill
with ice and shake until well chilled. Strain into a chilled coupe
glass or into a short tumbler or rocks glass over ice. Garnish with
the citrus wheel half.

VERT VERRE

Makes 1 cocktail

1 ounce (30ml) gin

1 ounce (30ml)
white rum

1½ ounces (45ml) freshly
squeezed lime juice

1 ounce (30ml) fresh
mint syrup (page 272)

6 fresh mint leaves, torn

Best-quality tonic
water, such as Archibald
(in France), Fever-Tree,
or Q

Mint sprig and lime
wheel, for garnish

This cocktail is named for the rejuvenating combination of lime
juice and green mint (*citron vert* and *menthe verte*), spiked with
the one-two punch of gin and rum and topped off with a thirst-
quenching splash of tonic, all in one *verre* (glass).

_____

Add the gin, rum, lime juice, mint syrup, and mint leaves to a
cocktail shaker. Fill with ice and shake until well chilled. Open the
shaker and strain through a mesh strainer or julep strainer into
a tumbler or Collins glass. Add a handful of ice and top with tonic
water. Garnish with the mint sprig and lime wheel.

AVIATION

Makes 1 cocktail

2 ounces (60ml)
London dry gin

¾ ounce (22ml) freshly
squeezed lemon juice

½ ounce (15ml)
maraschino liqueur

¼ ounce (8ml) liqueur
de violette or crème de
violette

I met Peter Schaf over a glass . . . actually, several glasses . . . of absinthe at La Fée Verte in Paris (see page 218) around the time that absinthe became legal again, after having been banned in France in 1915. Peter was preparing to launch Tempus Fugit Spirits, with the ambition of reviving lost liqueurs, bitters, and distillations, starting with the *fée verte* (green fairy), the nickname for absinthe. Peter and his business partner, John Troia, went on to bottle a highly regarded absinthe, and their crème de noyau, crème de menthe, crème de cacao, and liqueur de violette can be found in many of the best bars in the world nowadays. Liqueur de violette had largely disappeared from liquor stores before Peter and John, and others, started making it again. It's a necessary ingredient in an Aviation; the violet liqueur gives this cocktail its signature ethereal, and aerial, hue.

Add the gin, lemon juice, maraschino liqueur, and liqueur de violettes to a cocktail shaker. Fill with ice and shake until well chilled. Strain into a chilled coupe glass.

MÉNAGE À QUATRE

Makes 1 cocktail

¾ ounce (22ml) gin

¾ ounce (22ml) freshly
squeezed lemon juice

¾ ounce (22ml) Grand
Marnier, Cointreau,
or triple sec

¾ ounce (22ml)
Lillet blanc or Cap
Corse blanc

Like the classic Negroni, which has three ingredients sharing one communal space in equal quantities, this less-conventional four-way is equally alluring.

Add the gin, lemon juice, Grand Marnier, and Lillet to a cocktail shaker. Fill with ice and shake until well chilled. Strain into a chilled coupe glass.

ABSINTHE IN PARIS

When the French government lifted the ban on absinthe in 2011, after almost a hundred years, it caused a lot of excitement in France. Modern-day spirit-lovers rejoiced that the much-maligned drink, once a mainstay of cafés and bars, was back and here to stay, and there are several places in Paris where you can participate in the ritual that surrounds drinking it. *La louche*, as it is called, is performed by placing a cube of sugar in a spade-like perforated spoon resting across the top of a glass with an inch, more or less, of absinthe in the bottom. Ice-cold water is dribbled over the sugar cube from a footed fountain, which sweetens the drink and turns it cloudy. It also dilutes the absinthe, making the powerfully flavored, high-test spirit easier to sip.

To taste absinthe in an easygoing setting, stop by La Fée Verte (108, rue de la Roquette, 11th). This friendly Parisian café has a menu of absinthes to choose from, listed by maker and degree of alcohol, along with tasting notes.

In the still-gritty Pigalle neighborhood, guests at the Royal Fromentin hotel can opt for an *absinthe d'accueil*: a glass of absinthe to welcome you at check-in. Absinthe is also available in the hotel's salon, whose décor matches the hotel's "budget-friendly" status. It's open to anyone, including those who want to take a break from the hubbub of Paris's red-light district, where the hotel is located. (But don't worry, the only danger there is being lured into one of the "gentlemen's bars," where the shapely hostesses entice potential paramours to buy a ridiculously overpriced bottle of bubbly.)

A decidedly different experience can be had at Cantada II (13, rue Moret, 11th), which doubles as a heavy-metal bar, with the appropriate music playing, along with heavy-duty imagery swirling on the walls and bar. There's a back staircase leading to a room with stone walls, but I haven't made it down there yet. I doubt it's a dungeon, but still, I'm staying away. But not to worry; the staff and other patrons are friendly enough, and for those looking for a decidedly untouristy experience—or a shot of tobacco-flavored liqueur, or a plate of stag meat from their *cuisine médiévale* menu—or just a glass of absinthe, a trip to Cantada II is in order. If whatever you're drinking gives you the courage to go downstairs, if you make it back up, let me know what's down there!

L'Absinthe Café (54, rue de Turbigo, 3rd) is a hip café on the edge of the Marais with an expansive terrace, which is pleasant in the afternoon or on a warm spring evening. It offers up a concise menu of *les absinthes* as well as a few *absinthes fines*, for those who are a little more discerning.

MY TAILOR IS RICH

Makes 1 cocktail

2 ounces (60ml)
white rum

¾ ounce (22ml) Grand
Marnier or Cointreau

¾ ounce (22ml) freshly
squeezed lime juice

2 teaspoons honey
syrup (page 271)

Generous splash of
good-quality grapefruit
or lemon soda

When learning to speak English like an American, French people are told to clearly enunciate—each—and—every—word, and not to mumble. They're drilled with the phrase "My tailor is rich," which all of my French friends can say with a spot-on, pitch-perfect American accent, even if the rest of their English remains rudimentary.

I'm not a fan of very sweet cocktails as I prefer to save my sweets for dessert, but honey gives this drink a little well-tailored richness.

Add the rum, Grand Marnier, lime juice, and honey syrup to a cocktail shaker. Fill with ice and shake until well chilled. Strain into a chilled coupe glass. Top with the soda.

REVISED OBITUARY

Makes 1 cocktail

2 ounces (60ml) gin

½ ounce (15ml) dry
vermouth

¼ ounce (8ml) absinthe
or pastis

Fresh fennel frond or
dill frond, for garnish
(optional)

There are so many things I feel like I should do before I die. And every day, others add to my "should do" list, insisting, "You *should* come to Tasmania!" or "You *need* to go to Martinique!" or "You *must* eat at such-and-such bistro!"

My list is now so long that if I went everywhere I *should* go, and ate at every bistro I *should* eat at, I'd never be able to squeeze into an airplane or restaurant seat. (However, if anyone offers to fly me in one of those spacious business-class seats that turn into a bed, I'm available to go anywhere.) After I'm gone, I'm concerned that my tombstone won't say, "He did it!" but "He *should have* done it. . . ."

One thing I have done, however, is to up the amount of vermouth in this revised version of the classic cocktail. The hint of licorice-like flavor stands up to a botanically heavy gin, such as one from Distillerie de Paris (see page 222). If you like anise, you *should* like this, but I won't insist.

Add the gin, vermouth, and absinthe to a cocktail shaker. Fill with ice and shake until well chilled. Strain into a chilled coupe glass. Garnish with the fennel frond (if desired).

BLOODY MARY

Makes 1 cocktail

2½ ounces (75ml) vodka

¾ ounce (22ml) Noilly Prat extra-dry vermouth

½ ounce (15ml) freshly squeezed lemon juice

¼ teaspoon Tabasco sauce, plus more if desired

½ teaspoon Worcestershire sauce

Homemade celery salt (see Note)

Freshly ground black pepper

4 ounces (120ml) tomato juice

Lemon wedge

Celery stick, for garnish

Few people associate the Bloody Mary with France, but the cocktail was likely invented here. One story goes that Fernand Petiot, the bartender at Harry's New York Bar in the 1920s, was given a bottle of vodka by some Russian immigrants. Vodka wasn't well-known at the time, and he found it lacking in flavor. So he opened a tin of tomato juice, added some spices and seasonings, and called the drink Bucket of Blood. When he later went to work in New York City at the St. Regis Hotel, the name got changed to the less-*sanguine* Red Snapper. No one is quite sure how the drink finally became the Bloody Mary, but some say it's a reference to Mary I, known for her bloody reign.

There's no argument, however, that the Bloody Mary is the quintessential morning-after drink. This version is adapted from bartender Antonia Catton's recipe. She showed me around the Noilly Prat distillery (see page 96), and only after the tour was finished did I learn that my guide was also a bartender, when she got behind the bar and shook up her version of the Bloody Mary, adding vermouth to the mix. Although Antonia didn't use it, I sometimes add ½ to ¾ teaspoon of prepared horseradish to the shaker, and I finish the drink with homemade celery salt scattered over the top.

Add the vodka, vermouth, lemon juice, Tabasco and Worcestershire sauces, a big pinch of celery salt, a few turns of black pepper, and the tomato juice to a cocktail shaker. Fill with ice and shake until well chilled.

Make a slash in the lemon wedge and run it around the rim of a tumbler. Spread some celery salt on a saucer and dip the rim of the tumbler into the celery salt. Strain the cocktail into the glass, and then fill with ice. Taste, and add more Tabasco, if you wish. Garnish with the celery stick, additional celery salt, and another turn of freshly ground pepper.

NOTE

To make your own celery salt, wash and thoroughly dry 1½ cups (30g) celery leaves. (I spin them in a salad spinner and then blot dry with a kitchen towel.) Strew them on a baking sheet and dry them out in a 300°F (150°C) oven until brittle, 5 to 7 minutes. Don't overdo it, as you want the leaves to retain their bright green color, so keep an eye on them. Cool, then crumble with ¾ teaspoon flaky sea salt either in a mini-chopper or with your hands.

DISTILLERIE DE PARIS

One of the first streets I discovered in Paris was the rue du Faubourg Saint-Denis. Some people enjoy strolling down the grand boulevards of Paris and meandering through its many parks. Me? I prefer to snoop around the less-traveled parts of town, where I'm likely to stumble on interesting eateries and food shops that introduce me to cuisines I'm unfamiliar with. But I wasn't prepared for the gritty realness of the rue Faubourg Saint-Denis, an extension of the rue Saint-Denis, which is famous for its peep shows and women beckoning from curtained doorways. After moving my wallet from my back pocket to the inside of my jacket, I poked around the shops, which included an Eastern European pickle and sauerkraut vendor, a Kurdish sandwich joint where dough was being rolled out in the window and baked up with spiced meat fillings, and several Indian produce shops selling fruits and vegetables that were completely foreign to me.

I saw a few things for sale on the streets that I won't recount here, but my biggest surprise was a well-stocked specialty store with a cheese display featuring everything from creamy, ripe wedges of Brie to a giant pot of crème fraîche so thick that a metal ladle stood straight up in the center of it. Corsican sausages hung over a counter of cured hams wrapped in brine-stained netting, and there was a refrigerated showcase of French specialty butters. It even had a basket of fresh truffles, which I smelled as soon as I walked in the doorway. Off to the side was a small yet sophisticated wine *cave*. Telling friends about my discovery

a few days later, I learned that Julhès, run by Nicolas Julhès and his brother Sébastian, is a well-known fromagerie, charcuterie, and wine and spirits shop, and the family has been in that location for years.

The neighborhood has since evolved, and the biggest danger you face these days is getting smoked out by the beer-drinking *bobos* clogging the fronts of bars and cafés until late in the evening. (Doesn't anyone have to be at work the next day?) Julhès has expanded to two additional storefronts; one is a bakery and pastry shop, and the other is a *sandwicherie* and *traiteur*, offering food to go. Hidden behind this mini-empire of shops is a distillery, the first to open in Paris in more than a century. Nicolas Julhès told me that helping his grandmother make *chèvre* (goat cheese) first kindled his interest in transforming foods, and his knowledge of fermentation came from owning a bakery; a distillery seemed like the right place to combine his two passions. But it wasn't easy: It took five years of wrangling with the notorious French bureaucracy before the micro-distillery was able to start producing spirits in 2015.

With their scruffy, chiseled looks, Nicolas and Sébastian could have easily fallen into the hipster trap, slapped "Gin from Paris" on the bottles, and sold plenty of them, regardless of what was inside. Instead, they have taken their mission seriously, like everything they do (and sell) in their shops.

The distilling takes place in the back corner of a cobblestone alley, in a small room with a roll-up door and a very fancy (and hard-won) alembic still inside. Everything is done by hand, from adding the juniper berries and orange peel that flavor the lineup of gins to bottling the finished products.

The Julhèses' goal is to make spirits that taste handmade. Their gin begins with a neutral, grape-based distillate that is then seasoned with juniper, bergamot, coriander seeds, angelica, and quinine. When I took a sniff from a bottle, I was drawn in by the blend of juniper and citrus—not enough to overwhelm the delicate notes of lavender and jasmine, but enough to make this made-in-Paris liquor versatile enough for a classic Martini (page 97) or other gin-forward cocktails that would benefit from a bit of French finesse. The Julhès brothers have also made one-off batches of gin, experimenting with adding hops (from Deck & Donohue; see page 44) and quinine to make it even more gin-and-tonic-friendly. After expanding to four varieties of gin, they're now also making brandy, aquavit, rum, vodka, and whiskey, which are sold across France, including at their store on the now destination-worthy rue du Faubourg Saint-Denis, which I'm not worried about visiting anymore. In fact, it's become one of the most sought-after areas in Paris to live in. And with a distillery in the neighborhood, I suspect it's going to become a lot more popular.

A IS FOR ANANAS

Makes 1 cocktail

1 ounce (30ml) gin

1 ounce (30ml) unsweetened pineapple juice (jus d'ananas)

¾ ounce (22ml) sweet vermouth

¾ ounce (22ml) red bitter apéritif, such as Dolin, Campari, or St. George Bruto Americano

Sprig of fresh mint and wedge of fresh or dried pineapple, for garnish

France doesn't instantly come to mind when people think of gin, but that's changing; I see a new French gin every time I go to a liquor store. The popularity of the *gin tonic* has something to do with it, but much credit goes to cognac maker Alexandre Gabriel of Maison Ferrand distillery. Regulations mandate that cognac can be distilled only from November to March, so his stills sat empty the rest of the year. With a bit of perseverance, Alexandre was granted the right to distill gin in the off-season.

Citadelle gin became a hit worldwide, prompting people to pay attention to French gin as well as inspiring others in France to get in the spirit, including Laurent and Patricia Gaspard, two schoolteachers from the sunny South of France who started the Distillerie du Petit Grain in the Minervois, where citrus proliferates. They use local Buddha's hand citrons, kumquats, yuzu, and bergamot culled from the garden of a local chef. Feel free to use a citrus-forward gin in this cocktail, if one is available. (Pictured, opposite.)

Add the gin, pineapple juice, vermouth, and red bitter apéritif to a cocktail shaker. Fill with ice and shake until well chilled. Strain into a chilled coupe glass. Garnish with the mint sprig and pineapple wedge.

HEMINGWAY DAIQUIRI

Makes 1 cocktail

2 ounces (60ml) white rum

¾ ounce (22ml) freshly squeezed lime juice

½ ounce (15ml) freshly squeezed grapefruit juice

½ ounce (15ml) maraschino liqueur

Lime wheel, for garnish

The French have a deep love affair with rum, due to vacationing in the French Caribbean islands. Rum from Martinique is the most famous, and it has the coveted Appellation d'Origine Contrôlée (AOC) status. The Hemingway Daiquiri was inspired by one-time Paris resident Ernest Hemingway, who had a fondness for the spirit. After he tasted a daiquiri in Cuba, he noted that it would be better with less sugar— and more rum.

Add the rum, lime and grapefruit juices, and maraschino liqueur to a cocktail shaker. Fill with ice and shake until well chilled. Strain into a chilled coupe glass. Garnish with the lime wheel.

ROSEMARY GIMLET

Makes 1 cocktail

2 ounces (60ml)
London dry gin

¾ ounce (22ml) freshly
squeezed lime juice

¾ ounce (22ml)
rosemary syrup
(page 272)

Sprig of rosemary,
for garnish

My partner, Romain, introduced me to the Menthe à l'Eau (page 37), and I responded in kind by introducing him to cocktails, starting him off on the right foot with a Rosemary Gimlet. The combination of fresh lime juice, gin, and woodsy rosemary syrup is what he now considers to be the perfect cocktail. Unfortunately, he thinks every bar offers one (if only!), and perplexes bartenders when he orders one, because it's not quite a cocktail standard.

One bartender in Paris did his best to comply with the request, using a gin he had on the shelf that had some rosemary flavoring in it. But it wasn't quite right, and Romain told him so. (Which is probably why my texts and emails to the bartender requesting the recipe for the cocktail that I had enjoyed that night went unanswered.) Maybe someday the Rosemary Gimlet will become a classic served at cocktail bars in Paris and elsewhere, but until it does, I keep a batch of rosemary syrup on hand to shake one up for Romain whenever he wants one. Which is often.

Add the gin, lime juice, and rosemary syrup to a cocktail shaker. Fill with ice and shake until well chilled. Strain into a chilled coupe glass. Garnish with the rosemary sprig.

5 APÉRO SNACKS

It's no secret the French like to eat, but stroll down any sidewalk in France, from first thing in the morning to late into the night, and it's obvious the French enjoy having something to drink as well. The apéritif hour is when they get to do their two favorite things at the same time: eat *and* drink.

One of the largest and most diverse aisles in any French grocery store is "Les apéritifs," referring to the wide range of snacks, often called *les salées*, which translates to "salty," but includes the wide variety of savory things that are meant to be enjoyed with drinks. These range from bite-size dried sausages, smoked almonds, and anchovy-stuffed olives to pretzels, peanuts, and potato chips. But *les apéritifs* don't stop at the end of that aisle. Head over to the refrigerator section and there are Apéricubes, flavored cheeses that are individually packaged like foil-wrapped dice, from the folks who brought us La Vache qui Rit (Laughing Cow) cheese, and Boursin, spreadable cheese flavored with garlic and *fines herbes*. You'll likely come across prepared ruffles of Tête de Moine cheese, and an assortment of neatly trimmed vegetables ready to put on the table, with tubs of eggplant caviar, Duck Rillettes (page 242), and tapenade just a few steps away. (Sorry, but there's no French onion dip in France.)

Busy hosts rely on store-bought snacks (and a number of them head to their nearest Picard frozen food shop, where there's no shortage of *apéro* snacks either), but I prefer to pick up a bunch of fresh radishes with their leaves still attached from the market, as well as something from the local charcutier, such as thinly sliced *jambon de Bayonne* or a dried sausage studded with hazelnuts. Or I'll buy a mixture of olives

and heat them with olive oil, orange zest, and herbs (see page 265), which makes an intriguing accompaniment to a round of Za'atar Martinis (page 207). The Spicy Glazed Nut and Pretzel Mix (page 266) invariably appears on many of my *apéro* spreads, since it goes well with everything from RinQuinQuin Rickeys (page 102) to Americanos (page 58), which are especially appropriate when I dig into my stash of my Texas pecans to add to the nut mix. Cheesy Gougères (page 247) come together faster than you might think; serve them warm to friends, with a glass of Lillet (page 78), Pineau des Charentes (see page 82), or Kir (page 49).

French people are always appreciative of any extra effort a host makes. Everyone oohs and aahs when they see that I've made something, protesting that I really shouldn't have gone to the trouble—*"Oh-la-la! C'était pas nécessaire, Daveed . . . mais . . ."* ("It wasn't necessary, David . . . but . . .")—as they dive in.

Your guests will also appreciate a homemade *terrine facile pâté* (see page 236) that gets better when made a few days

in advance and served with an earthy Bonalgroni (page 94), or warm, gooey Baked Camembert (page 233) doused with a sharp whiskey *gastrique*, along with an apple-based D-Day Swizzle (page 215), doubling up on the flavors of Normandy. The *salées* in this chapter are dishes I often make for guests, and most can be made in advance, so that by the time your *invitées* arrive for the early evening *apéro*, you can relax and join them for a drink—and something to eat as well.

SALT SENSE

The recipes in this chapter call for "kosher or sea salt" and "flaky sea salt." The sea salt I use is gray and rich in minerals. It tastes less "salty" than fine table salt. The grains of the sel gris (gray salt) that I use are small enough to dissolve when mixed with other ingredients, but they're not as fine as standard table salt, which I find too harsh. (Fine sea salt, which resembles standard table salt, tastes too salty for me as well.)

If you only have fine table or fine sea salt, reduce the amount by 25 percent. You can add more, if necessary, to taste. If only

very coarse-grained sea salt is available, it can be ground in a mini-food processor, blender, or mortar and pestle. For kosher salt, I recommend Diamond Crystal. If using Morton's, reduce the amount by 50 percent.

Flaky sea salt is used for finishing. The wispy crystals or flakes have a mild taste and are suitable for sprinkling over Radishes with Radish Greens Butter (page 241) or Chicken Liver Mousse (page 238) just before serving. In France, I use fleur de sel; my favorite is from the Guérande. Maldon (England) and Jacobsens (Oregon) are others that can be used.

BAKED CAMEMBERT WITH WALNUTS, FIGS, AND WHISKEY GASTRIQUE

Makes 4 to 6 servings

6 dried figs
(1½ ounces/40g)

Boiling water

½ cup (125ml) apple
cider vinegar

½ cup (125ml) plus
1 tablespoon bourbon
or another whiskey,
plus more if needed

¼ cup (80g)
mild-flavored honey

⅓ cup (35g) toasted
walnuts, whole or
coarsely chopped

1 (5-inch/13cm)
round of Camembert
cheese, or similar-
size soft cheese

Crackers or toasted
slices of baguette,
for serving

True Camembert de Normandie is made in Normandy using raw milk from local cows. The real deal is hard to get outside of France, but similar soft-rind cheeses labeled "Camembert," "Brie," or ones that go by another name and are sold in similar-size disks, work perfectly for this recipe.

The rind of most soft cheeses is edible; the decision of whether or not to eat it is based on your preference, whether you like the taste or not, or whether (or not) it's going to negatively affect the taste of the cheese. The rind is usually stronger tasting than the rest of the cheese, and I love it. But if you don't, feel free to remove it with the aid of a serrated knife, cutting around the perimeter of the top and peeling off the top layer of rind after you bake the cheese, before pouring on the gastrique.

Trim the stem end off the figs. Quarter them and place in a heatproof bowl. Pour boiling water over them, cover, and let sit until the figs are softened, about 10 minutes. Drain well and set aside.

Bring the vinegar, ½ cup (125ml) of the bourbon, and the honey to a boil in a medium saucepan or skillet. Reduce the heat to a low but steady simmer and cook for 5 minutes.

Add the plumped figs and cook the gastrique, swirling the pan every so often, until the bubbles start to widen and the liquid is as thick as warm maple syrup, 6 to 8 minutes. Remove from the heat and stir in the walnuts. Set aside.

Preheat the oven to 350°F (175°C).

Remove any paper wrapping surrounding the Camembert and place the cheese back in the wooden box, if it came in one. If you're not sure if the box will hold together in the heat of the oven (for example, if it's glued together, it may come undone in the oven), tie butcher's twine around it to hold it together. Place the uncovered cheese in a small baking dish that will hold it comfortably. If it didn't come in a wooden box, unwrap it and place it directly in a small baking dish, with not much room around it.

continued

Poke six or seven deep holes in the cheese with a paring knife and spoon the remaining 1 tablespoon bourbon over the top.

Bake until the cheese is warmed through, 12 to 15 minutes. When you touch the center, it should feel soft, supple, and warm. Cheese can vary, so go for look and feel, rather than a strict baking time.

A few minutes before the Camembert is done, check the gastrique. It should be as thick as honey. If it's become too thick, add a spoonful or two of bourbon, and perhaps gently rewarm it, until it's pourable. If it's not thick enough, simmer it for another minute or so to reduce it until it's syrupy.

Remove the Camembert from the oven and scrape the gastrique, along with the figs and walnuts, over the hot cheese.

Serve in the baking dish with crackers or toasted baguette slices. This goes especially well with Pommeau de Normandie (see page 85), a calvados cocktail such as Stan's the Man (page 196), Pommes Away (page 97), or an apple-based D-Day Swizzle (page 215).

SMOKED SALMON PÂTÉ
À TARTINER

Makes 8 appetizer-size servings

4 ounces (115g) cream cheese, at room temperature

3 tablespoons (45ml) plain Greek yogurt

2 tablespoons minced fresh dill or chives, plus extra for garnish

2 teaspoons extra-virgin olive oil

2 teaspoons freshly squeezed lemon juice

1 teaspoon prepared horseradish

½ teaspoon kosher or sea salt

Freshly ground black pepper

Generous pinch of cayenne pepper

6 ounces (170g) smoked salmon, finely diced

The French eat a lot of salmon, either smoked or cured (see Gravlax with Mustard Sauce, page 253), as an appetizer or *apéro* snack. But salmon makes a very flavorful spread as well. Cream cheese, which is a recent addition to the French dairy aisle, has become very popular; it's sold under the now familiar Philadelphia brand and other brands are labeled "*fromage à tartiner*," or spreading cheese.

It's fairly quick to dice the smoked salmon by hand, and I like to see little morsels of salmon in the spread, but if you prefer a smoother paste, pulse it in the food processor a couple of times until the spread is the consistency you like.

Serve the spread with crackers, or make it fancier by spreading it in individual leaves of Belgian endive and top with fresh dill or minced chives. To gild the lily, top each with a small spoonful of salmon caviar. (Or sturgeon caviar, if you really like your guests.) The smoky flavor of this spread holds its own when served with a Grapefruit Rosé (page 61), a more bracing Cinq Cylinder (page 208), or The Yellow Cocktail (page 202).

In a medium bowl, mash together the cream cheese, Greek yogurt, dill, olive oil, lemon juice, horseradish, salt, a few turns of freshly ground black pepper, and the cayenne pepper.

Stir in the smoked salmon until it's well incorporated with the cream cheese and yogurt mixture. Scrape into a serving bowl. Garnish with additional fresh dill. The spread will keep for up to 4 days in the refrigerator.

VARIATION ——— To add a little smoky flavor, replace the salt with smoked sea salt and use chipotle powder or smoked paprika in place of the cayenne.

TERRINE FACILE

Makes 14 to 16 appetizer-size servings

6 to 8 ounces (170 to 225g) chicken livers

1 pound (450g) ground pork

1 pound (450g) ground veal, lamb, chicken, or turkey (if using poultry, use dark meat)

2 teaspoons kosher or sea salt

Freshly ground black pepper

2 tablespoons dry or fresh bread crumbs

2 large eggs

2 tablespoons heavy cream

2 tablespoons coarsely chopped capers

2 tablespoons cognac, Armagnac, or brandy

2 tablespoons minced fresh sage, tarragon, or other herbs (see headnote)

3 or 4 dried or fresh bay leaves (optional)

Cornichons and Dijon or stone-ground mustard, for serving

I was invited to a party in Paris and brought a crock of Chicken Liver Mousse (page 238) to share for the *apéro* hour. While everyone was taking second and third helpings of my mousse, I was lopping off slabs of a terrine that another guest had brought. He told me it was very simple, which aren't words normally associated with making terrines and pâtés. The next day, he sent me the recipe, which he had gotten from his grandmother. It was, indeed, very easy, but like a lot of French recipes, it left much to interpretation.

This recipe is very adaptable; I've converted *un peu de crème* and *un demi-verre de cognac* into specific measurements. The capers add a piquant touch, and I like to use sage or tarragon, or sometimes both, but chives, thyme, and parsley would work in their place. Add more herbs, or less, depending on how mild or present you want their flavor to be. Another option is to add a teaspoon of ground allspice or dried ginger. And if I'm using capers packed in brine, I sometimes tip a soupspoon or two of their brine into the mix.

Preheat the oven to 350°F (175°C). Grease an 8- or 9-inch (20 or 23cm) terrine mold or a loaf pan with duck fat, if you want to be really French, or butter. You can use nonstick spray, if you want to be more practical.

Clean the livers by trimming and discarding any visible fat, green parts, and membranes. Dice or coarsely chop the livers.

In a large bowl, mix together the ground pork, ground veal, chicken livers, salt, and a generous seasoning of black pepper. Add the bread crumbs, eggs, cream, capers, cognac, and minced herbs, and mix until everything is well incorporated.

Transfer the mixture to the prepared terrine mold or loaf pan. Use your hands to make sure it's even and to smooth the top. Press the bay leaves into the top, if using.

If your terrine mold has a cover, use that. If you're using a loaf pan, cover the mold or pan snugly with aluminum foil.

Bake the terrine until it feels firm when you press it in the center, 1 to 1¼ hours.

Remove the terrine from the oven and cool for 10 minutes, then remove the foil and let cool completely.

Once cool, wrap and store the terrine in the refrigerator for at least 1 day before eating. The terrine will keep for about 1 week.

To serve, remove the terrine from the mold and place it on a platter or cutting board. Serve with the cornichons and mustard.

WINE AND CHEESE, PLEASE

While the French are great lovers of wine and cheese, the two aren't normally paired together before meals—but after. Of course, there are exceptions. When I'm in the Jura, every dinner I go to in someone's home starts with a generous wedge of Comté, the local cheese, served with a glass of wine from the region, either Chardonnay or Savagnin, which can have a sherrylike finish, a quirk that grows on you the more you drink it. In Provence, fresh goat cheese is spread on garlic toasts, which helps the free-flowing rosé go down.

And while it has been an uphill battle, I've been working hard to change people's belief (including that of many cheesemongers I know) that red wine is a better pairing with cheese than white. I find that the strong tannins in many red wines can easily overwhelm nuances in cheeses, even in strong varieties like Roquefort. Sauternes, Barsac, and Muscat de Beaumes-de-Venise, with their non-cloying sweetness, balance the pungent *fromage bleu* much better.

The most renowned goat cheeses in France come from the Loire, so try pairing them with wines made close by, such as Sauvignon Blanc, Sancerre, or the underrated Muscadet, which Americans often confuse with Muscatel, a potent sweet wine that's best left on the shelf of the corner convenience store.

Soft Normandy cheeses like Camembert, Pont l'Évêque, and Livarot that have an enticing funk go well with a full-bodied Chablis or Mâcon. Or do like the locals in Normandy do, and pair cheese with sparkling hard apple cider or Pommeau de Normandie (see page 85), a friendly *mélange* of apple juice and calvados.

CHICKEN LIVER MOUSSE WITH ARMAGNAC AND PORT JELLY

Makes 10 to 12 appetizer-size servings

6 tablespoons (85g) unsalted butter, cubed, at room temperature

3 small shallots (90g), peeled and sliced, or 1 small onion, peeled and diced

1 pound (450g) chicken livers, trimmed of any membranes

1½ teaspoons kosher or sea salt

½ teaspoon freshly ground black pepper

2 tablespoons Armagnac, cognac, or brandy

Generous pinch of grated nutmeg or allspice

Pinch of cayenne pepper

1 or 2 dried or fresh bay leaves (optional)

3 tablespoons cold water

1 teaspoon (3g) unflavored powdered gelatin

⅔ cup (160ml) dry or tawny port

Sliced baguette or crackers, for serving

Flaky sea salt, such as fleur de sel or Maldon, for serving

The French never turn their noses up at liver. But let's face it, *mousse de foie de volaille* sounds a lot better than "liver spread." A shiny mirror of port-spiked jelly on top makes this irresistible to all. While it's not a typical apéritif in the United States, the French enjoy glasses of chilled white port, which would make a fine accompaniment to this mousse, as would glasses of Pineau des Charentes (see page 82), French vermouth (see page 95), or Lillet rouge served over ice (pictured, opposite).

Melt 2 tablespoons (30g) of the butter in a skillet (not a nonstick one). Add the shallots and cook over medium-high heat, stirring frequently, until they're soft and translucent, about 2 minutes.

Add the chicken livers. Sprinkle with the salt and black pepper and cook, stirring occasionally, until the livers are mostly cooked but still pink inside, 3 to 5 minutes.

Turn the heat off and pour the Armagnac into the pan, being very careful to keep your hands and face (and anything else) away, as it can flame up. Gently stir the Armagnac into the livers, then add the remaining 4 tablespoons (55g) butter and stir until the butter is melted. Let cool for a few minutes.

Combine the liver mixture, any juices in the pan, and the nutmeg and cayenne pepper in a food processor or blender and puree until as smooth as possible. Scrape the mousse into a decorative serving bowl or crock with a capacity of at least 1 quart (1L). Gently press the bay leaves, if using, into the top of the mousse and refrigerate while you make the port jelly.

Pour the cold water into a small bowl and sprinkle the gelatin over it. Let stand for 5 minutes. Heat the port in a small saucepan. When warm, pour the port over the gelatin and stir until the gelatin is dissolved. Remove the liver mousse from the refrigerator and pour the port mixture over the top of the mousse. Return the mousse to the refrigerator to set the jelly.

Serve the chicken liver mousse at room temperature, with baguette slices and a small dish of flaky sea salt on the side.

RADISHES WITH RADISH GREENS BUTTER

Makes 6 to 8 appetizer-size servings, ½ cup (115g) butter

4 cups (60g) loosely packed radish leaves

6 tablespoons (85g) salted butter, cubed, at room temperature

1 small or medium garlic clove, peeled and minced

½ teaspoon kosher or flaky sea salt, plus extra for serving

Freshly ground black pepper

Fresh radishes, trimmed

I'm *anti-gaspillage*, as the French say, or someone who doesn't waste food, like my in-laws who make a *soupe aux fanes de radis*, radish leaf soup, rather than tossing the still-tasty greens away.

To make this astonishingly green spread, make sure the butter is very soft. If your kitchen is on the cool side, put the butter in a warm (not hot) place to soften before mixing it with the radish leaves. Be sure to wash the greens thoroughly, in several changes of water if necessary, to ensure your radish butter is free from any grit. If you don't have a food processor, chop the radish leaves very finely with a chef's knife after they're cooked, then mash them into the butter with a fork. And if you can, make the butter in advance so the flavors meld together.

Bring a small pot of water to a boil. Fill a medium bowl with very cold water and ice cubes, and have a mesh strainer handy.

Add the radish leaves to the boiling water and leave them in the water until the leaves are wilted, about 12 seconds. Drain the leaves in the strainer and immediately plunge them into the ice water, which fixes the vivid green color. Once cool, remove the radish leaves and squeeze them as hard as you can to remove any excess water.

In a food processor, combine the radish leaves, butter, garlic, salt, and a generous amount of black pepper. Process until the leaves are completely incorporated into the butter. Scrape into a bowl and serve at room temperature with the fresh radishes, either whole or sliced in half, for guests to smear with a little dab of the butter. I make sure to have some flaky salt nearby, in case anyone wants to add a few flakes of that, too.

The radish greens butter can be made up to 1 week in advance and refrigerated. Let it come to room temperature before serving.

VARIATIONS —— Here are two more options for flavored butters.

To make Seaweed Butter, mix 1½ tablespoons furikake (Japanese seaweed seasoning, available at Asian markets) with ½ cup (115g) softened salted butter.

To make Smoked Paprika Butter, mix 1 teaspoon smoked paprika with ½ cup (115g) softened salted butter and add a sprinkle of salt.

DUCK RILLETTES

Makes 10 to 12
appetizer-size
servings

3 large garlic cloves,
peeled, plus 1 garlic
clove, peeled and very
finely minced

2 bay leaves

4 duck thighs (with
legs attached)

1 tablespoon plus
a scant ¼ teaspoon
kosher or sea salt

Additional duck fat;
you'll need a total of
⅔ cup (160ml)

2 teaspoons minced
fresh thyme

Freshly ground
black pepper

Freshly grated nutmeg

Generous pinch of
ground cloves

Freshly squeezed
lemon juice

Baguette slices or
crackers, for serving

NOTE

See Resources
(page 283) for a
suggested duck
products purveyor.

I don't mean to rub it in, but duck confit and duck fat are both readily available in France, even at the supermarket. They're right next to the chickens in the poultry aisle. For those of you who live elsewhere, I've included the quick version of my duck confit recipe from my book *My Paris Kitchen* that doesn't require gallons of duck fat, or days of work in the kitchen. Just be sure to salt the thighs 8 hours in advance for the most succulent flavor.

This recipe uses three duck thighs, but I always bake four so I have an extra thigh to snack on while preparing the rillettes. (I find it hard not to pilfer some of that tender duck meat while I'm shredding.) While you can save any fat from cooking the thighs to melt down and bind the rillettes, you'll still need extra duck fat, which you can use for frying potatoes or for making this tasty spread again.

Duck is often paired with orange, so you can serve this with an orange-based apéritif, such as Lillet (see page 78), Vin d'Orange (page 147), a Pousse Rapière (page 134), or something stronger, such as a Dubonnet-based Waterloo with bourbon and orange (page 190).

Place the 3 peeled garlic cloves and the bay leaves in a baking dish that will fit the duck thighs snugly. Rub the duck thighs all over with 1 tablespoon of the salt and place them in the dish, skin side up. Cover and refrigerate for 8 hours, or overnight.

To bake the duck, uncover and place in a cold oven. Turn the oven on to 300°F (150°C) and bake the duck for 2½ hours.

Remove the duck from the oven. Transfer the duck thighs and legs to a plate or bowl, along with the garlic cloves, if they aren't irretrievably stuck to the bottom. (If you can get them out, they're delicious added to the rillettes mixture.) Discard the bay leaves. Drain and scrape off as much duck fat as you can into a heatproof measuring cup (you'll probably have about ¼ cup/60ml). Add more duck fat until you have a total of ⅔ cup (160ml).

When the duck is cool enough to handle, shred the meat of 3 of the duck thighs and legs into a medium saucepan (refer to the headnote to learn what to do with the fourth!), and add any roasted garlic you've retrieved. Add the duck fat to the duck in the saucepan, along with the finely minced garlic and thyme. Warm over low heat, stirring occasionally, until the fat is melted and the duck is slightly warmed through.

Transfer the duck mixture to the bowl of a stand mixer fitted with the paddle attachment. Add the remaining scant ¼ teaspoon salt, a few generous turns of freshly ground black pepper, several swipes of grated nutmeg, the ground cloves, and a squeeze of lemon juice. Mix on low speed until the mixture forms a well-shredded, cohesive mass. Taste, and add more seasonings, if desired. Scrape the duck rillettes into a serving bowl or terrine.

The duck rillettes are best served at room temperature. They can be refrigerated for up to 5 days. Let them come to room temperature before serving. Serve with slices of baguette or crackers.

CHICKEN RILLETTES

Makes 10 to 12
appetizer-size
servings

2 pounds (900g)
chicken thighs with
legs attached, or
bone-in thighs

2 teaspoons kosher
or sea salt, plus more
if needed

Freshly ground
black pepper

½ teaspoon
cayenne pepper

1 tablespoon
unsalted butter, plus
4 tablespoons (60g)
unsalted butter, cubed,
at room temperature

1 tablespoon
extra-virgin olive oil

1 small onion, peeled
and diced

2 medium garlic cloves,
peeled and thinly sliced

5 sprigs fresh thyme,
plus 2 teaspoons
minced fresh thyme
leaves

1 cup (250ml) dry
vermouth or white wine

¾ cup (180ml)
chicken stock

2 bay leaves

3 small shallots,
peeled and minced

2 tablespoons minced
fresh tarragon

1 tablespoon
Dijon mustard

Rillettes don't have to be made with pork or duck. Easy-to-find chicken thighs to make a lighter, yet very flavorful version of this classic French spread. These go well with a glass of dry white wine, a round of Kir (page 49), or tarragon-based TNT cocktails (page 161).

―――――――

Preheat the oven to 300°F (150°C).

Rub the chicken all over (including under the skin) with 1½ teaspoons of the salt, black pepper, and the cayenne pepper.

Heat the 1 tablespoon butter and the olive oil in a Dutch oven over medium-high heat. Place the chicken pieces in the pan skin side down. (If the Dutch oven won't fit the chicken thighs in an even layer with some space between them, cook them in two batches.) Cook until well browned on one side, about 5 minutes, then turn and brown the other side. When the thighs are browned, transfer them to a plate.

Add the onion, garlic, and thyme sprigs to the pan, and cook, stirring frequently, until the onion is translucent, about 3 minutes. Add the vermouth and stir, scraping up any browned bits stuck to the bottom of the pan. Add the stock and heat until the liquid comes to a boil.

Turn off the heat and return the chicken pieces to the pot. Tuck the bay leaves between the chicken. Cover and cook the chicken in the oven for 45 minutes, turning the thighs over midway through the cooking time.

Remove the pot from the oven and transfer the chicken pieces to a plate. Set them aside until cool enough to handle. Strain the cooking liquid through a mesh strainer, discard the solids, and set the liquid aside.

Once the chicken has cooled, remove the skin and shred the meat from the bones.

In the bowl of a food processor, pulse the remaining 4 tablespoons (60g) room-temperature butter with ½ cup (125ml) of the tepid chicken braising liquid, remaining ½ teaspoon salt, and a generous amount of freshly ground black pepper. (You can also use a stand mixer

1 teaspoon freshly
squeezed lemon juice,
plus more if needed

Freshly grated nutmeg

Baguette slices
or crackers and
cornichons, for serving

fitted with the paddle attachment for this step.) Add the shredded chicken. Pulse the mixture about ten times, until the pieces of chicken are broken up a bit.

Remove the lid and scrape the chicken mixture off the sides of the bowl and into the center, if it's not mixed evenly. Add the shallots, tarragon, Dijon mustard, minced thyme, lemon juice, a generous dusting of nutmeg, and 2 more tablespoons of the chicken braising liquid. (Any leftover braising liquid can be refrigerated or frozen and used in a future batch of soup.) Pulse the food processor a couple more times until the mixture is a cohesive mass, but with discernible pieces of chicken visible.

Taste, and season with additional lemon juice or salt, stirring them in by hand so the rillettes don't get overprocessed. You want the mixture to be slightly chunky. Scrape into a serving dish and serve with slices of baguettes or crackers and cornichons.

The chicken rillettes can be refrigerated for up to 3 days. Remove from the refrigerator about 30 minutes before serving, so it has time to soften and become spreadable.

GOUGÈRES

Makes about
30 cheese puffs

1 cup (250ml) water

½ cup (115g) unsalted
butter, cubed

½ teaspoon kosher
or sea salt

¼ teaspoon
cayenne pepper

1 cup (140g) flour

4 large eggs

1¾ cups (5 ounces/
140g) grated Comté or
Gruyère cheese, plus
about 1 cup (3 ounces/
85g) additional grated
cheese for sprinkling
on top

Something I couldn't find when I arrived in France were spring-loaded ice cream scoops in different sizes. I used them a lot when I baked professionally, so I searched far and wide, only to come up empty-handed. Exasperated, I asked a salesperson at a pastry supply shop in Les Halles why they didn't carry them, as bakers use them for everything, especially for portioning cookie dough. Without missing a beat, he replied, "*Monsieur*, we do *not* scoop cookies in France." He was right, but I do know that most home cooks aren't comfortable using a pastry bag—if they even have one. A spring-loaded cookie scoop is the perfect tool to portion out these *gougères*, but a pastry bag fitted with a wide plain tip, or even two soupspoons, can be used to shape the mounds of dough.

These traditional French cheese puffs are shaped, baked until crusty brown, and served warm. I use full-flavored Comté or Gruyère in these, but another strongly flavored cheese, like Cheddar or Jarlsberg, would work well, too. I also top each with additional cheese before baking, which gives them extra flavor, and crispiness, on top. French Manhattans (pictured, opposite; recipe on page 180) and Gentian Fizzes (page 89) are efficient drinks to down the *gougères* with. If you have beer-loving guests, glasses of Picon Bière (page 48) will be popular with the cheese puffs, too.

Preheat the oven to 425°F (220°C). Line two baking sheets with parchment paper or silicone baking mats.

In a medium saucepan, heat the water, butter, salt, and cayenne together over medium-high heat, stirring occasionally, until the butter is melted.

Immediately add the flour all at once. Reduce the heat to medium and cook, stirring continuously with a flexible spatula or wooden spoon, until the dough forms a smooth ball and is no longer sticking to the sides of the pan.

Scrape the dough into the bowl of a stand mixer fitted with the paddle attachment and let it rest for 2 minutes, "bursting" the mixer (turning it on and off) a couple of times to help it cool. (If you don't have a stand mixer, the eggs in the next step can be added by hand,

continued

stirring them briskly into the slightly cooled batter, one at a time, so they don't "cook" while adding them.)

Turn the mixer on medium-high speed and add the eggs, one at a time, letting each one get incorporated before adding the next, and stopping the mixer and scraping down the sides after each addition. When the eggs have been incorporated, add 1¾ cups (140g) of the cheese.

Using a medium spring-loaded ice cream scoop or two soupspoons (or a pastry bag fitted with a wide plain tip), form rounded scoops of the dough, each about 1½ tablespoons, on the prepared baking sheets until you've used up all the dough. Each mound should be about 1½ inches (4cm) wide; leave at least 1 inch (2.5cm) between them.

Top each mound with as much grated cheese as will stick to the top. I make a tube shape with one hand and place it over each mound to guide the cheese, then use the other hand to drop the cheese through the "tube" so it lands on top of the dough.

Bake for 5 minutes. Turn the heat down to 375°F (190°C) and bake until deep golden brown across the top and up the sides, about 30 minutes, rotating the baking sheets from top to bottom and bottom to top and turning them 180 degrees three-quarters of the way through the baking time so they bake evenly.

Serve the gougères warm or at room temperature. If made in advance, they can be rewarmed in a moderate oven, uncovered on a baking sheet, before serving.

FONTINA AND SEED CRISPS

Makes 8 to 10 appetizer-size servings

¾ cup (105g) raw (untoasted) pumpkin seeds

¾ cup (105g) untoasted, unsalted sunflower seeds

½ cup (65g) sesame seeds

3 tablespoons (30g) flax seeds

3 tablespoons (30g) poppy seeds

¾ teaspoon kosher or flaky sea salt

¼ teaspoon cayenne pepper

2 cups (6 ounces/170g) coarsely grated Fontina cheese

2 cups (6 ounces/170g) coarsely grated Asiago cheese

I discovered these crazy-good apéritif snacks when I was on a book tour for *L'appart*, a memoir about the comedy of errors I encountered when renovating my kitchen in Paris—a two-month job that extended to two years. If there were ever a situation in my life when I needed a drink, it was then. One bright side of that experience was that it led me to discover these crunchy, crackly, seedy crisps. The bakers at Market Hall Foods in Oakland, California, began to notice how obsessively the staff plucked off the shards of stuck-on browned cheese and seeds that seeped out onto the baking sheets while baking their cheese and seed breads, and so they started baking just the cheese and seeds in large sheets, which they offer in their stores. They graciously sent me the recipe, which I adapted here, in portions that can be made at home. Fontina is a soft cheese that can be tricky to grate. I cut the block into several pieces, then put them in the freezer, uncovered, for an hour (shhhh, don't tell the French I freeze cheese . . .) before grating, which helps.

Bracingly dry drinks like the Suze & Tonic (page 89) and Sapatini (page 153), or an apéritif like La Découverte (page 73), go well with these nutty, cheesy crisps. (Pictured on page 72.)

Preheat the oven to 350°F (175°C). Line a rimmed baking sheet with parchment paper and spray it lightly with nonstick spray.

In a large bowl, toss together the pumpkin, sunflower, sesame, flax, and poppy seeds, the salt, and cayenne pepper.

Add the cheeses and mix very well with your hands. Strew the mixture over the prepared baking sheet in an even layer, so it reaches almost to the edges of the pan.

Bake until the cheese and seeds are golden all the way across the top, making sure any pockets of cheese are lightly browned as well so they'll crisp up when cool, 25 to 30 minutes. Remove from the oven and let cool completely. Once cool, break into pieces and serve. The crisps can be stored in an airtight container at room temperature for up to 1 week.

DEVILED EGGS WITH CORNICHON TAPENADE

Makes 6 appetizer-size servings

6 large eggs, at room temperature

¼ cup (30g) cornichons, drained, cut into ½-inch (1.5cm) pieces

¼ cup (35g) green olives, pitted

2 tablespoons chopped fresh chervil, parsley, or chives, plus more for garnish

1 tablespoon extra-virgin olive oil

1 tablespoon capers, rinsed and squeezed dry

1 or 2 anchovy fillets

1 teaspoon Dijon mustard, plus more if needed

1 dash Tabasco or another hot sauce

Freshly ground black pepper

¼ cup (60g) mayonnaise

Up to ¼ teaspoon kosher or sea salt, if necessary

Smoked or sweet paprika, for garnish

One day, an email arrived from an excited reader alerting me to a cornichon tapenade recipe on the website of a French mustard company that, admittedly, looked very appetizing. Since I always have a jar of cornichons on hand, I made it right away. But after one taste, I knew it wasn't going to be my new go-to tapenade recipe. The cornichons were too vinegary and overwhelmed the olives. Determined, I tried it a few more times, but I couldn't get the balance quite right. The idea was stuck in my head for a few days, and there were those several bowls of cornichon tapenade taking up valuable space in my refrigerator. . . . It needed something. But what?

Hard-cooked eggs, it turned out. Eggs are the perfect foil for strong, vinegary flavors, so I whizzed up the tapenade with the yolks of a few *œufs durs* (hard-cooked eggs), a generous dollop of mayonnaise, and some other seasonings, and prayed for the best. I had a friend coming for dinner that night, and another one of my prayers was answered when he brought a lovely bottle of Dom Pérignon vintage champagne for the apéritif. Some insist that eggs don't pair well with wine, but these very tasty *œufs à la diable* (deviled eggs) will change anybody's mind, and they were a big hit. You don't need to serve them with such extravagant bubbles, but they do go remarkably well with champagne or a dry crémant.

To hard cook the eggs, bring a medium saucepan of water to a low boil. Use a spoon to lower the eggs into the water, one at a time. Adjust the heat so the water remains at a steady low boil and cook for 10 minutes.

Drain the water from the saucepan and jerk the pan a few times to crack the cooked eggs a bit. Fill the pan with enough ice cubes to cover the eggs and add cold water to the pan to stop the eggs from cooking further.

In a food processor (if yours comes with a smaller bowl, or you have a mini-chopper, this is a good time to use it), combine the cornichons, olives, herbs, olive oil, capers, anchovies, mustard, hot sauce, and a few grinds of black pepper. Pulse, stopping the

continued

machine a few times to scrape down the sides, until the ingredients are coarsely chopped.

Peel the eggs. Use a sharp knife to cut each one in half lengthwise, wiping the knife blade clean with a damp paper towel between cuts. Carefully remove the cooked yolks and put them in the food processor. Arrange the egg whites on a serving plate, cut side up.

Add the mayonnaise to the food processor and pulse about ten times, or until incorporated. Taste, and add some salt, if necessary (depending on the saltiness of your other ingredients), and maybe a touch more mustard for some extra zip. Process until the mixture is almost smooth and creamy, but with slightly crunchy little bits of cornichon still visible.

Use a spoon to fill the cavity of each egg white with the mixture, mounding it up so there's a good amount in each. Garnish each egg with a sprinkle or sprig of fresh herbs and a bit of paprika.

GRAVLAX WITH MUSTARD SAUCE

**Makes about
24 appetizer-size
servings**

GRAVLAX

1 teaspoon
caraway seeds

¼ cup (45g) coarse gray
sea salt or Diamond
Crystal kosher salt
(see Note, page 254)

2 tablespoons sugar

1 teaspoon freshly
ground black pepper

1½ to 2 pounds (680 to
900g) salmon fillet,
preferably center cut
(the thickest part),
pin bones removed

1 large bunch dill

2 tablespoons gin,
cognac, vodka, or pastis

MUSTARD SAUCE

3 tablespoons neutral
vegetable oil

2 tablespoons
Dijon mustard

1 tablespoon distilled
white vinegar

1 teaspoon honey,
or 1½ teaspoons sugar

2 tablespoons finely
chopped fresh dill

When I bought a slab of salmon to make gravlax, my fishmonger was perplexed when I told him that I use gin, rather than cognac, the French standby, for curing. To my taste, the juniper flavor of gin is more *sympatico* with the fish, but he wasn't convinced. The French can be apprehensive about veering from tradition; my partner's mother from Brittany was astonished when I told her that you could cook oysters. Another way to go rogue, but still keep it French, is to use pastis (see page 164) in place of gin. But my guests don't seem to mind the gin, and they always reach for seconds. It doesn't hurt that I often use French gin.

This makes a generous amount of gravlax and is an ideal do-ahead appetizer. (You can also cut the recipe in half, using just 1 pound/450g of salmon. Leftovers freeze well.) In France, gravlax is served on sturdy rye or whole-grain bread or toast, with a spoonful of tangy mustard sauce (pictured on page 250). The French have an understandable fondness for Dijon mustard. It's their umami bomb, and the more mustard, the better. Just be aware that the sauce packs a wallop, and a little goes a long way. The recipe makes ½ cup (125ml) sauce, enough for *une lichette* (a dab) with each serving, but feel free to double it if you think you'll want more.

Bracing drinks are called for with cured salmon, such as the well-seasoned Za'atar Martini (page 207), a traditional martini (page 97), or the Vesper (page 79). Lighter choices would be Champagne Cocktails (page 65) or Grapefruit Rosés (page 61).

To make the gravlax, in a skillet over medium-high heat, toast the caraway seeds, stirring, until they smell fragrant, about 2 minutes. Cool, then crush them in a mortar and pestle or spice grinder, but not too fine. (They can also be placed in a sturdy ziptop freezer bag and crushed with a rolling pin.)

In a small bowl, mix the crushed caraway seeds, salt, sugar, and black pepper.

Place the salmon flesh side up in a glass, ceramic, or nonreactive metal dish that the fish will fit into without too much space around it. Rub half of the salt mixture over the top surface and the sides of the salmon.

continued

1 tablespoon chopped capers, rinsed and squeezed dry before chopping

¼ teaspoon kosher or sea salt (see Note)

Freshly ground black pepper

Thin slices of pumpernickel or other dark or dense grainy bread, or crackers, for serving

NOTE

Kosher salt can vary in strength and saltiness. While I use coarse gray sea salt in France, I've tested this with kosher salt and found Diamond Crystal salt to have a similar saltiness to the salt I use. (See "Salt Sense," page 231.)

Flip the salmon over so it's skin side up. Rub the skin with the rest of the salt mixture. Lay half of the dill over the skin and flip both the salmon and dill over, so the dill is underneath the salmon and the flesh side is up again. Spoon the gin over the salmon and lay the rest of the dill over the salmon. Flip the salmon over one last time so it's skin side up (there should be dill on both sides now).

Cover the salmon with plastic wrap and set a plate on top. Place something fairly heavy on top of the plate, such as a few big cans of tomatoes. Refrigerate for 48 hours.

Remove the plastic and the dill, and wipe the salmon with a paper towel to remove as much salt as possible. Place in a clean dish and refrigerate until ready to serve.

To make the mustard sauce, mix the oil and mustard together in a small bowl. Stir in the vinegar and honey, then mix in the chopped dill, capers, salt, and some freshly ground black pepper to taste.

To serve, place the salmon on a cutting board and slice it as thin as possible using a long slicing knife or a chef's knife. Drape pieces of the gravlax on the sliced bread or crackers, and spoon a bit of the mustard sauce over the salmon.

BURRATA WITH DRIED TANGERINES, OLIVE OIL, AND SEA SALT

Makes 2 to 4
appetizer-size
servings

2 or 3 tangerines

1 burrata (or fresh,
soft mozzarella)

Best-quality
extra-virgin olive oil

Flaky sea salt, such as
fleur de sel or Maldon

NOTE

Extra tangerine
dust will keep for
several months
stored in a jar in a
cool, dark place.

Anyone who thinks the French don't work hard hasn't watched La Buvette wine bar owner Camille Fourmont in action. Each day she rolls up the heavy metal front gate, sets up the bar, prepares the food, and then waits on customers, who begin trickling into this pocket-size *cave à manger* before she's even taken the chairs off the few tables. The rest of her night is spent refilling wine glasses and plating up food while chatting with friends and neighbors, who stop in to *boire un coup* (have a drink). Due to French law, Camille can't serve wine without food, which works in our favor. People come in thinking they don't want anything to eat. When they find they don't have a choice, they realize how lucky they are.

This burrata is one of her favorites. Camille showers it with a very fine dusting of dried tangerine peel, a souvenir of her childhood. After eating tangerines in the winter, French kids put the peels on the radiator to dry. Here she uses the fragrant rind to perfume the supple cheese, and finishes it with a touch of salt. It's a memorable combination.

The creamy cheese goes well with natural wines, as served at La Buvette. Check in your area to find a shop that carries them.

Peel the tangerines. (Reserve the fruit for another use.) Place the peels on top of a warm radiator and let them dry completely, until brittle. Depending on the radiator and the thickness and moisture of the tangerine peels, it will take about 24 hours. (If you don't have a radiator, you can dry them on a baking sheet in a 170°F/75°C oven until brittle. It will take between 1½ and 2 hours.)

Let the peels cool completely, then grind them to a fine powder in a spice mill or high-powered blender.

Place the burrata on a serving plate and drizzle with extra-virgin olive oil. Put a spoonful of the ground tangerine zest in a fine-mesh strainer and dust the top of the burrata with the zest, covering the cheese in an even layer. Sprinkle with grains of flaky sea salt and serve.

MUSHROOM-ROQUEFORT TARTLETS

Makes 24 tartlets

DOUGH

2 cups (280g) flour

2 teaspoons sugar

½ teaspoon kosher
or sea salt

1 cup (230g) unsalted
butter, cubed, chilled

4 ounces (115g) cream
cheese, chilled

6 tablespoons (90ml)
ice water

FILLING

1 pound (450g) wild or
button mushrooms

3 tablespoons (45g)
unsalted butter

2 small shallots, peeled
and minced, or 4 green
onions, minced

Kosher or sea salt

Freshly ground
black pepper

⅓ cup (80ml)
heavy cream

2 tablespoons cognac,
brandy, or dry sherry

3 ounces (85g)
Roquefort or another
blue cheese, crumbled,
at room temperature

3 tablespoons minced
fresh chervil or chives

These bite-size tartlets with sautéed chopped mushrooms and sharp Roquefort are perfect when my guests need something more substantial than just a nibble. Due to their buttery aroma, expect everyone to make a dive for the platter as soon as they get a whiff.

In the fall, I use the wild mushrooms that are at the markets, but these tartlets are also delicious with brown button mushrooms, called *champignons de Paris* because they used to be cultivated in catacombs under the city.

If you have only one 12-cup muffin pan (or two 6-cup ones), assemble the first twelve tartlets, then roll the rest of the dough into twelve squares and chill them while the first batch is baking. When the first tartlets are done, remove them from the pan and set them on a cooling rack. Let the muffin pan cool, wipe it clean, then bake the remaining twelve tartlets. If you want to use store-bought puff pastry, you'll need 1½ pounds (680g).

These little tarts go well with a red Bordeaux, or a fruity Gamay, Merlot, or Pinot Noir from Burgundy. The rich grape flavor of Byrrh in the Saint/Sinner (page 73), or simply a Byrrh on the rocks with an orange twist, works nicely with the *piquant* Roquefort.

To make the dough, mix the flour, sugar, and salt in the bowl of a stand mixer fitted with the paddle attachment or in a food processor. (You can also make it by hand using a pastry blender.) Add the chilled cubes of butter and run the mixer at medium speed, or pulse the food processor a few times, until the pieces of butter are well dispersed but still in large, discernible pieces.

Add the cream cheese and continue mixing until the butter and cream cheese are the size of peas. Add the ice water and mix just until the dough comes together. Remove it from the machine, shape into a rectangle, then wrap it in plastic wrap and refrigerate for at least 1 hour or up to 2 days before using.

To make the mushroom filling, finely chop the mushrooms. Melt the butter in a large skillet over medium-high heat. Add the mushrooms and shallots and season them lightly with salt and black pepper.

Cook, stirring frequently, until the mushrooms are cooked through and most of the liquid has evaporated, about 6 minutes. Reduce the heat to medium and add the cream, then the cognac, and continue to cook,

NOTE

These can be
baked in advance
and rewarmed,
uncovered, on a
baking sheet in
a moderate oven.

stirring constantly, until most of the cream is absorbed. (There should still be some liquid in the pan.) Turn off the heat and stir in the crumbled cheese until melted. Add the chervil. Let the filling cool to room temperature, or refrigerate until ready to use.

To bake the tartlets, preheat the oven to 400°F (200°C). Have two standard 12-cup muffin pans ready. (See headnote for other options.)

Using a chef's knife, pastry scraper, or pizza cutter, cut the rectangle of chilled dough in half lengthwise. Rewrap the other half of the dough and refrigerate it while you roll the first half. On a lightly floured countertop, roll out the dough to a rectangle about 8 by 16 inches (20 by 40cm), adding a little more flour as you roll if the dough sticks.

Position the rectangle of dough so the short ends are facing left and right. Cut it in half lengthwise to make two long pieces, then make one cut vertically down the center. You should have four pieces. Make four more vertical cuts, two on each side of the center cut, so you have twelve pieces of dough.

Using a rolling pin, roll one piece of dough into a 4-inch (10cm) square. (It doesn't need to be a perfect square as the dough will adapt itself to the shape of the muffin pan.) Drape it over one cup of a muffin pan and gently coax it to fit inside, with the four corners of the dough overhanging the edges. Continue rolling the rest of the dough pieces into squares and fitting them into the remaining indentations of the muffin pans.

Place a level tablespoon of the mushroom filling in the center of each square of dough. (It may not look like much, but the blue cheese and mushrooms are quite strongly flavored.) Use your fingers to bring the four corners of the dough together over the mushroom filling, pressing the four corners gently together. Bake, rotating the pans 180 degrees midway through baking, until golden brown, 22 to 25 minutes. Remove the tartlets from the oven, let stand for a few minutes, then run a butter knife or small spatula around the tartlets, remove them from the pan, and set them on a cooling rack. (If you need to reuse the muffin pan to bake any remaining tartlets, as mentioned in the headnote, cool and clean the pan, then repeat the process with the rest of the dough and the filling.)

The tartlets can be served at room temperature, but people really go for them if they're warm.

CORNMEAL, BACON, AND SUN-DRIED TOMATO MADELEINES

Makes about 18 madeleines

5 strips (2½ ounces/70g) thin-cut bacon

½ cup (60g) all-purpose flour or corn flour (see Notes, page 260)

½ cup (65g) stone-ground cornmeal

1 teaspoon baking powder, preferably aluminum-free

¾ teaspoon kosher or sea salt

½ teaspoon piment d'Espelette or smoked paprika

¼ teaspoon baking soda

¾ cup (175ml) buttermilk

2 tablespoons extra-virgin olive oil

2 teaspoons honey

¼ cup (12g) minced fresh chives

3 medium sun-dried, oil-packed tomato halves, well-drained, patted dry, and finely diced

You know a recipe is a hit when the normally reserved Parisians go back for seconds, and even thirds. Most will usually take one, maybe two, of something, then restrain themselves, knowing that taking too much is *un peu* (a little) "too much," which they say in English, because eating too much isn't a French concept. But they make an exception for these.

Madeleine pan sizes can vary, so you may get a couple more, or slightly fewer, than I did. Most pans are designed to bake twelve madeleines at a time. If you don't have two pans, use one pan to bake the first dozen, and then wash and dry the pan. Once it's cool, make the remaining madeleines in it. For best results, dice the bacon and sun-dried tomatoes into the smallest pieces possible.

These savory madeleines won't get the traditional hump that their sweet counterparts get, but they're very attractive baked in the scalloped molds. You can also bake these in mini-muffin pans (see Notes, page 260).

I like to serve drinks that are relatively straightforward with these madeleines, since they have a multitude of flavors in them. A French Manhattan (page 180), The Sunny Side (page 161), or a Sidecar (page 190) fall into that camp.

In a medium skillet, cook the bacon over medium heat until it starts to brown. Just as it starts to get crisp, transfer the bacon to a plate lined with a paper towel to drain. Let the bacon fat in the skillet cool a bit, then use a brush to generously grease eighteen indentations, and their rims, in two madeleine pans. When the bacon is cool, finely dice it.

Preheat the oven to 400°F (200°C).

In a medium bowl, whisk together the flour, cornmeal, baking powder, salt, piment d'Espelette, and baking soda. In a separate small bowl, mix together the buttermilk, olive oil, and honey.

Make a well in the center of the dry ingredients. Add the buttermilk mixture and stir until the dry ingredients are partially incorporated,

continued

but some of the flour is still visible. Add the diced bacon, chives, and sun-dried tomatoes, folding them in just until combined.

Fill the prepared indentations of the madeleine molds three-quarters full with batter. (I use a small spring-loaded ice cream scoop. Two soupspoons also work well.) Rap the madeleine pans on the counter a few times to settle the batter into the indentations. Bake for 7 to 8 minutes, until the centers of the madeleines spring back when you touch them. Let cool for 1 minute, then remove the madeleines from the pans and place on a wire rack. You may need a small metal spatula or butter knife to help release them.

These are best served the same day, but they can be kept in an airtight container for up to 3 days.

NOTES

Corn flour is very finely milled cornmeal. It's yellow and powdery; its texture resembles all-purpose flour. It's sold in natural food stores and well-stocked supermarkets.

If using mini-muffin pans, fill them three-quarters full. Make sure to grease the indentations especially well, including the rims. The baking time is the same as if baked in madeleine molds. Depending on your pans, you may need to run a sharp paring knife around the cakes to help release them.

CRESPÈU

Makes 8 to 10
appetizer-size
servings

10 ounces (285g)
(stemmed weight) kale

6 tablespoons (90ml)
extra-virgin olive oil

3 garlic cloves, peeled
and minced

Red pepper flakes

Kosher or sea salt

3 large eggs

½ cup (40g) finely
grated Comté, Gruyère,
or Swiss cheese

Flaky sea salt,
for serving

My introduction to *crespèu* came from Lulu Peyraud, via Richard Olney, in their book *Lulu's Provençal Table*. Her family winery, Domaine Tempier in the South of France, is known for its excellent Bandol rosé. I like it so much that I once overbid on a massive bottle of it at a wine auction, which became the subject of a lot of attention, and possibly some jealously, from the other métro passengers on the way home at the end of the event. A few weeks later, I filled my apartment with delighted friends to help me drink it because I knew I couldn't go through it all by myself. (Or could I?) It seemed only right that I make Lulu's *crespèu* to go with the wine.

Lulu's *crespèu* is an open-faced omelet. It's similar to a frittata, but with a much higher proportion of vegetables to eggs. I took a few liberties with the original recipe, using the same Provençal-approved amount of olive oil and garlic, but adding a sprinkle of red pepper for heat, a bit of cheese to make it heartier, and some kale—because no matter how long I've been in France, I will always be a Californian at heart.

This isn't at all difficult to make, but be sure to read through the instructions before starting, as you need to have a large serving platter or wooden board nearby when the *crespèu* is ready to be turned out of the pan. Using a nonstick pan helps the *crespèu* release easily. Like riding the métro at midnight with an oversize bottle of rosé on your lap, expect this *crespèu* to draw extra attention once cooked. I like to serve it with some wisps of flaky sea salt, such as fleur de sel or Maldon, sprinkled over the wedges.

This is perfect with rosé, or an apéritif, such as Suze (see page 86), Lillet blanc or rosé (see page 78), or sparkling Limonade (page 36).

Bring a large pot (about 4 quarts/4L) of lightly salted water to a boil. Add the kale and cook, turning it with tongs a few times, until it's soft and wilted. Tuscan kale will take 3 to 5 minutes; thicker curly kale will take 8 to 10 minutes.

When the kale is tender, drain it in a colander and run cold water over it while turning it with tongs. Once it's cool, working in batches, use your hands to firmly wring out as much water as you possibly can. Very finely chop the kale with a chef's knife.

continued

Warm 3 tablespoons (45ml) of the olive oil and the garlic in a 12-inch (30cm) nonstick skillet over medium heat until the garlic starts to sizzle. Stir for about 10 seconds, until the garlic smells fragrant, then add the chopped kale along with a few flakes of red pepper and salt to taste. Cook, stirring frequently, until the garlic and kale are cooked and well flavored, 4 to 5 minutes.

Mix the eggs in a medium bowl. Add the warm kale mixture to the eggs, stirring them constantly. (If you don't, you'll get bits of precooked eggs, which you don't want.) Once the kale is well mixed with the eggs, stir in the cheese. Clean the pan and dry it well.

Heat the remaining 3 tablespoons (45ml) olive oil in the pan over medium-high heat. Scrape the kale-and-egg mixture into the pan and immediately spread it with the back of a wooden spoon or silicone spatula so it's even across the bottom of the pan. As you're spreading it, jerk the pan back and forth a bit to keep the mixture from sticking.

Lower the heat, cover the pan, and cook the *crespèu* until it's one solid mass that moves as a round disk when you shake the pan, about 4 minutes. The center will still be runny, which is okay, and if you take a peek, the underside should be gently browned in places.

Run the spatula around the outside of the *crespèu*, shaking the pan as you go, to make sure it'll release from the pan. Lay a piece of parchment paper over the top of the *crespèu* in the skillet and set the bottom of a baking sheet over the parchment, so the baking sheet is right side up. (If you have a rimless pan, it doesn't matter what side you use, but if you place a jelly roll–style baking pan rim side facing down, it'll be a challenge to slip the *crespèu* back into the skillet later.)

Grasping both the baking sheet and the pan, turn them both over simultaneously, so the *crespèu* releases onto the parchment-covered bottom of the baking sheet.

Slide the *crespèu* back into the pan and cook until the underside is cooked, about another minute. When done, slide the *crespèu* onto a flat serving platter or wooden board.

Cut into thin wedges and serve warm or at room temperature, sprinkled with flaky sea salt.

SOCCA

Makes 6 appetizer-size servings

1 cup (130g) chickpea flour

¾ teaspoon kosher or sea salt

¼ teaspoon ground cumin

1 cup (250ml) water

1½ tablespoons extra-virgin olive oil, plus more for oiling the pan and brushing over the top

Flaky sea salt and freshly ground black pepper, for serving

When I first published a recipe for socca nearly fifteen years ago, most people outside of Nice had never heard of it. But it was a secret too good to keep quiet, and I felt compelled to spread the word. (I wasn't the first to share it, though. *La Cuisinière Provençale* by Jean-Baptiste Reboul, which was published in 1897, called the snack *vulgaire*, no doubt due to its provenance as "street food.")

Part of socca's newfound popularity is due to the fact that it's naturally gluten-free; it's made with chickpea flour, readily available in natural food stores and online. You want to use finely milled chickpea flour; some stores sell a coarsely ground version, which gives socca a rougher texture that I don't prefer.

Socca is always sprinkled with flaky sea salt and lots of black pepper, and it demands to be paired with the Grapefruit Rosé cocktail (page 61) or glasses of rosé with plenty of ice, another specialty of the South of France, where it's called a *piscine de rosé*—a "swimming pool" of wine.

In a medium bowl, whisk together the chickpea flour, salt, cumin, water, and olive oil until smooth. Cover and let rest for 1 hour at room temperature. (The batter can rest for up to 6 hours at room temperature if you want to make it in advance.)

When ready to make the socca, adjust the rack to the top third of the oven, place a 10-inch (25cm) cast-iron skillet on it, and preheat the oven to 450°F (230°C).

Remove the skillet from the oven (remember to stay aware of how hot the pan is, especially the handle) and carefully brush the bottom and sides with olive oil. Pour in the socca batter and, using an oven mitt to hold the handle, tilt the pan to spread the batter around so it's even. Bake the socca until it feels almost set, about 8 minutes. Remove from the oven and turn on the broiler.

Brush a little olive oil over the top of the socca. Place it back in the oven and broil until the top turns brown in patches, which will take 1 to 4 minutes, depending on your broiler. Watch it carefully. Remove the pan from the oven, run a spatula under the socca to release it from the pan, and slide it onto a cutting board. Brush with additional olive oil, slice the socca into wedges, and serve with a liberal sprinkling of flaky sea salt and black pepper.

WARM MARINATED OLIVES

Makes 6 appetizer-size servings

1½ cups (255g) olives

1½ tablespoons extra-virgin olive oil

1 or 2 small sprigs fresh rosemary, or 8 sprigs fresh thyme

3 wide strips orange or lemon zest

Freshly ground black pepper

Pinch of red pepper flakes

This is more a technique than a recipe, so you're welcome to improvise. I make these when I am pressed for time but still want to impress my guests. These always-popular olives can be prepared just before guests arrive and served warm. But they're also an excellent do-ahead dish for those hosts who are better prepared than I often am.

You can use green or black olives, but I like a mix of both. (If using unpitted olives, you might want to remind guests to watch out for pits.) My favorite varieties are Picholine, Castelvetrano, Nyon, Kalamata, Cerignola, and Niçoise.

Warm the olives, olive oil, rosemary, orange zest, black pepper to taste, and red pepper flakes to taste in a small skillet or saucepan, stirring until the olives are well coated with the oil and seasonings.

Remove from the heat and transfer the olives and seasonings to a serving bowl.

Serve warm.

SPICY GLAZED NUT AND PRETZEL MIX

Makes about
8 appetizer-size
servings

2 cups (200g) raw
(untoasted and
unsalted) mixed nuts
(see headnote)

1 tablespoon
salted or unsalted
butter, melted

3 tablespoons (40g)
dark brown sugar

1½ tablespoons
maple syrup

1½ teaspoons kosher
or flaky sea salt

¾ teaspoon cayenne
pepper or red chile
pepper powder
(smoked or unsmoked)

½ teaspoon
ground cinnamon

2 cups (100g) small
pretzel twists

This is the most popular savory recipe I've ever come up with. And I have to confess, it's one of my favorites, too.

This crunchy, salty, spicy mix (pictured opposite, at top) can be made with any variety of raw, untoasted nuts; I usually go with whole almonds and pecans, tending to be extra generous with the pecans since they're the ones that everyone reaches for first. (Since I get first dibs on them in the kitchen, I find myself reaching for them, too.) I recommend using the full amount of cayenne pepper, but you can use another red pepper powder if you want these to be on the less-spicy side.

I often shake or stir up cocktails that are more spirit-forward to stand up to the spices in this mix. A Le Piqueur (page 186), Toronto (page 184), or Boulevardier (page 179), if called into service, would do the trick, as would a glass of roguish Cap Corse rouge, over ice.

Preheat the oven to 350°F (175°C). Spread the nuts on a baking sheet and bake until they're lightly toasted, about 8 minutes.

Meanwhile, in a medium bowl, mix the butter, brown sugar, maple syrup, salt, cayenne, and cinnamon.

Remove the nuts from the oven and tip them into the bowl. Add the pretzels and stir until the nuts and pretzels are completely coated with the butter and seasonings.

Spread the mixture back onto the baking sheet and bake for 10 to 12 minutes, stirring several times during baking so they toast evenly. Remove from the oven and cool on the pan. When they are cool enough to handle, use your hands to separate any large clumps of pretzels and nuts.

The mix can be stored in an airtight container for up to 1 week at room temperature.

ROSEMARY BAR NUTS

**Makes about
8 appetizer-size
servings**

4 cups (400g) raw
(untoasted and
unsalted) nuts, any mix
of cashews, walnuts,
pecans, hazelnuts,
and almonds

¼ cup (6g) coarsely
chopped fresh
rosemary leaves

2½ tablespoons
unsalted butter, melted

1½ tablespoons light or
dark brown sugar

1½ teaspoons smoked
paprika or another red or
smoked chile pepper
powder

2 teaspoons kosher
or flaky sea salt

This recipe is inspired by the bar nuts served at Union Square Café
in New York City, a recipe that appeared many years ago in *Saveur*
magazine. I include some smoky paprika and adjusted the sweet/
salty ratio. Like many things in Le Big Apple, these are a hit in the
City of Lights as well. The salty, herbal punch of these rosemary-
scented nuts makes them a good candidate to go along with fruity
drinks like a Peach Smash (page 103), La Bicyclette (page 51), or
Strawberry Spiked Limonade (page 140). (Pictured on page 267.)

Preheat the oven to 350°F (175°C). Spread the nuts on a baking
sheet and bake until they're golden brown and crisp, about
10 minutes.

Toss the warm nuts in a bowl with the rosemary, butter, brown
sugar, paprika, and salt until they're thoroughly coated.

Serve warm or at room temperature.

The nuts can be stored in an airtight container for up to 1 week
at room temperature.

CHAMPAGNE TRUFFLES

Makes 35 truffles

½ cup (125ml)
heavy cream

10 ounces (285g)
bittersweet
chocolate, chopped

3 tablespoons (45g)
unsalted butter, cubed,
at room temperature

3 tablespoons (45ml)
cognac

½ cup (40g) unsweetened
Dutch-processed cocoa
powder

Some people think champagne truffles contain champagne, but they're actually flavored with cognac and named after the areas where the grapes for cognac are grown: the Grande Champagne and the Petite Champagne. French *truffes au chocolat* are meant to resemble the truffles that grow in the ground, not the fancy, precisely round ones you may see outside of France.

These are perfect after dinner, with coffee or a digestif such as eau-de-vie, calvados, or cognac. But champagne, the kind with bubbles, is also a *ne plus ultra* accompaniment.

Heat the cream in a small saucepan until it starts to bubble around the edges. Remove from the heat, add the chocolate, and stir gently with a whisk until the chocolate is melted and the ganache is smooth. Add the butter and cognac, and stir until they're completely incorporated. Pour the ganache into a shallow baking dish, such as a 9-inch (23cm) glass pie plate or a similar-size vessel. Cover and refrigerate until firm enough to scoop, about 1 hour.

Remove from the refrigerator. If the ganache is too firm, let it sit at room temperature for 5 to 10 minutes, until scoopable.

Line a dinner plate or small baking sheet with parchment paper or plastic wrap and have a bowl of very hot water ready. Dip a melon baller or small spring-loaded ice cream scoop into the hot water, then scoop out a 1-inch (2.5cm) round of the ganache and set it on the plate or baking sheet. Continue scooping the truffles, dipping the scoop in the hot water after each and shaking off any excess water before scooping the next one. Chill the truffles for 30 minutes.

Sift the cocoa powder through a mesh strainer into a shallow bowl or pie plate. Roll eight to ten truffles at a time in the cocoa powder to coat them. Lift them out, place them in the strainer, and shake off any excess cocoa powder, then set the truffles either in individual paper candy cups or on a serving plate. Repeat to coat the remaining truffles. (Any leftover cocoa powder can be reserved for another baking project.)

The truffles will keep in an airtight container in the refrigerator for up to 1 week. Let them come close to room temperature before serving.

KEEPING BAR SYRUPS

Most bar syrups can be stored in the refrigerator for up to two weeks. Some can be kept longer, and others will lose their vigor after the first week or so. (The fresh mint syrup on page 272 is best used within a few days.) It's hard to pinpoint precisely how long syrups will last, but those made with fruit won't keep as well as those made without it.

When in doubt, give it a taste. If the flavor has faded, it's time to make a new batch. Of course, if you see anything fuzzy or hazy on top, toss the syrup (without tasting it). Should you find yourself with extra syrup on hand after you've used it for a cocktail, add some to sparkling water for a tasty homemade soda.

SIMPLE SYRUP

Makes ½ cup (125ml)

½ cup (100g) sugar

½ cup (125ml) water

This 1:1 syrup is a standard ingredient in a number of cocktails, and it's good to have it on hand in the refrigerator so it's ready, and well chilled, when you need it.

Heat the sugar and water over medium-high heat in a small saucepan, stirring, until the sugar is completely dissolved. Turn off the heat and let the syrup cool to room temperature. Pour into a clean jar. Cool, then cover and refrigerate.

RICH DEMERARA SYRUP

Makes ½ cup (125ml)

½ cup (110g)
demerara sugar

¼ cup (60ml) water

Demerara sugar is a large-crystal cane sugar, and is called *cassonade* in France. When Napoléon ordered sugar beets to be grown in France, everyone could afford sugar, which previously was a pricey import. While times have changed, cane sugar still has a more highly esteemed status in France than beet sugar. To make this syrup, you can use natural demerara or turbinado sugar. I use it when stirring up a Toronto (page 184).

Heat the sugar and water over medium-high heat in a small saucepan, stirring, until the sugar is completely dissolved. Turn off the heat and let the syrup cool to room temperature. Pour into a clean jar. Cool, then cover and refrigerate.

NOTE

If the syrup crystallizes after being stored in the refrigerator, warm it in the jar (without the lid) in a microwave oven briefly until it liquefies, or scrape the syrup into a small saucepan and rewarm it on the stovetop, stirring, until it is liquefied.

HONEY SYRUP

Makes ¼ cup (60ml)

¼ cup (80g) honey

1½ tablespoons hot
(but not boiling) water

My preference is to make this syrup with a dark honey that has a little more intensity than a light-colored variety. In France, it's sometimes labeled "forest" or "mountain" honey; grocery stores elsewhere stock wildflower honey, which is a good all-around choice.

In a jar, shake together the honey and water until the honey is liquefied and the mixture is well combined. (Make sure the lid is well sealed so no hot water comes out when you shake it.) Cool, then refrigerate.

FRESH MINT SYRUP

Makes 1½ cups (355ml)

1½ cups (355ml) water, plus more for blanching the mint

2 cups (80g) loosely packed fresh mint leaves

⅔ cup (135g) sugar

To make this syrup, I followed the lead of author and bartender Jeffrey Morgenthaler, who, in his award-winning bartender's guide, *The Bar Book*, blends his syrup with blanched mint leaves to give it an attractive, long-lasting green color.

In a small saucepan, heat about a cup (250ml) of water until it boils. Turn off the heat and add the mint leaves, letting them blanch for 10 seconds in the hot water. Drain the mint leaves in a mesh strainer, discarding the liquid.

Heat the 1½ cups (355ml) water and the sugar in the saucepan over medium-high heat, stirring, until the sugar is dissolved. Remove from the heat and add the mint. Let steep until the sugar syrup is tepid.

Transfer the syrup and the mint leaves to a blender and blend at high speed for 1 minute. Strain through a fine-mesh strainer set over a small bowl, pressing on the mint leaves to extract as much flavor as possible. Pour the syrup into a clean jar. Cover and refrigerate. Shake well before using.

ROSEMARY SYRUP

Makes ½ cup (125ml)

½ cup (100g) sugar

½ cup (125ml) water

2 tablespoons coarsely chopped fresh rosemary leaves

This flavorful syrup is a base for the Rosemary Gimlet (page 227) and Ginger-Rosemary Lemonade (page 34).

In a small saucepan, heat the sugar, water, and rosemary leaves over medium-high heat, stirring, until the sugar is completely dissolved. Remove from the heat and let cool to room temperature. Strain through a fine-mesh strainer into a small bowl. Pour the syrup into a clean jar. Cool, then cover and refrigerate.

GRENADINE SYRUP

Makes 2¼ cups (560ml)

1 cup (250ml) fresh or bottled unsweetened pomegranate juice

1 cup (200g) raw granulated sugar or regular granulated sugar

2 tablespoons (30ml) pomegranate molasses

½ teaspoon orange flower water

½ ounce (15ml) vodka (optional)

Pomegranates are called *grenades* in French, which I'm sure is because it looks like a bomb went off in your kitchen after you rip one open. (So wear something you don't mind having splashed with red pomegranate juice when making this boldly colored syrup.) This recipe, used by professional bartenders worldwide, is adapted from barman and cocktail writer Jeffrey Morgenthaler, whom I've previously referenced, since he's the master of bar syrups. It can be made with freshly squeezed pomegranate juice or store-bought unsweetened pomegranate juice. POM Wonderful, available in France and the United States, works very well. The vodka helps to preserve it, but if you're planning on serving it to kids, in a drink like a Grenadine (page 37) or Diabolo Grenadine (page 39), you can leave it out.

In a nonreactive saucepan, warm the pomegranate juice and sugar over the lowest heat possible, stirring constantly, until the sugar is dissolved.

Turn off the heat and add the pomegranate molasses, orange flower water, and vodka (if using). Pour into a clean jar. Cool, then cover and refrigerate.

NOTE

Since this makes quite a bit more than you might need, you can either cut the recipe in half or store it in the freezer. Even frozen, it stays soft enough to dig out a few ounces as you need it.

SPICED TANGERINE SYRUP

Makes ½ cup (125ml)

2 teaspoons Sichuan peppercorns

½ teaspoon black peppercorns

⅓ cup (65g) sugar

Zest of 1 tangerine

½ cup (125ml) freshly squeezed tangerine juice

Two kinds of peppercorns back up this tangerine syrup. The fizzy heat of Sichuan pepper and the kick of black pepper are welcome counterpoints to the lush tangerine juice. They don't overwhelm when the syrup is used in a cocktail, such as The Sunny Side (page 161), but you can leave them out if you wish, or replace them with crushed allspice berries.

Lightly crush the Sichuan and black peppercorns in a mortar and pestle or in a ziptop freezer bag with a hammer or rolling pin. Warm the peppercorns in a medium saucepan over medium heat, stirring occasionally, until they smell fragrant, about 2 minutes.

Remove the pan from the heat and add the sugar, then stir in the tangerine zest and juice. Warm the mixture over medium-high heat until it just begins to boil, then reduce to a simmer and cook for 2 minutes, stirring occasionally.

Remove from the heat, cover, and let stand at room temperature for 4 hours. Rewarm the syrup, then strain it through a mesh strainer set over a small bowl, pressing on the peppercorns and zest with a flexible silicone spatula to extract as much flavor as you can. Pour the syrup into a clean jar. Cool, then cover and refrigerate.

RICH FRESH GINGER SYRUP

Makes 1 cup (250ml)

1 cup (200g) sugar

½ cup (125ml) water

4 ounces (115g) fresh ginger, unpeeled, sliced

Although this concentrated spicy ginger syrup from bar manager Zac Overman of L'Oursin in Seattle is used as a base for the Ginger Devil (page 110), it's also excellent stirred into a glass of sparkling lemonade (see page 36) or even to add some zip to a cup of hot tea.

In a small saucepan, heat the sugar and water over medium-high heat, stirring, until the sugar is completely dissolved. Turn off the heat and let cool to room temperature. Transfer the syrup and ginger to a blender and puree until as smooth as possible. Strain through a fine-mesh strainer into a small bowl. Pour into a clean jar. Cover and refrigerate.

GRAPEFRUIT SYRUP

Makes 1 cup (250ml)

Zest of 1 grapefruit

1 cup (250ml) freshly
squeezed pink
grapefruit juice

½ cup (100g) sugar

1 tablespoon (15ml)
freshly squeezed
lemon juice

1 star anise, crushed,
or 2 or 3 broken allspice
berries (optional)

I sometimes add a crushed star anise or a few broken allspice berries to this mix, letting the spice simmer with the other ingredients. They add a certain *je ne sais quoi* to the syrup.

———————

In a small nonreactive saucepan, combine the grapefruit zest, grapefruit juice, sugar, lemon juice, and spice (if using) and bring to a boil, stirring occasionally, until the sugar is dissolved. Reduce the heat and simmer the syrup for 5 minutes. Strain through a fine-mesh strainer into a small bowl. Pour into a clean jar. Cool, then cover and refrigerate.

BLACKBERRY SHRUB

Makes 1 cup (250ml)

1 cup (150g) fresh or
frozen blackberries

⅔ cup (130g) sugar

⅔ cup (160ml) apple
cider vinegar

A tangy component in the Blackberry Aigre-Doux (page 94), because it's so flavorful, a few spoonfuls of this shrub can also be added to sparkling water, along with ice and a lemon twist, for a satisfying nonalcoholic apéritif.

———————

Mix the berries and sugar together in a medium bowl, stirring and mashing the berries with the sugar to encourage juicing. When the berries are completely broken down, stir in the vinegar. Cover the bowl and let stand at room temperature for at least 8 hours, or overnight, stirring several times as the berries are macerating to encourage them to release their juices.

Set a mesh strainer over a small bowl and strain the berry mixture, pressing down on the berries firmly with a silicone spatula to extract as much liquid from them as possible. Discard the berry seeds. Pour the liquid into a clean jar, cover, and refrigerate. Unlike fruit syrups, the shrub will keep for up to 6 months in the refrigerator, due to the vinegar.

CANDIED AMARENA CHERRIES

Makes 1½ cups (350g)

1½ cups jarred sour cherries and their syrup (total weight 360g)

½ cup (100g) sugar

These are similar to the pricey Italian candied cherries sold in jars, and they are as delicious in cocktails as they are in desserts.

To get an accurate reading on your candy thermometer, I recommend cooking these in a saucepan that's not too wide, so the thermometer bulb is submerged in the liquid, unless you're using a digital thermometer. Whatever type of thermometer you use, if your saucepan is wide, tilt the pan when checking the temperature to get an accurate reading. Fortunately, these cherries aren't too fussy, and if you don't have a thermometer, simply cook the cherries and sugar until the liquid is reduced to the consistency of warm honey, and the cherries darken and start to shrivel.

In the United States, jarred sour cherries are sold at well-stocked grocery stores, Trader Joe's, and shops that specialize in European foods.

In a small nonreactive saucepan with a candy thermometer attached (if you have one), heat the sour cherries and their syrup along with the sugar until the mixture comes to a boil.

Reduce the heat to maintain a low boil and cook until the syrup starts to look foamy, tilting and swirling the pan as the temperature inches closer to 225°F (107°C). Make sure the syrup isn't caramelizing; you want to cook the cherries until they are deep, dark red and slightly shriveled. Transfer the cherries and the liquid to a clean jar and let cool until tepid. Cover and refrigerate. The cherries will keep in the refrigerator for up to 1 year.

BONNES ADRESSES À PARIS
(FAVORITE SHOPS IN PARIS)

Paris is a paradise for picking up anything drink-related, from iconic *café au lait* bowls and bistro *café express* cups, to French liqueurs and apéritifs. Below are some of my favorite places in Paris to shop. But if you meander around the city, especially in the outer neighborhoods (what are called the double-digit arrondissements), you'll likely come across smaller shops, tucked away on side streets, specializing in foods and spirits from various regions of France (most notably, mountainous regions like the Auvergne and the Savoie) that you won't find outside of the country.

Wine stores in France generally have a serviceable selection of French spirits. But even more fun are *les supermarchés*, where French liqueurs and apéritifs cost a fraction of what they go for elsewhere. I get a kick out of seeing fully stocked shelves of Amer Picon (see page 98) and watching people fill their shopping baskets with pastis, gentian liqueur, and absinthe while I'm filling mine with eggs, flour, and butter.

Note that the selections in the listed shops can, and will, change. Most *caves* and liquor stores aren't large, so they rotate their offerings frequently to keep things interesting.

LIQUORS AND SPIRITS

A'Rhûm

This *cave à rhum* specializes in rum from the French colonies and the Caribbean, with selections from Africa, Cuba, Haiti, and Tahiti rounding out the collection of nearly 1,300 kinds of rum. The store offers tastings and cocktail classes, if you want to expand your knowledge of rum and rum-based cocktails. Their nearby shop, G43.3 (34, rue de Grenier Saint-Lazare, 3rd), focuses on gin, mezcal, tequila, and tonic waters, including French-made Archibald.

203, rue Saint-Martin (3rd)
www.arhum.fr

Caves Bossetti

A must-stop for fans of Chartreuse, the vivid green herbal liqueur made by monks in the French Alps (see page 198). Passionate *caviste* Philippe Beaudet stocks the elusive Chartreuse elixir, little bottles of extra-strength Chartreuse that come tucked into a wooden box; Génépi *intense*, an infusion of alpine herbs bottled in a handy hip flask; and nearly a dozen other variations of Chartreuse, including a showcase of old and rare bottles. They hold an annual get-together of the Club des Fous de Chartreuse (Club of People Crazy for Chartreuse) at their shop in the Marais, which is open to all, during which they pour several types of Chartreuse from oversize bottles, including varieties not normally available to the public.

34, rue des Archives (4th)
www.caves-bossetti.fr

Caves du Panthéon

It's no wonder people come from all over the city to shop in this neighborhood wine and liqueur store. This *caviste* changes its stock depending on what's available, but you might find a verveine liqueur made in the Loire Valley; Gabriel Boudier *crème de cassis de Dijon*, one of the original black currant liqueurs from Burgundy; or eaux-de-vie from the Distillerie du Petit Grain in the Languedoc (see page 224), which are distilled from apricots, barley, and pears, as well as gin. A local liquor distributor (who operates WOS, a friendly spirits pub down the street that's also worth stopping in) supplies them with a caramel liqueur spiked with French sea salt, as well as Xuxu, preblended strawberry vodka liqueur, which sounds like something I'd normally avoid, but surprisingly packs a bright, fresh strawberry flavor.

174, rue Saint-Jacques (5th)
(no website)

Christian de Montaguère

Every kind of rum you can imagine is in this shop just off the beaten path on the Left Bank. According to the manager, there are 1,500 kinds of rum in the boutique, inspired by the spirit of the Caribbean. You'll find premium rums, spiced rums, overproofed rums (one was 70 percent alcohol, or 140 proof!), and beautiful bottles of *rhums arrangés* (see page 154) infused with fresh fruits and flavorings, like kumquat-coffee, mango–passion fruit, and vanilla, and one in a bottle packed with macadamia nuts. The shop hosts several tastings a month.

20, rue de l'Abbe Grégoire (6th)
www.christiandemontaguere.com

Julhès

This family-owned stalwart has been a fixture on the suddenly hip rue du Faubourg Saint-Denis for years. Fueled by the recent cocktail boom, they have expanded to include a shop devoted solely to liqueur a few blocks away, on the Boulevard Sebastapol, and a satellite in the 11th arrondissement. The Julhès brothers have a distillery (see page 222) behind the store on the rue du Faubourg Saint-Denis, and sell their gins, rums, and pre-batched cocktails from the Distillerie de Paris in their shops. You'll find a closely curated selection of spirits, liqueurs, and apéritifs in all three locations. The stock changes frequently, but there are invariably French specialties like Cap Corse, Pommeau de Normandie, Chartreuse, and even Périque *liqueur de tabac* (tobacco liqueur, when available), which may be unique to France.

56, rue du Faubourg Saint-Denis (10th)
59, rue du Faubourg Saint-Martin (10th)
129, boulevard Voltaire (11th)
www.julhesparis.fr

La Maison du Whisky

There are two locations of La Maison du Whisky: an imposing boutique near the Place de la Madeleine (on the rue d'Anjou), dedicated exclusively to whiskey (with many upper-end bottles), and a second shop in the Carrefour de l'Odéon on the Left Bank, with a vast collection of spirits, including their own line of rums, French gins, whiskeys, vodkas, cognacs, bitters, and Armagnacs. The Left Bank shop is also a great place to scope out French vermouths, apéritifs, and curiosities like Byrrh Rare Assemblage, wormwood-based Dolin Génépi liqueur, La Quintinye, a vermouth that's fortified with Pineau des Charentes (see page 82), and *liqueur de sapin* made from wild spruce tips.

20, rue d'Anjou (8th)
6, Carrefour de l'Odéon (6th)
www.whisky.fr

Lavinia

This multilevel emporium of liquor carries an impressive selection of wine, but there are also plenty of French spirits to peruse: Metté eaux-de-vie from Alsace, Suze à l'ancienne (barrel-aged gentian liqueur), the hard-to-find Suze bitters, Lillet Grand Réserve, Dolin white and dry vermouths, as well as Macvin and Floc de Gascogne. Particularly interesting are the unusual crèmes and liqueurs, such as those made with roses, lavender, chestnuts, and blackberries, in addition to rosé Pineau des Charentes. In the lower-level *cave* are more than a dozen vintages of Château d'Yquem and Barsacs, the glorious sweet wines of Bordeaux. For those who want to taste, you can buy a card at the register that allows you to wander through the store, grab a glass, and swipe the card at various machines loaded up with bottles, which distribute a measured sip of whatever you select. (Sorry, d'Yquem is not included.)

3–5, boulevard de la Madeleine (1st)
www.lavinia.fr

Legrand Filles et Fils

Known for its extensive wine selection, Legrand Filles et Fils also has an unusually charming collection of French candies. But the wooden cabinets at the shop hold some truly unique spirits, which change depending on availability or what the staff feels is most interesting to stock at the moment. One curiosity I've found here is Houlle, a grain-based distillation infused with juniper berries. Another time I found slender bottles of emerald-green verveine (lemon verbena) liqueur from a *petit producteur* who makes only a thousand bottles per year. Eastern France is well-represented with eaux-de-vie distilled from cardamom, Mirabelle plums, quince, and *sorbier*, a red berry similar to rose hips. There's also the French version of limoncello, made from the famous lemons of Menton, near Nice. And although I've never gotten up the gumption to buy it, I've wondered about a curiosity called Hypocran, which the clerk explained to me was wine *à l'ancienne* (old-fashioned), sweetened and flavored with cloves, rose petals, and ginger.

1, rue de la Banque (1st)
www.caves-legrand.com

Les Caves du Roy

Above the fray of the lively Goutte d'Or neighborhood is the highly regarded Les Caves du Roy, which has shelves and wooden nooks filled right up to the ceiling with bottles of wines and spirits from across France. There's quite a selection of absinthes (including a red one from Czechoslovakia), but I focus on the liqueurs and hard-to-acquire apéritifs, like Maurin Quina and Salers gentian liqueur, available here in three degrees of alcohol, as well as *crèmes* made with figs, geraniums, and peppers. Treasures are tucked in everywhere, so it's worth spending time to look around . . . and up and down.

31, rue Simart (18th)
www.cavesduroy.fr

Oogy Wawa

In-the-know Parisian cocktail fans head to Oogy Wawa for shakers, mixing jars, absinthe fountains, and barware. But the store also stocks an unusual selection of liquors that "you won't find at the supermarket," one of the owners told me. Indeed, you'd be hard-pressed to unearth curiosities like licorice syrup or liqueurs made with smoked tea and *pêche de vigne* (red-fleshed peaches) elsewhere. Because they named their store Oogy Wawa, you can probably guess that

owners François Fayard and Antoine Moncet have a special place in their hearts for tiki drinks, so there are some fun glasses and cups to help you get your tiki on. The Ali Baba–like *cave* is full of very cool glassware, with a full-on bar that's used for cocktail classes.

4, rue Auguste Dorchain (15th)
www.oogywawa.net

Ryst-Dupeyron

Best known for a comprehensive selection of Armagnacs, some dating back to 1868, Ryst-Dupeyron's in-house brand of ports (J. W. Hart) is well-respected, too. You won't find a more knowledgeable and helpful staff than theirs, and they keep a table of open bottles for impromptu customer tastings. Other things to look out for: Pousse Rapière (see page 137), meant to be mixed with sparkling wine. (The shopkeeper confided that a dash of the liqueur is also excellent in a glass of white wine, similar to a Kir.) There's also inky-purple *crème de mûre*, made from wild blackberries, for yet another twist on a Kir. If your budget (and your luggage) isn't big enough to bring a full bottle of Armagnac home, the store offers Armagnac in 400ml (a little shy of 2 cups) bottles and minis, to stash away for yourself or for gift-giving.

79, rue du Bac (7th)
www.maisonrystdupeyron.com

The Whisky Shop

This shop has a carefully curated collection of whiskeys from around the world, with France well-represented. Armorik whiskey, from Brittany, is the oldest whiskey distiller in France, and there's Elsass from Alsace and La Rouget de Lisle, made in the Jura, where Comté cheese is made. (Not surprisingly, it goes well with the whiskey.) The knowledgeable clerks can steer you to the right bottle, and the shop offers master classes as well as free tastings.

7, place de la Madeleine (8th)
www.whiskyshop.fr

DRINKING ACCOUTREMENTS

A. Simon

The imposing selection of *verrerie* (glassware) and barware at A. Simon covers a full wall, and if you're looking to pick up a French café drinks tray, or a holder for *l'addition* (the check), you'll find those in stock as well. On the opposite side of the store are shelves of porcelain ware, with very sturdy (and not inexpensive), top-quality *café au lait* bowls from Pillivuyt, made in central France. There are dozens of champagne and cocktail glasses, as well as wine carafes, serving trays, and small pitchers for steamed milk, exactly the kind used in French bistros and cafés. (Note that prices at A. Simon and Verrerie des Halles, below, may be listed as HT, or *hors taxes,* meaning tax isn't included. Don't be surprised if a VAT, or value added tax, of roughly 20 percent is added at the register.)

48, rue Montmartre (2nd)
(no website)

La Vaissellerie

It may take a moment for your eyes to adjust, but once they do, you'll find yourself amidst brightly lit shelves packed with a well-organized jumble of wine and cocktail glasses, drink tumblers, pitchers, shot glasses, pourers, French wine carafes, coffee cups, and footed *café au lait* bowls. Best of all, prices are modest; most items are just a couple of euros, and if you're traveling, the helpful staff packs things well.

(The store has multiple addresses in Paris.)
www.lavaissellerie.fr

Porcelaines M.P. Samie Blanc & Décor

This direct-from-the-manufacturer store offers up French porcelain ware, from plain to decorative, just a few métro stops from the city center. Sort through the shelves and crates to find teapots, terrines, *café au lait* bowls (plain and decorated), and colorful coffee cups at this multilevel shop.

45, avenue du Général Leclerc (14th)
www.porcelainesmpsamie.fr

Verrerie des Halles

Tucked in a courtyard, Verrerie des Halles specializes in glassware. The store is geared toward professionals, but anyone is welcome to browse and poke around the well-worn wooden shelves packed with crockery, *café au lait* bowls, apéritif dishes, and French café-style coffee cups. The *verres* (glasses) are up front, and range from glasses with the characteristic bulge used for drinking Menthe à l'Eau (page 37) to French cocktail coupes, useful for Boulevardiers (page 179) and other drinks. If they don't have what you're looking for, ask and they'll order it, or it may be stocked in back. Especially interesting are the thick absinthe glasses, which cost a fraction of the price of vintage ones.

15, rue du Louvre (1st)
www.verrerie-des-halles-paris.fr

RESOURCES

Alambic Bourguignon

Mathieu Sabbagh's distillery in Burgundy, where he produces gentian spirits, eaux-de-vie, and brandies.

www.alambic-bourguignon.com

Astor Wines & Spirits

This New York institution carries a broad and remarkably varied selection of French apéritifs, liqueurs, and spirits at their store in Manhattan, with mail order available.

www.astorwines.com

Audemus Spirits

Small-batch French spirit maker, creator of Sepia *amer*, a bitter in the spirit of Amer Picon. Their bold Pink Pepper gin is worthy of the rave reviews it garners.

www.audemus-spirits.com

Bigallet

French-made syrups, spirits, crèmes, and liqueurs. Bigallet's China-China *amer* is an excellent substitute for Amer Picon, and available in the United States.

www.bigallet.fr

Byrrh

Makers of Byrrh Grand Quinquina, a wine-based apéritif. Their website includes information on visits to their historic wine caves, close to the Spanish border.

www.caves-byrrh.fr

Chartreuse

The history and finesse of Chartreuse, the renowned herbal liqueur made by monks in the French Alps for four centuries, is explained on their comprehensive website.

www.chartreuse.fr

Clear Creek Distillery

American-made eaux-de-vie and aged apple brandy (similar to calvados).

www.clearcreekdistillery.com

Cointreau

A classic French orange liqueur, distilled from sweet and sour oranges.

www.cointreau.com

D'Artagnan

Duck fat and fresh duck thighs, as well as pre-prepared duck confit and rillettes.

www.dartagnan.com

Deck & Donohue

Craft beer brewed a short distance from Paris.

www.deck-donohue.com

Distillerie de Paris

Located in the heart of Paris, this small-batch distillery creates various gins, vodka, pre-batched cocktails, and more.

www.distilleriedeparis.com

Distilleries et Domaines de Provence

Distillery based in the South of France, makers of pastis, Noix de la Saint Jean (walnut liqueur), thyme liqueur, and RinQuinQuin peach apéritif.

www.distilleries-provence.com

Dolin

The makers of the original *vermouth de Chambéry*, their lineup also includes Bonal Gentiane-Quina apéritif and liqueurs made from local strawberries, mountain herbs, and other botanicals.

www.dolin.fr

Dubonnet

The flavor of this American-made version of the French aromatized wine (which is still made in France, by a different manufacturer) was recently reformulated to hone closer to the original apéritif.

www.doyoudubonnet.com

Fee Brothers

Offers orange, chocolate, and other cocktail bitters, in addition to green "crème de menthe" mint syrup, to use in café drinks.

www.feebrothers.com

Giffard

French distiller specializing in flavored syrups (including mint), crèmes, liqueurs, and rum infusions. (The Caribbean pineapple is a favorite.)

www.giffard.com

Golden Moon Distillery

American-made *crème de violette*, Amer dit Picon (their version of the French Amer Picon), and other spirits.

www.goldenmoondistillery.com

Grand Marnier

Renowned French liqueur made from Seville oranges with a cognac base.

www.grandmarnier.com

Haus Alpenz

American-based distributor of international spirits, with a focus on France. No direct sales, but their website is a wealth of information on the spirits.

www.alpenz.com

Hella Cocktails

Maker of orange, aromatic, eucalyptus, apple blossom, and other cocktail bitters.

www.hellacocktail.co

Kalustyan's

Carries za'atar and other spices.

www.foodsofnations.com

K&L Wine Merchants

California-based seller of French liqueurs, apéritifs, and spirits, with mail order available.

www.klwines.com

Lejay

Home of the original *crème de cassis de Dijon*, Lejay also makes a mono-variety crème de cassis, using only the choice Noir de Bourgogne variety of black currant.

www.lejay-cassis.com

Lillet

The classic orange-based apéritif from Bordeaux, available in white, red, and rosé.

www.lillet.com

L.N. Mattei

Family-owned producer of Cap Corse, a quinine-based apéritif from Corsica.

www.capcorsemattei.com

Local Harvest

Offers French green walnuts, seasonally available, for making Vin de Noix (page 163).

www.localharvest.org

Maison Ferrand

Best known for its outstanding cognacs, as well as Citadelle gin, superb dry curaçao (triple sec), and fruit-based liqueurs.

www.maisonferrand.com

Marx Foods

Fresh spruce tips for Gin de Sapin (page 153) and Vin de Sapin (page 149).

www.marxfoods.com

Monin

French-made flavored syrups, including green mint syrup.

www.monin.com

Noilly Prat

Classic French vermouth, made in the South of France.

www.noillyprat.com

Royal Vallet

Bitters crafted in Mexico, Fernet-Vallet and Amargo-Vallet are the creations of a French distiller who settled in Mexico in the 1860s.

www.royalvallet.com

Salers

Gentian-based apéritif, produced in the Auvergne.

www.gentiane-salers.com

Scrappy's Bitters

Aromatic, cardamom, chocolate, and lavender cocktail bitters.

www.scrappysbitters.com

Spruce on Tap

Fresh spruce tips for Gin de Sapin (page 153) and Vin de Sapin (page 149).

www.spruceontap.com

St. George Spirits

Producer of French-inspired distillations and eaux-de-vie as well as absinthe, Bruto Americano (an excellent red bitter apéritif, similar to Campari), coffee liqueur, and a barrel-aged apple brandy, made in the spirit of calvados.

www.stgeorgespirits.com

Suze

Popular French gentian apéritif, available in several varieties.

www.suze.com

Tempus Fugit Spirits

Top-quality crème de noyau, liqueur de violette, crème de menthe, and absinthe.

www.tempusfugitspirits.com

The Depot

American makers of Amer Depot, a re-creation of an "(Amer) Picon-style liqueur," as they say.

www.thedepotreno.com

The Meadow

Extensive collection of salts and cocktail bitters.

www.themeadow.com

Torani

Mint and other flavored syrups (including green mint), as well as Torani *amer* (an Amer Picon substitute), which isn't listed on the site, but can be found online at liquorama.com.

shop.torani.com

Védrenne

Mint and fruit syrups, crèmes, eaux-de-vie, and apéritifs, including elderflower (*fleur de sureau*) liqueur, made in Burgundy.

www.vedrenne.fr

ACKNOWLEDGMENTS

The vast subject of French drinks has fascinated me ever since my first visit to France. It is exciting to share what I learned, discovered, and drank. Along the way, I was fortunate to have such generous and talented people help me.

Thanks to my friends at Ten Speed Press, especially my editor, Julie Bennett, for graciously allowing me to expand this book, and for nurturing it (and occasionally me) from start to finish. To Aaron Wehner for keeping tabs on things, Kim Keller for her keen eye and production assistance, Betsy Stromberg for designing yet another beautiful book, Jane Chinn for book production, and Ed Anderson and George Dolese for creating photographs that capture what I love about French apéritifs, cocktails, and other libations . . . and for making the process even more fun. To Brandon Clements of The Saratoga, Ethel Brennan, and Laurie Furber of Elsie Green for adding their touches of France. And to my agent, Bonnie Nadell, for guiding me in the right direction, and to Austen Rachlis, for being a supportive associate. Special thanks to Comstock Saloon for the use of their bar.

To bartenders, spirit makers, chefs, and friends Miko Abouaf, Adrien Angeli, Matt Armendariz, Franck Audoux, Joe Boley, Antonia Catton, Frédéric Chambeau, Quentin Chapus, Clifford Colvin and John Reuling, Emmanuel Delafon, Chris Elford, William Elliot, Joshua Fontaine, Camille Fourmont, Antoine Goldschmid, Eric Goujou, Guy Griffin, Julia Grossman, Mike Higdon (for his encyclopedic knowledge of Picon Punch), Steve Horton, Stanislas Jouenne, Roberta Klugman, Margot Lecarpentier, Matthew Levison, Carlos Madriz, Olivier Magny, Tim Master, Romain Meder, Jim Meehan, Jeffrey Morgenthaler (who allowed me to graciously crib several of his recipes and techniques), Robby Nelson, Zac Overman, Jake Parrott, David Phillips, Christiaan Röllich, Peter Schaf, Eric Seed, Heidi Swanson, and John Troia for sharing their recipes and *savoir-faire*.

To Brad Thomas Parsons for being a *ne plus ultra* drinking buddy and opening doors in the cocktail community for me. To Cindy Meyers for testing recipes and providing invaluable feedback, Jeff Galli for helping me learn what it takes to stand behind the bar, and Forest Collins of 52 Martinis for joining me on spirited sojourns around Paris. And to Emily Cunningham for helping taste-test the recipes and keeping the rest of my life in order.

Merci to David Flynn and Thomas Lehoux of Belleville Brûlerie Cave de la Chartreuse, Caves Byrrh, Thomas Deck of Deck & Donohue, Nicolas Julhès of Distillerie de Paris, Mathieu Sabbagh of Alambic Bourguignon, Noilly Prat, Pierre-Olivier Rousseaux of Dolin, and Tristan Simon of Védrenne for showing me their passion for what they do.

To Alain Ducasse au Plaza Athénée, Belleville Brûlerie, Café Charbon, Café Méricourt, Café Rhum Marin, Combat, Fédération Français de l'Apéritif, Gallopin, La Bague de Kenza, La Bourgainville, La Buvette, La Fée Verte, La Fontaine de Belleville, Le Dôme, Legrand Filles et Fils, Le Mary Celeste, Le Plein Soleil, Le Saint-Sébastien, and Red House for letting us photograph there, with special thanks to Cravan, Le Petit Vendôme, and Poulette restaurants for telling me to consider their restaurants and bars *comme chez toi*, as if they were my home, when shooting this book.

And to Romain Pellas, *merci pour tout (comme toujours)* . . . *à ta santé, mon chéri.*

INDEX

Copyright © 2020 by David Lebovitz
Photographs copyright © 2020 by Ed Anderson

Photo on page 95 by David Lebovitz

All rights reserved.
Published in the United States by Ten Speed Press, an imprint of Random House, a division of Penguin Random House LLC, New York.
www.tenspeed.com

Ten Speed Press and the Ten Speed Press colophon are registered trademarks of Penguin Random House LLC.

Library of Congress Cataloging-in-Publication Data
Names: Lebovitz, David, author. | Anderson, Ed (Edward Charles), photographer.
Title: Drinking French: the iconic cocktails, apéritifs, and café traditions of France, with 160 recipes / David Lebovitz; photographs by Ed Anderson.
Description: California: Ten Speed Press, [2020] | Includes index.
Identifiers: LCCN 2019019161 | ISBN 9781607749295 (hardcover)
Subjects: LCSH: Cocktails. | Aperitifs—France. | LCGFT: Cookbooks.
Classification: LCC TX951 .L428 2020 | DDC 641.87/4—dc23 LC record available at https://lccn.loc.gov/2019019161

Hardcover ISBN: 978-1-60774-929-5
eBook ISBN: 978-1-60774-930-1

Printed in China

Design by Betsy Stromberg
Food and drink styling by George Dolese
Prop styling by David Lebovitz and George Dolese

10 9 8 7 6 5 4 3 2 1

First Edition